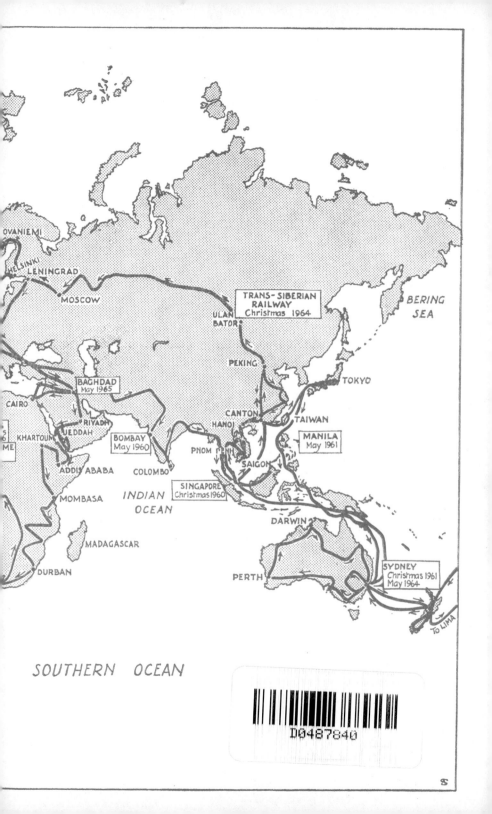

SEVEN LEAGUE BOOTS

SEVEN LEAGUE BOOTS

The story of my seven-year hitch-hike
round the world

by

WENDY MYERS

HODDER AND STOUGHTON

*To my mother and father,
and to all my families
throughout the world without
whose love, understanding
and help nothing could have
been accomplished.*

Printed in Great Britain for Hodder and Stoughton, Limited, St. Paul's House,
Warwick Lane, London, E.C.4, by Cox and Wyman Limited, London, Fakenham
and Reading

CALENDAR

1960
   London   The Far East
   Turkey

1961
   Japan   Australia
   The Philippines   New Zealand

1962–3
   South America

1963–4
   North America   Laos
   Fiji   North Vietnam
   New Zealand   South Vietnam
   Australia   China
   Sarawak   Russia
   Thailand

1964–5
   Europe   The Middle East

1965–6
   Africa

1966–7
   Europe   London

Chapter 1

April 1960–May 1960

I'm not sure how, or when, or why it really began; whether it stems from a desire for knowledge, a curiosity about people, or some deeply-buried nomadic streak in my family; but I've always been an explorer. As a child I used to dream, as children do, that I was a sort of Marco Polo, an adventurer travelling for the love of it, finding what I could find, seeing the squalor alongside the beauty. It was this sense, I think, of the necessity of seeing things for myself, rather than through the second-hand accounts of television or Fleet Street, that made me take the first steps; and, once those were behind me, it was impossible to stop.

When I left school at seventeen and a half I joined a bank. There I was, dressed in a blue overall and sitting in an office with a horde of other teenage girls. I'm not saying that there wasn't a lot of fun and laughter during those hours from nine till five each day, but somehow I felt quite dissatisfied as I punched away at a machine or tried to decipher illegible signatures. While the other girls chatted about new clothes, boyfriends and television programmes, my mind wandered through other lands, in an adult imitation of my childhood dreams.

Whitsuntide came around, and we were all discussing where we would be going for the short holiday. "Brighton," said one girl, "Blackpool," said another, "Paris," said I. Then, as the girls were still exclaiming over this exotic notion, I suddenly realised that, having said so, I would really have to go. That was my first trip to the continent completely alone, and when I got there I discovered that I felt perfectly at ease, in spite of a foreign language, fresh Frenchmen, and a limited budget. I triumphantly returned to London and the office girls, with a bottle of cheap champagne and

7

some very happy memories which whetted my appetite for more.

That year I spent six and a half months in travelling all over Western Europe and Morocco. During that time I gained a knowledge of Italian, my French improved tremendously, and I got used to hitch-hiking, staying in Youth Hostels, and sleeping under the stars. When, on returning home, I told mother and father of my aspiration to travel all over the world, they heartily approved.

I wasn't surprised. They are a down-to-earth, sensible Yorkshire couple, and not in the least narrow-minded. "Go and see the world before another war starts and we blow it up," said mother. "You're right in deciding to do this thing while you are young, and not married with responsibilities to tie you down." My father added that I had already won my spurs by looking after myself in fourteen foreign countries and that by the look of the number of murders which had appeared in the newspapers of late, I would probably be safer in the mountains, forests and deserts of the world.

My parents then told me that as I was mature enough to travel alone, I should be able to see that my passport was in order, arrange my visas for various countries, and choose my clothes and equipment on my own initiative. I already had a passport, and upon 'phoning to some of the embassies of the countries to which I knew that I would be likely to travel, I discovered their visa requirements to be often so complicated that I decided to get most of my visas in the countries immediately preceding those for which they were necessary.

Clothes and equipment were not difficult to choose. A shirt, trousers, windcheater, socks, underwear and strong shoes would be my travelling apparel, while in my knapsack was a complete change of travel clothes, plus a sweater against the cold and a blouse and skirt. My first diary, a water-bottle, toilet articles, water-purifying tablets, and anti-malaria pills completed my equipment, bringing the weight of my luggage up to thirty-six pounds.

Since my preliminary tour around Europe I had been working and saving hard. I had bought traveller's cheques with some of the money, and the rest my shrewd Yorkshire mother had sewn into my bra as a reserve. I was to start my journey with one hundred pounds sterling. I intended to work whenever funds ran low, and my parents insisted that they should send me a little money from time to time, to help with boat passages whenever the need arose.

For my date of departure I chose April 4th. On this date most of the Youth Hostels would be open after the winter, and I could hope for some spring sunshine to cheer up my hiking days. The year was nineteen hundred and sixty, I was eighteen years old and an ardent lover of life in all its absorbing aspects.

I bade my parents farewell and received their blessing; my journey that was to take me all over the world was about to begin. Standing at the rail of the ferry from Dover to Ostend, I watched the white cliffs of Dover diminish to a blur on the horizon. I had no idea that the next time I should be setting foot on England's shores would be seven years to the day.

I travelled rapidly across Western Europe, hitch-hiking during the day and staying in Youth Hostels at night. Late one evening, I arrived in Istanbul. Tall minarets and domes of all shapes and sizes were silhouetted against a starry sky, lit by an orange moon. My heart pounded with excitement and tears of pleasure filled my eyes, at the calm, majestic beauty of the scene before me. This was my first and most beloved impression of the Middle East.

Traffic over the mountains between Istanbul and Ankara seemed most infrequent, maybe because the pass was dangerous and still covered with snow. I decided to take the cheapest form of public transport along that route, which happened to be a very overloaded and ancient bus. When I mentioned my intended journey to a friend, I sensed a certain lack of encouragement. "Mobile coffins!" he bellowed. "Before they set off, the drivers drink to keep out the cold, and you'll see the rusting frames of overturned buses all along the way." Sitting right at the front, I was squashed between the driver and an enormous fellow in a thick fur coat. A whiff of alcohol pervaded the air, and we set off into the night.

In Erzurum, a Turkish town in a military zone, the chief of police introduced me to an American doctor and his family who offered me a lift with them right to Tehran, which I gladly accepted.

We drove away through mountainous country, stopping to have a picnic in the snow. Rather appropriately, we feasted on tinned turkey, with turkish delight to follow. Mount Ararat, where Noah's Ark is said to have been stranded after the great flood, rose up before us, and a moslem rider stopped his horse and prayed towards Mecca in the setting sun. Nearer to Tehran the country was sandy and gently undulating, covered with a coarse grass.

Not only were the villages which we passed through picturesque and often interesting historically, but even their names were like poetry to me: Mianah, Zanjan, Qazvin, I would repeat them over and over again in delight.

Then, Tehran, nestling on the slopes of the great range of Alburz mountains. It is Iran's capital city, and although I saw such symbols of modern life as the college of agriculture, the double-decker buses and some statues of the Shah, I also saw women doing their washing in the gutters, the rows of towels hanging up to dry outside a communal bath, and the thin, flat Irani bread hanging over shop doorways waiting to be sold.

The very best way to get to know about a country, I decided, would be to stay with a family, and my first opportunity to do this came when I delivered a letter from an Irani girl, Kheaban, whom I'd met in London, to her parents in Meshed, a village in the north-east of Iran and, as I was later to learn, one of its very holiest places of pilgrimage.

Upon my arrival in Meshed, I wandered around the sandy streets, and some people directed me to the place where Kheaban's family lived. I was welcomed enthusiastically into the house by her parents, sisters and brother, Ahmed. The house was a two-storied, commodious affair, set in a garden which contained a goldfish pond. Cooking was done downstairs, but we ate, relaxed and slept in the upper rooms, where the open windows sometimes introduced the suggestion of a breeze.

Ahmed and his sisters were studying English at their high-schools, so we chatted together easily, as the evening meal was being prepared. While we talked, we sat cross-legged on the thick, Persian carpets which extended for about three feet up each of the walls, giving the most luxurious effect. Eliha, one of the sisters, ran out of the room for a moment and returned carrying a chador, a full-length veil which Irani women wear. She gave it to me to put over my legs as the other girls did, so that we could sit at ease yet retain the careful modesty which is demanded in a strict moslem household.

As is the case in moslem countries, Irani boys and girls don't usually mix on social occasions, and while in Meshed, I attended a girls-only party. Without any males around, the girls really let their hair down, casting away their chadors – under which many of them were wearing short, European-style skirts and dresses.

One girl played an accordion, another banged on a tamborine, and the rest of them danced animatedly and sang impromptu songs. It wasn't long before they hauled me to my feet to join in, and soon I was vigorously rendering my impressions of a belly-dance, also glad that there were no men around to goggle. At last, tired and laughing, we flung ourselves down on to some soft cushions and took our fill of nuts, cakes and fruit, washed down with cool, curdled milk.

Zahidan was my next destination, and the whole of Kheaban's family came to see me off on their friend's ramshackle old bus, Eliha placing a little gold chain with 'Allah' in Arabic hanging from it into my hand as a parting gift.

Five times a day, the bus would stop with a jerk and the driver would shout 'namoz' – the signal for all the faithful to file outside, face Mecca, and say their prayers. For meals, we stopped at rest-houses along the way, all of the same Irani style, with cooling stone floors and no windows. Stone benches were built around the walls, covered with hand-woven Persian rugs, on which we sat cross-legged to eat and drink our tea.

From Zahidan I set out sitting on a narrow wooden seat in the third class of a train. We moved slowly over sandy wastes towards the Pakistan frontier.

It was suggested to me that instead of travelling right to Quetta and continuing to Lahore from there, I should climb into a train bound for Lahore which was due to cross us at any moment. The trains would only be stopping for a few minutes, so, as the other train approached, I stood at the door of the carriage clutching my knapsack. "Hurry up!" somebody shouted, and I quickly jumped into a compartment of the Lahore train. We moved off almost at once, and I spent that night on a luggage rack in the ladies' compartment of the third class.

Arrived in Lahore, I wandered light-heartedly along when a little boy came pedalling up to me on a bicycle. "My father wants to speak to you," he said, and pointed to where his father and another man were standing in the doorway of a shop across the street. The boy's father introduced himself as Mr. Khan. He asked me numerous questions about myself and my journey, then he said, "You must be very hot and tired. My wife and I both enjoy meeting and entertaining foreigners, so I wish to tell you that you are quite welcome to stay with us."

Mr Khan, it turned out, was the owner of an ice-cream factory, just the sort of place that I'd dreamt about on that stuffy train. The Khan family lived in a beautiful house beside the factory, and had many servants.

Mr Khan was very anxious to have my opinion on his ice-cream, which in that climate I was more than happy to give. I was soon seated, feeling like a connoisseur, before an enormous trayful of ice-creams, each one of a different flavour. Steadily working through them, I discovered them all to be scrumptious, with the mango and almond varieties gaining first place in my estimation.

Chapter 2

"Of course, we get the best of both worlds," said the Anglo-Indian in the car beside me. He had offered me a lift from outside Lahore and we were heading for Amritsar, a town not many miles within India's north-western border. "We are able to appreciate both the European and the Indian cultures," he continued, as he steered carefully along the narrow, shady roads where buffalo roamed at will. I nodded in agreement, saying that it must make life most interesting to have a foot in both camps, so to speak. When we arrived in Amritsar, the Anglo-Indian invited me to his home, and there I really began to understand what he had been trying to explain to me. His wife switched on an overhead fan in a lounge which one could have found in any English suburb, discussed all the latest activities of the British royal family, and poured tea from a fat brown pot with a cosy.

Impatient to see the famous Taj Mahal, I stopped only for a brief look at Delhi, India's capital, on the way. In old Delhi, the narrow, crowded streets were lined with tiny food shops, tailors and bookstalls, and rows of barbers sat at the roadside waiting for clients. Cows meandered in among the crowds, and half-naked beggars were either sleeping or cooking on the dusty pavements. Even though New Delhi was also swelteringly hot, it formed an astonishing contrast to what I had just seen. I was most favourably impressed with how well it had been planned, sporting wide, shady avenues and spacious, flower-filled parks. There were drinking fountains everywhere, and houses were all set together in neat little blocks, each with a children's playground at the front.

Visiting the Taj Mahal was an impressive and unforgettable experience. Built by a moslem emperor as an immortal tribute to the memory of his beloved wife, it houses the cenotaphs of him and his queen beneath a pearl-white dome. For several hours I sat on some grass gazing up at the Taj, and as the moon rose, the white marble dome and minarets became even more breathtakingly beautiful, illuminated against the dark sky. The awful majesty of the scene was faithfully reflected by the still waters in a garden set before it.

By this time it was quite late, and I started to feel sleepy. Wandering along through Agra's now quiet streets, I wondered where I could pass the night. Then I remembered the railway station, and soon discovered that I wasn't the only person who had had that idea. The floor of the station was covered with a mass of sleeping people, a lot of them red-shirted coolies, who snored away in bedraggled looking rows. Lying down at the end of one of these rows, I used my anorak as a pillow and went to sleep.

A sikh family gave me a lift to Bombay, and I was walking along its Marine Drive enjoying the fresh, salty tang of the sea, when a large car stopped beside me. The owner invited me to accompany him to his air-conditioned office, where I would be able to cool off for a while. Some minutes later, I was sitting in his office, telling him all about myself. Mr Bhanu then said that my impression of India would not be complete unless I had stayed with an Indian family, so when lunch-time came around, he took me home with him. At the house I was introduced to Mrs Bhanu, her sister, Pritty, and a baby son. I was to sleep with Pritty, so I put my knapsack in her room, then showered and changed my clothes. Servants seemed to appear from every corner as if by magic, taking my travel clothes away to wash, cleaning my shoes, ironing my skirt and later showing me to the dining room.

That day, I was to eat my first hindu-vegetarian meal. I took my place with the family at a table, upon which was a silver tray for each person and various silver bowls. The cook himself served the meal, putting each variety of food into a separate bowl and huge mounds of rice in the middle of the trays. As he came to each of us in turn, I noticed that the cook was especially careful never to brush against our arms or any part of our clothing. When he had left the room, Mrs Bhanu explained why. "Our cook is a Brahmin, which is the highest caste in our hindu society. We are proud to have him to cook for us, but even I must not enter into his portion of the kitchen or touch his utensils. If he had accidentally touched one of us while serving the food, he would have washed himself all over and not eaten for the rest of the day. Eggs must not be brought into this house," continued Mrs Bhanu, "as we are all vegetarians, and he would be most offended if we broke the rule. Therefore, when I wish to give eggs to my little son, I take him out to a restaurant. All my family have tasted eggs, but never meat or fish," she concluded. We ate the meal with our hands, except for the buttermilk soup and the mango juice, which we drank from the bowls. Curds, groundnuts and goat's cheese helped to provide us with vegetarian proteins and I couldn't help noticing just how robust and healthy everyone looked on their diet, including the cook, who was a wiry old man with half an inch of grey stubble around his chin.

Mr and Mrs Bhanu were wonderful hosts, taking me to see many places even outside Bombay, such as the famous cave temples of Elephanta Island, Ellora, and Ajanta. My last meal in that sumptuous Bombay house was eaten sitting cross-legged on the kitchen floor, with a cheerful Mrs Bhanu serving us all. "It's the cook's day off," she said, with a twinkle in her eye. "No red carpet for you, you're one of the family now."

When I left Bombay it was early in the morning, and in the fields around the city people were squatting thoughtfully, their cans of water beside them. This common toilet isn't such a bad idea, I thought; after all, they were fertilising the land. Traffic on some of the south Indian roads was very scanty, and by nightfall that day I had covered at least forty miles on foot. Tired and footsore, I wandered into a tiny hamlet. The people there were extremely kind and hospitable; they greeted me like an old friend, took me straight to one of their huts and shared some sort of cake with me by the light of a candle. Suddenly I realised just how appropriate the cake was, for today I was nineteen years old.

In Cape Camorin, situated in the densely populated state of Kerala, I met an Italian doctor of sociology who invited me to go with him when he visited one of the fishing villages. Cape Camorin, or Kanya Kumari, is the 'land's end' of India. Here, the Arabian Sea, the Indian Ocean and the Bay of Bengal converge to send huge, white-crested breakers crashing noisily over jagged grey rocks. As I walked along the seashore with the doctor, I watched the frail-looking fishing boats setting out over the rough sea, some of them consisting of nothing save three planks joined together. People rushed to greet us as soon as we arrived at the village. Women wore cloths and men wore loin-cloths; both sexes were naked to the waist. Children ran around us quite naked, with air-filled paunches, scraggy limbs and hungry eyes. Many of the older people were going blind or covered in open sores. One youth came up to us leading a very old man in chains. "That's his father who they say is mad," explained the doctor, who spoke the local lingo. "These people are almost starving as it is not yet quite the fishing season," he continued. "I have had some surplus maize-flour delivered here, and now I am going to show the women how to make a sort of porridge with it." I followed the doctor into one of the two-roomed mud huts, which was about twelve feet square. "About fifteen people have to sleep in here when it rains," said the doctor. "In fine weather, they can sleep out on the beach." The hut was soon full to overflowing, as most of the women in the village had gathered around us for the cookery lesson. A wood fire was lit, on which to boil water, and it wasn't long before all our eyes were streaming in the smoky atmosphere. When the pot of water started to boil, the doctor added some of the maize-flour and stirred it into a paste, adding oil and salt later to make it palatable. The women nodded their heads in approval, and the children started to wail hungrily at the smell of the porridge. We left the hut and I asked the doctor why the villagers couldn't eat the enormous coconuts which grew on trees all around the village. "They all belong to rich merchants and are counted," answered the doctor. "If the fisherfolk were to pick them they would be thrown into jail for stealing." As we were saying goodbye to the villagers, one of the women ran up to me and thrust a baby into my arms. "She wants money for it," explained the doctor. "The money which she might get for selling this baby could be used on her others." Putting some rupees into the baby's little hand, I passed it gently back to its mother. My eyes filled with tears as I turned away and walked pensively back along the sands beside the professor, where dark-skinned fishermen were mending their nets, ready for the next battle with the sea. Before we reached the road I looked back, and my last view of that South Indian fishing village was a cluster of huts on a golden beach beside an azure sea, looking microscopic against the towering purple mountains behind them.

Soon I was on my way again, heading for 'the Pearl of the Indian Ocean,' — the island of Ceylon. Night fell, and I found myself on a deserted stretch of road not far from the coast. Making my way to the seashore, I came to a patch of sand which was shaded from the bright moonlight by a cluster of palm trees. I lay down, and was sent to sleep with a soothing lullaby, caused by a fresh breeze which made the palm trees sway and rustle against the song of the waves.

On the following morning I crossed on the Adam's Bridge ferry from India to Ceylon. I was feeling light-hearted and full of anticipation as I briskly covered my first few Singhalese miles.

My last lift to the capital was with a prosperous looking Singhalese who sported a white shark-skin suit. He told me that although he was very occupied with business, he would like to help me in any way that he could, as I was a foreigner in his country. When I told him of my wish to get to know lots of Singhalese people, and, if possible, to stay with a Singhalese family, he was delighted. "My own family are spread out like rabbits," he laughed. "I suggest that you go down to Matara immediately, where my Uncle Musa will be your host and introduce you to Singhalese village life; then when you are ready to return to Colombo you may stay with my cousin Khalid." Without more ado we went straight to an office from where we telephoned to Uncle Musa, warning him of my imminent arrival. Then this amazing gentleman popped me on to a bus, handed me a ticket, and wished me a good journey.

I found Matara to be a large village on the southern coast of Ceylon. The bus driver obligingly drove me right up to the door of Uncle Musa's house, where he and his family were waiting to greet me like a long lost sister. Uncle Musa, although unmarried, was the head of the household, as both his parents were dead. He was striving to be a good mother and father to his younger brother, Hasan, and his sisters, Aishah and Fatima. The two brothers had a gem-cutting business and a shoe-shop, and their sisters stayed at home to do the cooking and look after the house.

During my stay in Matara, while the family were busy, I would often take long walks along the beach, to meditate, read the Koran or practise reciting some newly acquired phrases in Arabic. How familiar that stretch of Singhalese coast gradually became to me, with its golden sands stretching far into the haze, interrupted every so often by smooth, red rocks about which the waves swirled and threw their white foam. Coconut palms swayed against an ever-changing sky, crowding raggedly down to where the beach began. As I climbed over the rocks and jumped down on to the firm sand, hermit crabs would scuttle out of my way, and a group of old fisherwomen always waved a cheery greeting to me, as they worked at softening up damp coconut husk with stones so that it could be made into rope.

How quickly the time seemed to pass in that friendly little Singhalese village. A week flew by like magic and then four, so that I was surprised one day when I received a note from cousin Khalid, telling me that his family were impatiently waiting for me to come and stay with them in Colombo.

Monsoon rains were turning the Colombo streets into rivers, as a family friend drove me to cousin Khalid's house. Enormous waves crashed over the sea-front, and I watched a marooned turtle swimming frantically along a gutter. Khalid's servant was away sick, and I was happy to discover that I could assist Sarah, his wife, in many ways, such as mopping up the water which had leaked through the roof, washing clothes and dishes, and taking Hatim, their three year old son, out for walks when the weather permitted.

"We're going to a place called Kataragama," called Sarah from the kitchen next day. "It is a sacred place not only for moslems, but for hindus and buddhists as well." There was no question at all as to whether I should become a pilgrim or not, as one of the family; everyone said that the pilgrimage would do me good. That night, an animated family conference concerning the trip kept us all wide awake until the early hours, but resulted in everything being arranged.

It was late afternoon when our convoy, a fourteen-strong mixture of family, friends and servants reached Kataragama, and after parking the cars, we walked straight to the centre of the activities. Entering the moslem section, we soon found the trustee of the mosque. When the others told him that even though I was English, I could recite many verses of the Koran in Arabic, he blessed me profusely and invited us all to spend the night in one of the rooms on the mosque premises.

18

"And now we are all going to go down to the river to make our ablutions before the evening prayers," said Khalid. By family vote, it was decided that I should not appear before the hundreds of pilgrims who would be washing, wearing my scanty, European bathing costume. "It is advisable that you cover your legs," said Sarah. "You can bathe in a sarong, as we Singhalese women do, pulling it up to beneath the armpits and securing it with a little twist." Nobody had a spare sarong with them so I wore her brother-in-law Jaleel's, and he wore the skirt of his wife's sari around his waist. Off we went to the wide, brown river, which was already crowded with pilgrims having their ceremonial wash. The water was cool and delicious, though in no place more than two feet deep. For the first few moments I splashed blissfully around, then suddenly forgetting all about pilgrims, little twists in sarongs, and the rather strong current, I plunged forward and started to swim. How heavenly! I sighed, and idly watched a sarong float swiftly past me downstream. There goes a familiar-looking sarong, I thought dreamily, and then with a jerk I realised that I should have been inside it. The eyes of about two hundred male pilgrims may have been thinking 'how heavenly', as they gazed at my naked body, for there was a noiseless interval in the ablutions. Suddenly I was rushed upon and surrounded by a throng of chattering women, and in the midst of their shielding bodies I was transported swiftly to the river bank, where Sarah had my own bathing costume all ready for me to put on. "Better with that than with nothing at all," said Delilah, a friend of Sarah's, prudently, and in the circumstances I think everyone agreed with her, as we made our way back to the river.

Before retiring to the mosque premises, we had a last look around at the still lively activities. Walking along an avenue lined with limbless beggars, some covered with leprosy, we came to the moslem section again. Drawn towards a crowd of spectators, we watched an elderly imam split open the flesh of a writing boy's stomach, with a large, bloodied knife. "To prove that faith overcomes all," whispered Sarah calmly by way of explanation. The imam terminated the operation by sticking some leaves over the wound he'd made. Wondering how it would heal, I turned my head, just in time to watch another man thrust a sharp dagger into his own throat so that it came out from the other side. While all this was going on, old men sat around, incessantly chanting verses from the Koran. Feeling as if I was floating in a weird, unearthly dream, I followed my friends to the mosque premises.

All fourteen of us slept on mats on the floor of our room, after saying goodnight to the trustee of the mosque. I only woke once during the night, to see Jaleel standing over his wife and Delilah saying, "The next one who giggles, I'm coming to get them." Then I remembered no more.

We had a comparatively uneventful drive back to Colombo, though arriving a little later than scheduled. This was probably due to the fact that both cars had had punctures, and because we lost Jaleel's party for three hours just outside Hambantota, when one of the servants had leapt out of the car to vomit and had got lost in the darkness.

"My cousin Ali is a mechanic at Radio Ceylon," Khalid told me one day. "If you would like him to show you around the station, I'll warn him to expect you."

My tour of the radio station was most interesting. I was taken to see the control room, the studios, the record making room and the theatre, being introduced by Ali to all sorts of fascinating people on the way. One of the announcers introduced himself as Cecil Pannasara, was the darkest Singhalese I've ever seen, and spoke English with an authentic Oxford accent.

Our conversation was interrupted for ten minutes while Cecil read the news, then he told me that I simply must give a talk about my travels over the air. Some voice tests ensued, and I was introduced to a Mr Gamini Amarasuriya who said that he would be happy to produce me. Mr Amarasuriya sat me in his office and bombarded me with questions concerning my overland journey to Colombo. Then he told me that if I would be willing to write a series of articles about my adventures, I could read them over the air on his teenage programme and so start to earn some money. I was delighted to accept this offer, as my funds were getting rather low. At that moment into the office walked the principal of the Buddhist Ladies' College, and soon I was promising to deliver a lecture to her young ladies on the following day.

My lecture at the Buddhist Ladies' College was a huge success, and after signing hundreds of autograph books, I was invited to have a bite with some of the parents and staff. One charming lady, a Mrs Maude Dahanayake, gave me a prompt invitation to stay at her home for the rest of my time in Ceylon. "You haven't yet stayed with a Singhalese buddhist family," she pointed out, her black eyes twinkling.

When I told Sarah and Khalid of my invitation that evening, they said that much as they would be sorry to lose their English sister, I must not miss such a wonderful opportunity to get to know another section of Colombo society. So the following morning, promising to keep in touch, I bade them goodbye, and Jaleel drove me away to Mrs Dahanayake's house.

My new hostess had decided that I must be able to write my scripts for Radio Ceylon to the best of my ability, and so had prepared for me a quiet, comfortable room at the top of her house, with her typewriter installed there for my use. Soon I was tapping away, and when I read over my first script to Mr Amarasuriya, he seemed to be quite delighted with it. Then he asked me. "Would you by any chance be interested to meet the world's first woman Prime Minister?" "Oh yes!" I cried, and before I knew what was happening I had an appointment to visit Mrs Sirima Bandaranaike at her home in Rosmead Place.

I talked with the Prime Minister for three-quarters of an hour and enjoyed every minute of it. She asked me all about my adventures on the way to Ceylon, and then she enquired jokingly, "How would you like to be the Prime Minister of Ceylon?" "Oh, I'm not very good at wearing a sari," I replied. "Never mind about that," laughed Mrs Bandaranaike, "you would make a nice change in a blouse and skirt."

Five and a half months flew by and I was still having a glorious time on that tropical island. Broadcasting regularly, giving my first blood donation, acting in plays put on by the International Theatre Group, there was never a dull moment. As the curtain fell at the end of an I.T.G. play one evening, I realised that so must the curtain fall on my happy stay in Ceylon; time would not wait for me, and I had so many other countries to visit. A quick departure left less time for sad fare-wells, and soon I was back in India again, heading up the east coast this time, from Madras to Calcutta.

I had a letter of recommendation from friends in Ceylon for a Mr Gajra in Calcutta, and was not a little surprised when he turned out to be a millionaire, owning, among other things, a few coal mines. "Would you care to stay with a very wealthy Indian family, or with a more typical one?" asked Mr Gajra as we sat in his air-conditioned office. "Oh, with a typical one, please," I replied, and half an hour later I was being introduced to a most charming Indian couple and their children. The eldest son, Balu, said that he would be delighted to show me the city, and off we went that same morning, after a good solid meal of rice with raisins, roti, and prawn curry. Balu's family were non-vegetarians but Mr Gajra's family were, I gathered, and both families were hindu.

The following morning, Balu awakened me early, as we were going to the big market to buy some goat's meat for lunch. We chose a fat goat, which was slaughtered for us while we waited. "Now we can be sure that the meat is fresh," Balu muttered. Fish, also, were being kept alive until the last moment, in buckets of water beneath the counters. Vendors sat cross-legged, smoking bidi cigarettes while waiting for customers, seeming to be lost in silent meditation and oblivious of the noisy atmosphere around them. We carefully stepped over a crateful of leopard cubs which were on sale, and, for a few annas, bought some fried grams to munch on the way home.

Even though I was living in Balu's house, I spent many happy days with Mr Gajra and his family, riding polo-ponies at dawn, playing croquet on green, well-watered lawns, and often going out to dine and dance in the evenings. During this time, I was also busy tripping around to the various shipping offices with Balu, enquiring about boats to Rangoon, my next destination. When Mr Gajra heard about this, he summoned me to his office. "You will fly to Rangoon and Bangkok," he said kindly, "don't worry about the money. My business colleagues and I are overcome with admiration for a girl who is attempting to do what you are doing and has got so far. We shall consider it a great pleasure to be able to help you in this way." I left the office, feeling overwhelmed by such generosity.

When the day of my departure arrived, I sat in the modern and comfortable waiting room at Dum-Dum airport, gazing at the massive, gleaming planes which stood on the concrete out-side. I had said my goodbyes and had time for a last-minute chat with Balu, who did most of the talking. "Do you remember that beautiful girl with whom we had some tea one day, in the house next to mine?" asked Balu in a low voice. "Well, I have been asking her parents for her hand in marriage for two years now. Her parents are far poorer than mine, and as she is not a strong girl, she may need expensive medical treatment later on. We love each other and I would give anything to be able to marry her, but I can't." "Why not?" I asked. "Because her family are of a higher caste than mine," explained Balu sadly.

The jet engines roared and I peeped out through the curtained window for a last look at India, far below, Balu's recent words still preying on my mind.

Chapter 3

December 1960–February 1961

A wave of hot air invaded the plane as the doors were opened at Mingaladon airport, about nine miles north of Rangoon. First to brave the heat, I stood on the steps of the plane, blinking in the brilliant sunshine. Before I knew what was happening, a man had dived up the gangway and pinned a large, purple orchid on to the fraying lapel of my shirt. A camera flashed and I smiled, wondering who on earth I was supposed to be. Just when things could have become rather awkward, I followed eyes which were staring past my shoulder and saw a fair young maiden who wore a coronet of lighted candles on her golden hair, a long, white dress and a disappointed expression. No wonder, that orchid should have been hers.

I didn't wait around to see how they sorted that one out. Wearing the sort of look which said that I was as used to receiving orchids as other people were handshakes, I skipped down the gangway and over to the air-terminal building to await the unloading of my knapsack. "That was meant for the 'snow-queen' from Sweden," said an airlines officer glumly, eyeing my orchid which was already wilting from the heat.

One of the airline's buses dropped me at a Rangoon cinema where a friend of Mr Gajra's was the manager. He introduced himself as U Khe Myint and his friend, U Tun Da. After showing me around Rangoon for a while, my new friends took me back to the cinema. "Ah, now you can meet Myiut Naung," said the manager gaily. "That's his mistress," whispered U Tun Da, "she also happens to be a successful Burmese film star."

Myiut Naung was exceedingly beautiful. She had long, blue-black wavy hair, shining, almong-shaped eyes, full red lips and sensuous, slightly flaring nostrils. She was well built,

24

bosomy and with honey-coloured skin. A gay cotton cloth was wrapped around her waist in Burmese style, and above it she wore a blouse of the softest silk. "I am so happy to have an English sister," exclaimed Myiut, and she kissed me on both cheeks. That evening we watched a film in Japanese with Burmese and English sub-titles, before returning to U Khe Myint's house. During the interval I put a question to Myiut which had been on my mind for some time. "Why do all Burmese men's names seem to begin with the letter U?" I asked. She gave a peal of laughter and then replied "'U' is just the equivalent of the 'Mister' which you use in the English language," she said, "it doesn't stand for anything at all."

That evening I ate my first Chinese meal, with my host and Myiut. "And now you will learn to use chopsticks," said U Khe Myint firmly. So, my lesson began. How patient were my teachers, and how elusive was that food! Shakily, I would just manage to get a piece of pork or a few grains of rice as far as my lips, and then splosh, my chopsticks would open and it would fall, usually into my glass of water or down the front of my blouse.

Then in a flash I found that I could do it, just as though I had been using chopsticks all my life. The others laughed at my enormous pleasure as I proudly demonstrated how I could pick up even the smallest piece of meat and get it right into my mouth.

Still due to the generosity of my friends in Calcutta, I had an air ticket in my pocket from Rangoon to Bangkok. Compared with my sojourn in India and Ceylon, my stay in Burma had been extremely short, yet I felt in my heart that one day I should like to return to that country, when changed circumstances would allow me to travel freely all over it and to absorb its beauty and culture to the full.

A Mr Thongchai Inkatanuvat met me at Bangkok airport. "U Khe Nyint sent me a telegram to tell me to meet you," he said. "I have arranged for you to stay with a lady friend of mine whose husband is away at the moment."

My hostess was a charming woman who said that although she was out at business most of the time, she would be delighted to have me to stay in her home. Mr Inkatanuvat left me in her care.

Early the following morning, a gentleman who introduced

himself as Mr Nai Vutthithornnetiraksa came to the house. He said that Mr Thongchai had told him about me and as he had to take some other visitors to see the floating markets that morning, thought that I might like to join them. "Oh, yes please! Mr Vutti . . . Vuttihi-thorn . . . er?" I began. "There is no need for you to attempt to pronounce my second name," said the man with a chuckle. "Here in Thailand we put the 'Mr' before our first names, hence, I am 'Mr Nai' – which is a little easier for you, isn't it?" "Yes, Mr Nai," I replied with some relief, and followed him out to where his car was waiting with two other visitors to Thailand perspiring in the back seat.

We went by boat up the river to the markets, passing under a drawbridge and then into a small canal. The banks of the river and the canal were crowded with wooden houses, where people sat munching their morning rice.

The 'floating markets' consisted of many small boats selling an enormous variety of things. I noticed fruit boats, vegetable boats, butchers' boats, coal boats, and even a boat which sold hot coffee and buns. In and out of these 'shop' boats wove women in smaller boats, doing their morning marketing. Most people were wearing large, round, flat-topped hats, which were an ideal protection from the hot, bright rays of the sun as the day wore on. Farther up the canal we came to some large cargo-cum-houseboats, whose owners sent their children to special riverside schools.

On the way back, we stopped to look at some long, narrow ancient boats, which had ferocious dragons' heads carved upon their prows, through the mouths of which pointed cannons. "These boats used to be employed in fighting long-ago battles," explained Mr Nai, "and were manœuvred by many oarsmen. Now they are used to transport our king on state occasions. He sits on a golden chair in the centre of one of the largest boats, shaded from the sun by a big umbrella."

One of the last things which I did before leaving Bangkok was to visit the Temple of the Emerald Buddha with my hostess. "It is said that anyone who has looked upon this Buddha will definitely return one day to Thailand," she said. "I'm sure that I shall," I replied, and really meant it.

One lift took me most of the way to Singapore, with three Malayan schoolteachers. The Malayan countryside was varied and interesting, with wide open spaces, rugged, rocky hills, or forests of palm-oil trees and rubber plantations. In Ipoh, we had a delicious lunch of sweet rice which had been cooked in a bamboo stem. Farther south, in Kuala Lumpur, we ate a truly Malayan breakfast. Lightly boiled eggs were served in glasses, and we spread our bread with a 'jam' made from a mixture of eggs, sugar and coconut. As we set out on the last stage of our journey to Johore Bahru and Singapore, somebody switched on the car radio. Suddenly the air was filled with the peaceful strains of 'Silent Night' and I realised that tomorrow would be Christmas Day. Yes, even out here, when it's eighty in the shade and the sun is setting over palm trees.

The name on my letter was Chi-Ching Chang, and I discovered its owner to be a plump, genial Chinese sitting in a luxurious office. After reading the letter of recommendation he said, "Your problems are now over in Singapore. From this minute you will be in the hands of my friends and myself, and we will help you in any way that we can. First of all we must find somewhere for you to stay." Chi-Chin Chang made a short telephone call in Chinese. "All settled," he said as he put down the receiver. "You will be staying with a girlfriend of mine, Katy Tseng-Wang. She lives in a house not far from my office with her parents and many brothers and sisters. I am sure that you won't be lonely," he added.

I wasn't. Not even at nights. When I went to bed with Katy in what I thought to be her room, sixteen other members of the family of various ages and sexes joined us. As the beds became full to overflowing, people unrolled mats and slept all over the floor.

The next morning, Katy said, "I'm not working today, so I'll show you around the 'China-town' of Singapore, and Tan, one of my brothers, will accompany us." When I wandered along the overcrowded streets of 'China-town' and saw the poles of drying washing stuffed through almost every window of each house, I came to the conclusion that sixteen people sleeping in one room might easily be considered to be comparatively few. "What are those houses without any washing hanging from the windows?" I asked Katy as we walked along. "Death houses," she replied casually. "It is there that the very poor Chinese put their dying, so that they won't get in the way of the living." Well, that's one way of looking at it, I thought, and noticed that next door to the 'death houses' there were usually

27

carpenters' shops where coffins were being hammered together, and other 'houses' where bodies were put to wait if there wasn't one ready in time. As if to round off this little sequence of events, a Chinese funeral procession came marching up the street. The men were wearing white hats and the women were wearing white robes with hoods covering their heads, the holes cut out for their eyes to peer through giving them a ghost-like appearance.

During my next week in Singapore, I earned a little money doing an interview for 'Woman's Hour' at the Rediffusion station. This led to my giving a talk on horse-riding and choosing six records for 'Shipwreck', a programme rather like the English 'Desert Island Discs'. I was kept quite occupied with all this, as well as with expeditions to the Tiger Balm Gardens, the Chinese Swimming Club and other places, with Kathy and my other new friends, which was great fun.

When New Year's Eve came around, Chi-Chin Chang said to me, "This evening we are all going to a special dinner at the Chinese Club, and then to a party afterwards." That dinner was unforgettable. There were roast geese, trout, oodles of noodles, mushrooms, prawns, crabs, salad and melon, cooked in its own skin and all mixed up with bamboo-shoot soup. For dessert we ate boiled yams and lychees, washed down with strong, green tea. After two and a half hours of solid eating, we all went off to the party, collecting Katy and Tan on the way.

Leaving our shoes at the door, we padded into the drawing room of Mr and Mrs Shen Shan, who were our hosts. I quickly made some new friends among the guests, one of whom had a tape-recorder and we made some mock interviews with it which were most amusing. Ng Ting Shih introduced me to a Mr Robert Wong who had flown over from Hong Kong for a couple of days, and who kindly invited me to be his guest when I went to the island.

At five minutes to midnight the sounds of Chinese fire-crackers came up through the open window. We all linked arms and sang 'Auld Lang Syne', which sounded very good in Chinese, Malay and English. Drinking games followed in which people were required to 'choose their weapon', then they had to drink it straight down while all the others chanted a short song.

When my ship sailed into the port of Hong Kong, I remembered that the words meant 'fragrant harbour' and I sniffed. A heterogeneous mixture of smells pervaded my nostrils, not quite what I should have described as 'fragrant', yet somehow very inviting. Robert Wong had kept his word and had come to meet me from the boat.

On the following day, after we had breakfasted on a sort of savoury porridge with lumps of meat in it, Robert dropped me where his friend Mrs Wai Chung Yee's motor launch was moored, and I found her already on board. In a few minutes she was taking me on a fascinating private tour of Hong Kong harbour, and I was soon to realise what an enormous number of the island's population spent almost the whole of their lives afloat. We came to an area where there was an unbroken mass of boats. "There are hundreds and thousands of them," said Mrs Wai Chung Yee as she stood beside me at the prow of her launch. "You will see shop boats, school boats, a hospital boat, and even a floating church among them."

Brian, Robert Wong's brother, not only spoke English better than I did, but when he discovered that my father was a member of the masonic brotherhood, he exclaimed, "Now I must be like a good uncle to you, because I am a freemason myself, and my sister here will be your Aunty Polly." Uncle Brian and Aunty Polly ran a transport company together and worked in the same office in a building in Queen's Road, so I used to pop in and chat to them quite often. They were always as sweet and kind as any real aunty and uncle could have been, especially when disaster befell me and I was really in need of their help.

The disaster came when I was standing in one of Victoria's tramcars during the Hong Kong 'rush hour' period. I had my money and passport in a shoulder bag, and was holding my hand firmly over the zip across the top, just in case. A few stops later, some people descended from the tram and I managed to get a seat. I had felt nothing, but when I sat down, I saw several articles whch I recognised to be mine, scattered over the floor of the tram. My money and passport were not among them. Fortunately, my traveller's cheques were safely in Robert's house, but I was horror-stricken with the thought that as a British subject abroad without a passport I might be sent straight home in disgrace. With tears streaming down my cheeks, and clutching my shoulder bag which had been slit down the side with a sharp instrument, I made my way to Uncle Brian and Aunty Polly in their office. When they heard my woeful tale, they calmly told me to cheer up. Aunty Polly gave me all the money that she had in her purse and said, "Now take this and stop crying. Money and passports are always being stolen in the colony. Didn't my brother Robert ever tell you about the pickpockets?" I nodded my head and she continued, "Go with Uncle Brian immediately to see an immigration officer who is a friend of ours, and I am sure that he will help you to get a new passport." Still sniffing sadly and feeling sick with worry, I followed Uncle Brian out of the door. Happily, Aunty Polly had been right. The kind immigration officer asked me some questions, then looking me sternly in the eye, he said, "If you'll stop crying this minute, I'll have a new passport for you by tomorrow morning." I did.

One morning, I decided to explore some of the tiny back streets of Victoria. I had my first ride in a sedan-chair up one very steep alley, and then continued the rest of my way on foot. Suddenly, I realised just how saturated with people Hong Kong island was. Those back streets were positively teeming with life. Little boys were cooking food with babies slung to their backs, old men puffed away at long, bamboo-cane pipes, and one woman sat at a pavement hairdressers, having her hair cut and wearing the same sort of expression that I'm sure she would have worn if she had been in a chic Paris salon. A lot of people sat eating, perched upon small wooden stools which had been placed on top of benches, so that their feet could rest on the benches and be right off the ground. There were cocks crowing from a crate beneath a pile of boxes, Mah-jongg tiles rattling, and children shouting gleefully as they painted hard-boiled eggs in different colours, preparing for the coming Chinese New Year. People, people, and more people, I thought, as I gazed around me. But these were only the healthy ones. Some minutes later I was making for the Red Cross Blood Bank of Hong Kong.

"We're glad of all the blood we can get here," said the nurse as she stuck a needle into my arm. "All the blood which we take in one day will be used up within twenty-four hours." As I was about to leave the blood bank, I asked the nurse if there was any other way in which I could help. "Come along on Monday morning," she said, "a pair of extra hands will be most useful."

Early the next Monday morning, I arrived at the Red Cross

Blood Bank to find Jane, the nurse, in quite a flap. "The official transport hasn't arrived yet," she said. "We mustn't be late, so we'll have to take a taxi." I didn't have time to ask where we were going, I just donned the spare uniform which Jane had put out for me, helped her to pack up the transfusion equipment, and hugging some of it, jumped into the taxi beside her. We sped off to the docks, and suddenly, there was H.M.S. *Hermes* looming up in front of us. "She's an aircraft-carrier," explained Jane. "We're going to take blood transfusions from the men on board." We went straight down into one of the dormitories, and while we got busy unpacking bottles and cutting up Elastoplasts, the first batch of 'victims' lay down on the bunks and rolled up their sleeves. "Any questions?" asked Jane, heading towards the first, rather anxious-looking man with a needle. "Yes, how can I get out of here?" wailed a forlorn voice from the corner. We all laughed, and any tension which there had been at once disappeared.

On the following morning, we were back on board H.M.S. *Hermes* again, continuing the same procedure as before. When we had completely finished, and were putting the bottles of blood into the refrigerator at the blood bank, Jane said in a satisfied voice, "We have taken over two hundred pints of blood in two days." I think I must have been as pleased as she was.

The Chinese New Year drew very close, until it was only one week away.

"What a pity that you cannot be with us for the New Year," said Aunty Polly, and her brother heartily agreed. "It is the time when we eat lots of delicious, special food, go every night to the cinema, and have a really wonderful time!" I was sorry too, but my boat passage to Japan was booked for the following day, and as there would not be the chance of another for some time I felt I must go – I had spent a month in Hong Kong already.

So the New Year's Eve found me somewhere in the East China Sea, and the Chinese lady who shared my cabin gave me a doll for a New Year's gift. I loved my little Chinese doll and called her 'Fat Choy'. That name isn't as uncomplimentary as it sounds. It means 'New Year' in Cantonese.

Chapter 4

February 1961–March 1961

My first few days in Japan were not spent with Japanese, but with an Irani family, who had been passengers with me on the boat from Hong Kong. They took me to their house in the country, somewhere between Kobe and Osaka. After spending a couple of days with these kind Irani people, I told Mr Riahi that I would be hitch-hiking to Tokyo on the following morning. My host instantly looked quite alarmed, saying that the weather was still far too cold for hiking. That evening, when he came home from his work, he pushed a train ticket into my hand. "You can do the same for me if ever I come to England," he said with a smile.

The journey to Tokyo took ten hours by express train. I sat looking out of the window for a long time, gazing at the snow-covered countryside, from which russet-coloured trees stood motionless against the blue sky. The train sped on, beside the Pacific Ocean wide and blue, to the port of Yokohama. Darkness fell and soon milliards of lights came into sight. We had reached the city of Tokyo.

A few minutes later I was standing in the Ginza, the main street, trying to spot somebody in the crowds who looked as though he spoke a little English. My shoulders began to go numb with the weight of my knapsack and, shifting its position, I started to walk. When a group of young men who were unmistakably students of some sort stepped jauntily out from a cinema I asked them in simple English if there happened to be a Y.W.C.A. in the city. They were most polite and helpful, not only saying that there was one, but taking me right up to its door.

I rang the bell, and a Japanese girl of about my own age peeped out. She invited me into the hostel, and was most

32

Setting off to cross Saudi Arabia

On a rusting 'ship of the desert' . . .

. . . and more modern transport

Minding the
flock outside
Baghdad

Breakfast in an
Adeni palace

Red Sea in
the sunset

intrigued to learn that I was English and travelling all over the world to get to know about life in other countries. "I'm glad now that I was kept working late tonight," she said, smiling warmly. "My name is Nagako Ishikawa. If you would like to, you may come home with me and stay with my family. I shall be going to the U.S.A. next year to study, and it would be a great help to me now to have someone around with whom to practise my English. And you could learn something of our Japanese customs," she added.

I happily accepted Nagako's kind invitation, and we went by tube train to the suburb of Tokyo in which she lived. We were both too tired to eat very much, and soon were lying down in the darkness between Nagako's already sleeping sisters, on mats made from rice straw. Soft eiderdowns kept us warm and soon we too were asleep.

The next morning I awoke to find myself in a square room with walls made from a kind of paper. I blamed myself for being only half awake when, as I watched one of the walls, I saw it slowly begin to move to one side. Then a sleepy voice beside me said, "This house is built in the typical Japanese style, Wendy. The outside is made of wood and the inner walls are paper screens, which open by sliding to one side, so that no inside doors are necessary. This is so that if ever the house falls down during one of our not uncommon earthquakes, there will be less chance of us all getting buried alive."

Breakfast was raw fish on boiled rice, washed down with green tea. We ate with chopsticks, which Nagako said were called 'hashi' in Japanese, all kneeling back on our heels around a very low table. Nagako's mother wore a gaily coloured kimono, and her father a dark brown one.

We spent the morning sight-seeing, wandering around the big stores in Shiboya and on Ginza Street, stopping at a tiny restaurant for a snack of noodles which cost forty yen. "That's about tenpence in your money," said Nagako.

When I had been staying at Nagako's house for about three weeks, and she was going through a particularly busy stage at her office, I decided to look up a gentleman whose name had been given to me by Chi-Chin Chang. Following the directions which Nagako had written for me on the back of an envelope, I had no trouble in finding the office of Mr Soryo Toyoda.

Mr Toyoda was a man of about forty, tall, slim, and knowledgeable. He was delighted to hear that I was already staying with a Japanese family and enjoying learning about the customs of his country. After a nice lunch together of eel and rice, we had our coffee on the roof of the Maruzen department store building, where there was a putting green, and some of the store's employees were busy putting in a round or two before going back to work. "Just call me Soryo, instead of Mr Toyoda," said my new friend, and soon we were discussing a very wide variety of subjects, as though we had known each other for years.

By the time that we had finished our fifth cup of coffee, it was all arranged for me to pack my things and to meet Soryo at his office on the following morning to visit the Hakone hot springs.

The road to Hakone wound through hilly, wooded country, and then along beside the Pacific Ocean.

"The baths in this hotel are all fed from hot springs," said Soryo, "so you will notice that the water tastes and smells of sulphur. If you wish, you can bathe in the big bath with me and my friends, which would be quite acceptable, here in Japan. However, as the only girl present, you might feel a little awkward with so many naked men around you." When I said that I thought I would, Soryo continued, "In that case, take your bath in a private bathroom beside the room in which you will sleep, and I shall come and call you in time for dinner."

In my room I found two kimonos, an over one, made from brown, thick material and a cotton lining, in green and white stripes. Later, after a long soak which almost had me fainting, I climbed out of my hot, sulphur-smelling bath, and donned the kimonos just as Soryo was coming to tell me that dinner was being served.

We dined on 'tempura', which was fried prawns, meat and fish, cooked in batter and eaten on top of boiled rice. There was also a lot of 'sushi' and some seaweed soup, the last course being tangerines and green tea.

When everything had been cleared away, a host of smiling geisha girls appeared, to entertain the men. However, when they caught sight of the pink-faced stranger at the end of the line, they all flocked towards me, and in delightful, broken English, asked me all kinds of questions about myself and my country, until the men began to complain about their lack of attention and to call for some saké, a potent rice wine, which would be brought to them hot.

The geisha girls hurried away gracefully, returning with piles of small, porcelain bowls, into which they poured hot saké for everybody. Having already tried some of this Japanese liquor, I knew that it had quite a kick, so I kept on passing my bowlsful to Soryo, who obligingly drank them for me. By this time, a group of the geishas were dancing in the centre of our circle, using their eyes most expressively all the time, and others were singing to the music of a kind of Japanese lute. All through the evening, our bowls of saké kept being replenished by the nimble geishas, and the men were becoming more convivial and relaxed.

Yet another time, my bowl was full of hot saké, and fearing that Soryo would never survive the evening if he had any more, I beckoned to a young, jolly-looking geisha girl and offered it to her. She drank it, probably out of politeness, and then knelt down in front of me to have a chat, telling me that her name was Yukiko and that she was nineteen years old. As we talked, my saké bowl kept being refilled, and I would automatically hand it over to my new friend, who would drink it, just as automatically. Gradually, Yukiko's already rather shrill voice became louder and her conversation became more personal. "I don't like the Japanese, only foreigners," she suddenly exclaimed with a most ungeishalike belch and passed out. As she was being hauled away, amidst the unsuppressed giggles of the other geishas, I smiled sheepishly at Soryo, for I knew that I had been partly responsible.

The following morning I asked Soryo about the geisha girls who'd danced for us the night before. "Is that all they do in life?" I enquired. "Well, sort of," he said, adding with a smile, "If a man wants one of them to entertain him in other ways he has to pay for it very dearly. Yes, those girls are far more refined than prostitutes and to become a geisha, they have had years of hard training. We'll take you to a proper geisha house now if you like."

The geisha house stood on the banks of the river, surrounded by a large, Japanese garden. An elderly lady opened the door and led us into a fourteen-mat room. "She's the 'mama' of the geisha girls," explained Takuya, a friend of Soryo's who had come with us, and with whom I was going to stay. We removed our shoes and sat cross-legged on the mats, and then, one by one, the girls came in. They were all very pretty indeed, wearing their long, black hair piled up on to their heads, with decorative pins holding it in place. Their kimonos were of so many different hues that I could imagine them to be like variegated butterflies fluttering around us. I realised just how thoroughly these girls had been taught to entertain their clients, and to make them feel comfortable in so many different ways. One geisha brought us soft arm rests and placed them beneath our elbows. Another came into the room carrying platefuls of enormous strawberries which she set down before us. Yet another one bore in jugs of steaming saké, and some dried fish for us to nibble as we drank.

We sat enjoying the food and drink, while the geisha girls, who all spoke some English, hovered around us and chatted to me about my journey, finding it almost incredible that a young girl like them could have travelled so far alone. Then one of them asked me to sing them an English song. This I did, and they were so delighted about it that they got up immediately and began to dance for us, holding weird and amusing masks in front of their faces. "Would you like to join in?" asked one of the geishas when the dance was over. "Of course!" I replied, as they chose two simple dances that were easy for me to follow. One was called 'The Baseball Dance', and the other was translated as 'The Roadworker's Dance'. Both of them contained a lot of mimicry, and I simply followed the others. When we had finished off the last giant strawberry, Soryo said, "I am going to invite five of these geisha girls to come out to supper with us, so we must leave now, before it gets too late."

As we drove around the city, I saw nothing of the bright lights and bustle – being squashed firmly into the back seat of Soryo's car, with two heavily perfumed geisha girls on either side of me.

After supper we took the geisha girls home and then Soryo dropped his friend Takuya and me at Takuya's house, and disappeared into the night. "Meet Michiko, my wife," said Takuya, as a smiling, beautifully dressed lady opened the door of the house and bowed low. "I am so pleased to meet you, Wendy," said Michiko, as we sat in the Kobayashis' very European looking drawing room. "As you can see, the downstairs of my house is Western, but upstairs, it is decorated in the Japanese style. But now you must be very tired, so I shall show you to our guest room. Tonight you will be sleeping in a bed, instead of on a mat!" she concluded with a warm smile.

On one of the many entertaining evenings I spent with Takuya and his wife, having thoroughly enjoyed a visit to the theatre we had dinner in town and then went for a walk through some of Tokyo's narrower streets. "What a lot of amusement arcades they have here!" I remarked, as the clatter of slot machines became deafening. "They're 'pachinko parlours'," explained Takuya. "People put money into a slot, metal balls spin round and round, and if they drop into the right hole the prize is candy." "No money?" I asked. "No, only candy," confirmed my host. Great crowds of Japanese were grouped round the machines. Looking as though they were playing for their very lives, the gamblers pushed their yen into the slots, and, still without the ghost of a smile, would gather up their candy—if they were lucky.

During my stay in his house, Takuya Kobayashi found out all about boats for my next destination, the Philippines, and one day he told me that it was all arranged, and that I would be leaving Japan from Kobe harbour on a Japanese cargo boat which usually accepted a few passengers.

On the following day, I went aboard the twenty-five year old Japanese cargo boat that for the next twelve days would be my home. I stood leaning over the rail, watching boxes of wireless sets, cameras, and other Japanese goods come on board, bound, as I was, for the Philippines.

Our first port of call was Wakamatsu, where the ship's radio officer, who spoke better English than any other member of the crew, told me, "Here, we have the world's second longest tunnel under the sea. It is called the Kammon Tunnel." I went with him right through the tunnel and back on an express bus, while we were in port, 'just for the experience'.

Moji was our next stop, and some hours later, we were moving steadily through the choppy waters of the East China Sea, heading in the direction of Taiwan. Uncle Syoji, as the radio officer was called, had lost no time at all in introducing me not only to his captain but to every member of the crew, who were all very polite, yet with a wonderful sense of humour.

That evening after dinner, I went up on to the bridge and found the first officer doing his watch. He was busy looking at the stars through a sextant, trying to plot an accurate course.

"This ship has no mechanical course-finder," he said, when he caught sight of me watching him. With the help of three stars and a lot of trigonometry, he finally plotted our route, and then we stood looking down at the black waves, sipping green tea and munching the 'pachinko' candy that I had won from a Tokyo slot machine.

My first glimpse of Taiwan was a mysterious-looking island, with forested mountain peaks, towering upwards through an early morning mist. Soon, we were entering the port of Keelung. After lunch that day, Uncle Syoji accompanied me on shore, and we meandered along the crowded streets of the old seaport.

Night seemed to fall very quickly, and as the streets became full of puddles and soldiers, the latter due to a recent scare that there might be an invasion from communist China, Uncle Syoji suggested that we board one of the old buses and get back to the quayside.

On the following morning, I stood watching the dock-workers as they unloaded bags of flour, soya beans and metal sheeting, during the heavier showers of rain. They were dressed in thick sacks and round hats, but their feet were bare, which seemed to be highly practical in that warm, wet climate. Seated on the edge of the jetty was the captain, patiently fishing with a small hook and line.

The next day we arrived in Kaohsiung harbour, where we were given a thorough inspection by the immigration authorities and as I had noticed several American gunboats and destroyers standing in the port, I guessed that the threat of a communist invasion still prevailed.

At last the final crate of oranges swung up on to the deck and was stored safely next to some Coke which we had loaded from Keelung. With a whistle, we were off. I stood at the rail, watching Taiwan disappear into a heat haze, and soon a rasping cough told me that my Japanese uncle was at my side. "You're lucky that our captain isn't superstitious," he remarked. "The Chinese agent in Kaohsiung told our captain to leave you behind, saying that it is very unlucky for a ship to carry only one girl on board, for it could make King Neptune angry and then he would cause the ship to perish in a storm."

The closer we came to the Philippines, the more festive was the mood which prevailed among my shipmates, for they were all looking forward to a night out in Manila. The purser took to appearing regularly in white shorts and a Hawaian-type shirt, the first officer gave me a hair shampoo, and the captain told me that if I wished to wash my clothes before we came into port, I could dry them quickly in the ship's funnel. On the evening before we arrived in Manila, the purser made a colossal goodbye pineapple pie for me and we shared it all around the ship.

Tall, white buildings were our first glimpse of the Philippine capital, from across a calm blue bay. When we drew into the quayside, the customs check was so lengthy that I absent-mindedly began to play with two revolvers which the police had found and confiscated. Suddenly I realised that everyone was looking at me, including the chief customs officer, thinking that the weapons were mine.

A nasty situation might have arisen, if it weren't for the fact that at that precise moment a handsome Filipino bounced into the room, wearing a sunny smile and a brilliant red shirt. "Where is Miss Wendy Myers?" he called, and when I stepped forward he explained that Soryo Toyoda had wired him from Tokyo, telling him to take care of me during my stay in Manila. "My name is Mauro Ortega," he said, "and I am an old friend of Soryo." After giving a brief explanation to the now smiling police in Tagalog, Mauro said, "If you'd like to accompany me, my car is waiting on the quay."

Sadly, I bade farewell to the kind officers and men on board that sturdy, Japanese boat, saying a special 'thank you' to poor Uncle Syoji, who was at that time lying on his bunk, suffering badly with his liver.

As Mauro's spacious, shining car took me quickly away from the docks, I turned my head and looked back, just once. Above the warehouses fluttered a white flag, charged with a red sun. "Sayonara, Nippon Koku," I whispered. "See you again, Land of the Rising Sun."

Chapter 5

March 1961–June 1961

"You're just in time to come with my family to our farm near Batangas where we'll be spending Easter," said Mauro. "I am a lawyer, which is often arduous work, so I like to get away to the farm and relax whenever I have the opportunity." "Are you a pure Filipino?" I asked. "There's no such thing!" said Mauro with a laugh. "The Philippine Islands are a melting-pot of many races, Malays, Chinese and Spanish being the main ones. That's why we all look so different. Some are fair-skinned and Spanish looking, some are as dark as southern Indians, and some are like Chinese. We are mostly Roman Catholics, having been under Spanish rule for about three hundred years. However, there are some tribes of Moros in the south who are moslems, and some pagan tribes in the north." "But are you independent now?" I asked. "Oh yes," replied my friend, "we have been an independent republic since July 4th, 1946."

Mauro's wife, Lydia, was young and charming, and we took to each other immediately. "Jose, Norma and Elsa, come and meet your new sister," she called up a wide, marble staircase. A door banged somewhere above, and small feet were soon pattering down into the hall. "Jose is ten, Norma is eight and Elsa is five," Lydia informed me. "Batangas! Batangas!" suddenly shouted little Elsa and danced around her father. "They can't wait to be off," Mauro laughed, and turning to his wife, asked gaily, "Are all the things packed, darling?"

Soon we were all climbing into Mauro's car. There were eight of us, as my host had a driver, and Lydia had brought a maid along to help look after the children. The drive to Batangas took us two and a half hours and was most interesting. Horsedrawn carriages trotted up and down the country roads, pigs would run squealing out of our way, and behind one plantation of waving coconut palms we saw a high mountain, crowned with fluffy clouds.

That evening after a large supper, Lydia left the children in the care of her maid, and she and her husband took me to see what they called 'our village'.

We sat in a wine shop, Lydia and Mauro swapping news with their friends for a long time. "They say they're looking forward to the cockfight on Saturday," said my host, when at last we stood up to leave. "And the bear-baiting?" I enquired solemnly. "No," said my host, half stifling a guffaw, "but anyway, even if, as I suspect, you normally disapprove of blood sports, I'm going to take you along on Saturday and show you this ancient pastime of the Filipinos!"

Enthusiasm tends to be contagious, and when Saturday morning came, I found myself looking forward to the afternoon cockfight as much as the others. We all rode until lunch-time, and after an early meal, went straight to the cockpit which was already swarming with hopeful gamblers and their cocks. A lot of shouting and betting was going on. I bet two pesos – about three shillings and eightpence – on a black, tough-looking bird, and soon the fights began. The owner of the black cockerel brought it down close to the cockpit where the brown opponent which he'd chosen for it was waiting in its owner's arms. The owners removed sheaths from the steel spurs of their birds. "The natural spurs of cockerels vary so much in size that they are all equipped with steel spurs of equal length to fight with," said Mauro, "also, it makes the fight more humane by getting it over quicker."

Soon the cocks were struggling and lunging towards each other, eager to begin their battle, and the handlers placed them gently on the ground. With necks outstretched and hackles ruffled, the enemies began by feinting at each other with leaps off the ground. Suddenly, the black cock flew at the neck of his brown opponent, who quickly ducked, so that the black cock went whizzing over its head. The brown cock then had the advantage, and although its rival turned sharply, it wasn't sharp enough and with a kick the brown cock sank his spur deep into the breast of its enemy. However, by some strange reflex action, the black cock's leg came back with unexpected force, impaling the throat of its adversary with a shining spur. Quickly the handlers lifted up the two bleeding cocks and held them face to face. "In the rules of cocking the winner must always give its opponent two last pecks," Mauro informed me, "to show that it is still willing to fight." The black cock was. Raising its head it lunged.

One morning not long after our return to Manila, I sat down to breakfast and exclaimed, "It's my anniversary today!" "Oh, I didn't know you were married," said Lydia brightly. "I'm not," I laughed, "but it's April 4th, 1961 today, and my first anniversary of setting off to travel all over the world." "Then we'll be taking you out on the town tonight," said Mauro, and left for his office.

That evening, after the children had been put to bed, Lydia, Mauro, his mother and father, whom we usually referred to as 'Lola' and 'Lolo' as their grandchildren did, and I, got into Mauro's car and headed towards town.

"It's all strictly illegal," Lydia told me, as I entered a casino for the first time in my life. It was strange to step out of a dark street, walk through a dim lobby, and then arrive in such a place, dazzling with lights, bustling with life and colour, full of smoke and suspense. The red carpets were soft and thick, and upon the walls, scenes from Monte Carlo's famous casino had been painted, to help strike the right atmosphere.

Lydia, Mauro and Lolo were soon engrossed in a game called Blackjack, which looked like pontoon and didn't interest me very much. Taking a tenderloin steak sandwich from one of the trays, I walked around, looking for a game which had a bit more life to it.

At one side of the casino stood a long table, and whatever was happening there seemed to be attracting a lot of attention, so I threaded my way over to it. This other game, I found, was being played with dice. Players placed their bets on numbers which were marked on the table-top. Then a man called a 'shooter' threw the dice, and people were winners if their numbers came up.

Eager for a bit of exercise, I took the dice and started throwing, and judging by the whoops and yells around me I was lucky, so lucky that after my first ten throws or so the man whose job it was to dole out the winner's chips started to grumble, saying that I was losing too much money for the house, though with a twinkle in his eye. 'Beginner's luck' seemed to be mine that evening, and when Lydia and the others came and told me that it was time for us to go home, I had a pile of chips in front of me which amounted to sixty-seven pesos, about six pounds in English currency. We exchanged our chips for notes with the cashier, and stepped out into the night.

Towards the end of May, I thought I'd better start finding out about boats which could take me to Australia. I spent many hours traipsing around various shipping offices and always received the same reply to my question: "Nothing until the end of the year."

One of the shipping agents in an office I visited was very keen to hear all about my travels and expressed great interest in the fact that I was travelling alone. "But how does a young girl like you protect herself?" he enquired at last. "With words," I replied. "My mother always said I could talk the hind leg off a donkey." "Well, in my opinion that's not enough," said the Filipino, firmly. "I'm going to practise judo tomorrow evening, would you like to come and try it?" Judo! I thought excitedly, Japanese judo! "I'd love to," I said, "and how wonderful that I shall be starting it on my birthday. It's May 25th tomorrow and I shall be twenty years old." "That's fine," exclaimed my new friend, who introduced himself as Crispin Cacnio. And so the judo was arranged, which was, in a later stage of my journey, to help save me from 'that fate worse than death'.

On the following evening, Crispin took me to the dojo, carrying a T-shirt and a spare kimono for me. "You'll have to wear a brown belt, I'm afraid," he laughed, "I lost my white one years ago!" "As long as nobody forgets that I'm only a beginner," I said, aware that the status of 'brown belt' was high on the scale of judo efficiency. "As a black belter, I have the right to instruct," Crispin informed me as we limbered up with the other judocars. "I often help the chief instructor here, if he has to go on holiday or something." On that first evening, I learned how to fall which was important as I was to do a lot of it, how to roll, which I rather enjoyed, and how to throw Crispin over my hip, which gave me an enormous thrill. Then we did a bit of grappling and close combat, during which I forgot for a moment that this was judo and not a 'free for all' and kicked Crispin hard, in the chest. He was rather cool for a while after that, but being a good teacher, he patiently continued my lesson and at the end, after our final bows, he told me that I was very strong for a girl and should

43

take up the sport seriously. "Now you'll be stiff as it's your first time," Crispin added, "so before we leave the dojo I'm going to give you a massage. Lie down." When I lay down on my stomach, my teacher walked all over me, until I felt as if all the breath had been squeezed out of my body. However, as my muscles tightened and then relaxed, I discovered that this new form of massage had an exhilarating effect, removing any aches which had lingered after the many falls I'd taken.

Throughout the rest of my stay in the Philippines, I practised judo three times a week, and one evening Crispin introduced me to a friend of his named Benjo who was a newspaper reporter. Benjo told me of a coming religious fiesta which would be taking place at Obando, a coastal village of the Bulacan state. "A lot of press and television people will be going," he said. "You must join us and see some very old customs."

On the day of the fiesta, Benjo met me at the Ateneo University, and with many actors, artists and television folk, we climbed into a special bus and set off. The streets of Obando were gaily decorated with coloured flags, and once off the bus, we threaded our way through the bustling market to the ancient church. As my eyes became used to the dimness within, I could make out throngs of people who were paying homage to the saints by crawling on their hands and knees from one end of the church to the other, and then kissing the feet of some statues at the altar. Other groups of people were burning wax candles which had been moulded to form different parts of the human body; arms, legs, hearts, heads, etc. I nudged Benjo. "Why are they doing that?" I asked. "Well," he explained, "if their arm is sick they burn an arm, and if their foot is sick they burn a foot, and so on. When the candle has burned away, then they believe that they will be cured."

We left the church and wandered around the market for a while, lunching on local foods from the stalls. I ate a lot of shrimps and shared a huge lobster with somebody from the press. A camera flashed and a photograph was taken which later appeared in a Manila newspaper, along with an article all about my various exploits on the way from England to the Philippines, for I had been interviewed by one of their reporters some time before my birthday.

One day an uncle of Crispin's, a man called Solero Lingad,

told me that he was going to drive out to a small village in the country the next week to stay for a few days with his brother Manuel, who owned a cattle ranch there. He asked me if I'd like to go with him, and I gratefully accepted, eager to see more of Philippine country life.

From the moment I saw it I loved that friendly wooden house that lay in a green river valley surrounded by forested hills. Dogs came and barked their greetings to us, with Manuel running along behind. He embraced his brother and then welcomed me warmly, saying that the ranch was my home for as long as I wished. Very soon I was being shown all over it, and the contented-looking carabaos, cows, bulls, ponies, chickens and baby calves filled me with delight. The days that followed were some of the most enjoyable of the whole of my seven years abroad: hunting wild pigs at night, going for long, wonderful rides over the hills on Manuel's ponies, riding the carabaos, the 'water buffaloes', to the water-hole and back, feasting on goat or sheep in the evenings, or just standing in a high place, looking down over the ranch, the pineapple plantation, and the rolling green hills to the deep, hazy blue of the South China Sea beyond.

It was on the ranch, too, that I had one of the most memorable meals of my travels. Talking to Jaime, the cook, in the outside kitchen, I had come across a dead dog lying behind a sack of rice. "Oh, the poor thing!" I exclaimed. "How did it get here?" "Manuel bought it in the market this morning," replied Jaime. "We're going to have it for dinner." Robert Wong, in Hong Kong, had fascinated me when he'd said that I would have the opportunity of eating dog's meat in the Philippines; but somehow, seeing it lying there, skin and all, it didn't seem quite the same as buying half a pound of it at the butcher's shop. There, animals cease to be 'our dumb friends' when they turn up as 'cutlets', 'a joint', or, better still, 'mince-meat'.

As Jaime started to cook the dog, I sat and watched. After removing the skin he boiled it. Then he threw the water away and put it to boil again, this time adding coconut wine, garlic and onions to the water to make a tasty soup. "The first lot of water is always thrown away, as dog's meat is very strong," he explained, when at last he dished it up, liberally daubed with a piquant, blood-coloured local sauce over huge mounds of rice.

I must say I found it delicious, and not unlike the goat's meat with which I was by now so familiar.

My last day on Manuel's ranch came far sooner than I would have wished, but as Solero had some pressing business affairs to attend to in Manila, and I had to see about my ship for Australia, it could not be postponed.

I'd only been back in Manila a few days when I received the news from a shipping office agent that, owing to an important convention of the Rotary Club, an extra P. and O. boat would be sailing for Australia, and I would probably be able to book a passage on it. My ticket cost about fifty pounds, and as I paid him, the shipping agent smiled and said, "Nice ports, handsome stewards, good food. What more do you want?" which made me laugh, but I knew I'd have to find a job as soon as I got to Australia as my funds were now very low. The money which I'd won at the cockpit and in the gambling casino had helped, along with the cheque which my parents had sent me for my birthday. Above all, the hospitality of the wonderful people whom I'd encountered on my journey so far, had helped my original one hundred pounds to diminish at the very slowest possible rate, but now the wallet which held my traveller's cheques was thin indeed.

My ship came into port, and when at last the time came for me to go aboard her, I was by no means alone. Such a procession of friends had never seen me off before! Crispin held my passport, Jaime carried my knapsack, another friend clutched a bag of Filipino provisions (in case I should have lost my taste for English food), Benjo waved passes for himself and Mauro (nobody else seemed to have one), Solero was helping his niece to jump over rain puddles, and I trailed behind them all, trying to remember who had my ticket.

When they had all gone away, I stood alone in a corner of the deck, with odd reminiscences from my past three and a half months in the Philippine Islands rushing through my mind like a film. A wonderful ride with the Ortega family at the Manila Polo Club, and a changing room called 'mares', a swim from a beach at Cavite in the Manila Bay, and leaping out of the water in sudden pain from the stings of hundreds of tiny jelly fish. A dance at the village of Antipolo on a hot afternoon, and sipping halo-halo while watching laughing children bathe beneath a silver waterfall, and those numerous afternoons when

I'd eat with a group of friends discussing religion, politics, life and love, over an afternoon tea of passion fruit and boiled dog.

The ship's whistle blasted into my thoughts, warning everyone that she would soon be off, and the little lights of Manila twinkled a friendly goodbye. Then from somewhere on shore, the words of a Spanish song wafted out to us across the water, saying '*Vaya con Dios*'.

Chapter 6

June 1961–1962

The sea was a deep surging blue, lifting up foamy wave-crests as our ship passed beside the Great Barrier Reef, and the biting cold added to the choppiness of the waters kept most passengers below decks. I leaned over the rail, gazing out on to the bleak sea-scape. Four days later, Sydney, said to have the finest harbour in the world, came into sight. The ship glided slowly through a 'gateway' of rocky headland, against which crashed thundering waves. It was early morning, and as I watched, the brilliant lights which had illuminated the Sydney Harbour Bridge faded in the brightness of the dawn.

When we docked, I heaved my knapsack on to my back and made my way to the Commonwealth Employment Agency to find work. Unsuccessful there, I decided to specialise, and made for the Nurses' Employment Agency, where a plump, cheerful soul asked me a lot of questions, gave me the address of a hospital and wished me luck.

Nursing, I was soon to discover, was hard work. All our patients were over sixty, and most of them had reached their dotage, having to be fed, bathed and changed just as if they were babies again. The hospital was quite a large one, and there were three other assistant nurses on the staff, plus two trained nurses and the matron.

Soon, I was 'dug in' to the daily routine, washing dishes, linen and bottoms, emptying bed-pans, shaving the male patients and doing the hair of the female ones, wearing a white overall and a cap which I had starched so much that it had cracked in three places. Every job was new and interesting to me, and all the patients, I found, had different personalities and were often very lively.

My Sydney days passed quickly, with matron scolding me

Crossing bridges in Ceylon

In 'Sunday best' with a
Ceylonese sister

Going gay in Punjabi costume in Calcutta

Crossing the East China Sea

Behind a Burmese harp

Outside Nagako's house in Tokyo

every so often, or 'going crook', as the Australians would say. By the end of two months I had a useful amount of money in the Post Office savings bank, so when matron told me one morning that the girl whose place I'd been taking had come back to work, I trotted off to the employment exchange once more. The woman at the desk said there was a vacancy for a girl to work at a ski-ing motel up in The Great Dividing Range.

A few days later I had booked my boat passage to New Zealand and Peru for the following January, and was travelling towards Mount Kosciusko, 7,328 feet and the highest mountain in Australia.

My new boss met me in Cooma, the nearest town to the motel, which was forty-seven miles away up the mountain. The lights of his property looked cosy that evening as we approached it through a blizzard of snow, and after a good meal and a hot bath I retired to the bunk I'd been allocated in a room with three other girls. One of these, Diane, was an Australian, the other two were 'pommys', or English, like me.

The motel was designed especially for city people who wanted a ski-ing holiday sometime during the snow season, from about July to September, *en famille*. Each family lived in a separate cabin but ate in a common dining room attached to the main building. Our work was to clean the cabins and make or change the beds each morning, wash the dishes, and serve the meals. We worked long hours but the food was good, and most afternoons we would be free to go ski-ing, taking lessons without charge from Wolfgang, the motel's specially imported ski instructor.

The first day I was to ski dawned clear and sunny, after a heavy snowstorm during the night. There was always an assortment of boots, skis and alpine stocks at the motel for the use of the guests, and Wolfgang helped me to choose equipment which would fit and therefore be safe. His little car was soon packed with other skiers, and we drove up the mountain to a place called 'Smiggin's Hollow' where there were ski-lifts and a small restaurant. While Wolfgang organised his class I stepped gingerly up small slopes, ski-ing down them at what seemed to me a terrific velocity, for I was completely without control.

Living in that isolated ski-motel was rather like working on board a ship, earning good wages but with nothing to spend them on. I earned twice as much money there as I would have in Sydney, as most girls wanted to work in or near the towns, so the high wages were used as bait. The balance of my savings in Cooma quickly mounted up, and would be used to pay for my journey across the Pacific.

But things slowly began to decline as the snow melted and the guests became fewer. One day Diane and I were informed that everybody but us would be getting the sack. We two were being kept on to clear up the place before it was closed for the summer.

On November 2nd I left Mount Kosciusko, lucky to get a lift with my boss and his wife as far as Albury. We left the motel at seven o'clock in the morning, and as I watched white cockatoos pecking around in the green fields and brightly coloured parrots squawking amorously to one another in the gum and wattle trees, I knew that spring had really arrived. We drove along the Alpine Way, where snow lay only on the highest peaks, passing the village of Thredbo, and climbing even higher to the steep Geehi Wall, which curved up to 3,000 feet. Then down we came through the brilliant green country-side, where weeping-willow trees leaned over the first stream of the Murray River.

The following morning I started to walk in the direction of Melbourne, thankful that my washing-up days were over for the time being, and glad of the fat wad of traveller's cheques pinned into my pocket. I had reached the Victorian border and was taking a rest, idly watching half-inch long 'sugar-ants' go about their business, when a truck with at least 300 sheep on it stopped for the fruit-fly inspection, and the driver offered me a lift to Melbourne.

I hitch-hiked through the South Australian wheat country with a chimney-sweep, and spent the night on a pile of wool sacks in a sheep-shearing barn which had tattered streamers hanging from its rafters, decorations from past barn-dances, I supposed. At five-thirty I awoke, shivering with cold, and a large, slow-moving truck took me to Adelaide.

Then it was 'Sundowners' country, and small fishing villages where Aborigines solemnly did their shopping, wearing smart shirts and trousers. I was now on the edge of the Nullarbor Plain. At Iron Knob a huge truck pulled up for me, and when the driver told me where he was going I could hardly believe my ears. "Perth," he said. Over 1,500 miles across the desert. I jumped aboard.

That night we arrived at Wudinna and washed with some rain water at a house the driver knew. "This might be our last wash for some time," he remarked, "we'll need every drop of our water for drinking from now on." His truck was the largest I'd ever seen, and was loaded with wheel rims and Holden car bodies. "You can go up on top and sleep on one of the car seats," the driver suggested, "or you can sleep in the cabin with me on a mattress. My name is Otto, by the way, and I'm a German — as you've probably guessed from my accent."

I decided to sleep in the cabin, for Otto had been summed up in my estimation as a man who was rather lonely and sad, who would enjoy my company but not take advantage of it. We lay side by side like brother and sister, and Otto told me of his personal troubles while a dry wind moaned outside from across the temperate table-land of Western Australia.

Breakfast the next morning was tinned rice-cream. As we ate, a seven-foot-long snake slithered across the road and fat wombats hopped around, looking like small kangaroos. After Penong came an Aborigine reserve, where we weren't allowed to stop or turn off the road. I was busy reading out the names of villages from my map. They were all printed in large letters as if to indicate their importance, but in reality, these places got smaller and smaller as we penetrated the desert. "Nullarbor," I called out, looking around. "We passed it half an hour ago," said Otto calmly, "it was just one house in the scrub, and a sign saying, 'No petrol here'."

We were on our way at six-fifteen the following morning, along a road which was all but crowded with kangaroos, salamanders, a fox or two, and even a wild cat. Then the wheels began to churn through thick sand, and for many miles Otto had to use all his skill to keep us moving over this hazardous surface.

Beyond Coolgardie the temperature stuck at 110 degrees in the shade, and Otto told me that a Pole had just been found dead in the bush, not far from the road. "The barman told me he died of thirst. It hasn't rained here for many years, that explains why we can't get a glass of water anywhere now." This news was particularly worrying to me as my bottle was empty and Otto's water-bag leaked. The long afternoon wore on.

Suddenly, there on the road in the far distance was a notice, wavering in the heat-haze. As it came nearer, Otto pronounced the words on it slowly, carefully, and with unconcealed ravishment. "Ice – cold – beer – here." His eyes followed an arrow which pointed to a tiny hotel. Swinging quickly off the road, he drew the truck up to its entrance and we jumped out.

The barman pushed a beer and a Coke towards us over the counter with the remark, "This is Karalee, the only hotel between Coolgardie and Southern Cross. We're on the railway line, but it's the only place within 116 miles where you can get a drink."

From Perth, I set off along the red dust road towards Mount Magnet. I soon got a lift with a man who told me that he was a gold miner cum taxi-driver, but was very discreet about which was the more lucrative profession. I stayed overnight with him and his mother at Payne's Find, and the next morning at dawn found me sitting on the roadside practising Spanish from a text-book I'd brought along.

In a few minutes a pick-up came bumping along, and off I went, past Mount Magnet to Meekatharra, the last town before Marble Bar, said to be one of the hottest places in the world, with a temperature which often climbs up to 130 degrees Farenheit.

I slept in the pick-up that night, and the next morning waited on the dusty road. I waited, the sun rose high, and, half to pass the time, half to provide myself with some shade, I built a little house with some dead branches. All that day I waited in my little house, for any form of transport going in any direction to show up, but none did, until, as the sun dipped behind a boulder, a truck rattled up and stopped. The driver told me that he was on his way to Mount Magnet. "If you want to continue up north, better for you to come with us, and then to go to Geraldtown and around the coast," he said. "There'll be nothing bound for Marble Bar for three days or even longer, that's for sure."

I had been advised to get up to the north before the rivers started to run, so I pushed on from Geraldtown to Northampton, and from there got a lift with a couple who lived on an iron mine, and invited me to spend the night with them there. When he heard that I was making for Darwin, the husband said, "I think there's someone in town who's driving a Land-

Rover up to Wyndham. If you like, I'll go and see whether he's still here." He left me having some supper with his wife and daughter, and some time later the phone rang. Henry Smith would be collecting me in half an hour.

"Well, I never thought I'd be getting a lift for over 2,270 miles tonight," I told Henry as we set off. "It was a stroke of luck for me too," he replied. "It's a long road to travel alone. I wouldn't be doing it, only this new Land-Rover had to be delivered to one of my offices in Wyndham and I offered to take it up there – but I'll be travelling back to Perth in comfort, by air!"

It was a bright, moonlight night when we pulled up to sleep, and after brewing us some tea in his billy, Henry unfolded a stretcher and put it up on the roadside, while I curled up on the front seat of the Land-Rover.

The next morning we drove through the last of the coastal wheat country and the vegetation became nothing but scrub and mulga again, as on the Nullarbor plain.

Long, hot days of driving took us to Carnarvon, Port Head-land and Darby. We had almost reached the Fitzroy Crossing when there was a terrific thunderstorm and rain gushed down from a turbulent sky. It was then that we discovered that our Land-Rover was not waterproof. As I was trying to evacuate our luggage from beneath streams of water, the engine coughed, spluttered, and stopped. "S . . . !" said Henry, "no gas." There was no question of our spending the night where we were, as a storm such as this could start the Fitzroy River running at any moment and there was no bridge. Our spare petrol we usually pumped from a drum at the back of the Land-Rover, but on this particular night the hand-pump chose to break.

Then a flash of lightning illuminated my water-bottle which had fallen out on to the road, "Of course!" yelled Henry, and soon we were siphoning petrol out of the drum through a rubber tube to my bottle. When it became full, Henry would clinch the end of the tube as I emptied the contents into the petrol tank. Soon we were on our way again, and thankful to find the Fitzroy River still dry, we prudently camped at the far side of it.

Those last 250 miles to Wyndham were the worst. Some of the creeks were now full of soupy-looking water, the countryside became rocky, and often the 'road' disappeared into nothing, forcing us to stop and take careful bearings in order to keep travelling in the right direction. Kangaroos, emus, and goats kept darting across our path in the most unnerving manner. "If one of those goes through our radiator we've had it," muttered Henry, swerving just in time. "There is no hope at all of you continuing to Darwin by road," he said, when at last we were having supper in Wyndham's 'six-mile' hotel. "However, as payment for your help with the petrol and for your interesting company, I will buy you a ticket to travel there on tomorrow's plane."

The following morning, after flying over desert land, table-mountains and salt lakes, I left the Fokka-Friendship plane and was walking through the airport at Darwin when a very tanned young man asked me if I were looking for anyone. He introduced himself as Carlos, a half-Philippino pearl diver, transport-driver and crocodile hunter. When I told him that I hoped to visit Alice Springs, he said, "Don't worry about the transport, I know some truckys who are going there tomorrow."

After sight-seeing in Darwin, Carlos took me to the caravan where his sister-in-law lived, and there we had a fine rice and curry meal, after which I stayed with his family for the rest of the day and the night.

My truck for Alice Springs was even larger than Otto's. This one had thirty-four wheels on the ground. "We can only run these long fellas on this road to Alice," explained the driver. "She's bitumen all the way, built by the Yanks during the last war, and straight as they come, except for the first stretch."

Near to Darwin the land was flat, becoming hilly just before the Katherine Gorge, until white posts along the sides of the road warned us of steep drops to thundering rivers below.

The following morning we passed through Barrow's Creek, coming to a rocky area of country where there were some fascinating and natural formations made by the huge rocks. "Look — Sir Winston Churchill!" shouted the driver, and sure enough, there in front of us was a projecting rock face which had formed almost exactly the features of the famous man. Someone had even stuck a thick stick into its mouth.

Then began a desert of red sand, with hills, crags and winding paths. The silvery foliage of desert willows and the white bone-like branches of the ghost-gum trees stood out against a brilliant blue sky. When we came to Alice Springs I could see that, rather surprisingly, water was not too scarce, for many of the houses had beautiful gardens, with flowers, shrubs and green lawns. "Yes, there are plenty of wells here for water," said the driver, "and between December and March, rain is not uncommon." That night I slept in a transport driver's house, in that town surrounded with red hills – the very heart of the Australian continent.

The next afternoon I was bumping along on the back of a truck heading for Mount Isa – 703 miles north-west of Alice. After passing Tenant Creek we entered a stone desert. I stood up and gazed around me when the driver pulled to a halt to cool the engine. In all directions as far as my eyes could see there was nothing but stones, the bleached bones of cattle, and one or two dried up wells. It was hard to imagine that this spot was on the same earth which gave us green fields, lakes, mountains and seas. I felt as though I had suddenly been transported to the face of another planet.

The road to Mary Kathleen was not called 'the horror section' for nothing. However, what the road lacked in smoothness it made up for in a wild sort of beauty, weaving through bare hills where camels wandered. Uranium was Mary Kathleen's importance, with a well-protected mine a few miles away.

On the way from there to Richmond I got a lift with a cattle drover who could neither read nor write. He told me all about the farm on which he was working and the horses and dogs that he loved. Every time we came to a signpost on the roadside he would stop the car for me to read out what it said, listening as intently as if it had been the final chapter of a thriller.

Through table-lands, jungle and tobacco country, I travelled northwards as far as Cairns, and then up to Mossman, where the east coast road came to an end, the road up to Cooktown running inland. Then, southwards again, down the coast through Townsville, and the fruit and tobacco lands, towards the Blue Mountains and Brisbane.

Then it was Sydney once more – greeting old friends, collecting a nice tax-refund of nineteen pounds ten and enjoying a sweltering Christmas. It was one of the nicest Christmasses I've ever spent abroad, and was followed by a touching marriage proposal on New Year's Day, 1962.

"I can't say 'Yes'," I said, looking into my friend's dark eyes. "I know that I am not yet ready to marry, to settle down, have children, stay in one place. I wouldn't be happy and therefore

I couldn't make you happy either. Don't wait for me. Find yourself the right girl and marry her." I decided not to keep in touch with him, as that would only draw out the pain of parting for us both even longer. However, he insisted, so I wrote to him from many places during my travels. "I will wait for you," he told me before I sailed away, and for three years he did, becoming engaged just before my journey brought me unexpectedly back to Australia again.

On January 10th I sailed for New Zealand, where I would be spending about a month before continuing my journey to Peru. "Welcome to 'windy Wellington'," smiled a customs official as I stepped off the boat on to the shores of New Zealand's capital. Gulls and gannets screamed above the harbour, and little white-sailed yachts scudded across the choppy waters.

I didn't mind the wind, but as I set off, heading for the famous Rotorua hotsprings, rain began to fall, and only the squelch of my shoes kept me company along the grim deserted road. Then an old car came up to me and screeched to a halt. "Where are you going?" asked the voice. "All over the North Island," I replied. "Well hop in," said the voice, which belonged to an elderly gentleman of about sixty years, rather deaf but quite charming. "I'm on a three-week holiday myself," he told me. "I hope to tour around to many places in the North Island, and if you're willing to help me with the driving, you may join me for as long as you wish." This arrangement was agreeable to both of us. Mr Williams had company, while I had a guide and a chance to practise my driving.

Rotorua was on a lake, like Taupo, and we smelled it long before we saw it, a strong, sulphurous effluvium, not unlike bad eggs. The hotsprings gushed and steamed from amidst yellow sulphur rocks, and I stood watching the fascinating scene, feeling the warm vapour on my legs. The pools of boiling mud enthralled me most, gurgling, spitting, bubbling and hissing; quite hell-like, I thought.

The following morning we travelled northwards to Te Aroha and across the Waihou River to Waitakaruru, then to Auckland with its beautiful harbour and vast surburbs.

Waitomo was our next stop, 120 miles south of Auckland, where the caves are famous for their glow-worm grotto. We went down into a cave and found a boat bobbing on the surface of a still, black river. Sitting in the boat we were pulled over the water by a guide using a wire rope. "This water's alive with trout, and rats," said Mr Williams. "Shush," whispered the guide, "the glow-worms will extinguish their lights if they hear a noise." Then suddenly, above us, were thousands of shining pin-points, appearing in the inky blackness like so many constellations on a starry night. The guide showed us some of the little glow-worms close up, and I noticed that each one had several sticky threads hanging from it. "Those are their 'fishing lines'," he expounded. "The 'fish' in this case are midges which breed on the water, and their 'bait' is the glow-worms' phosphorescent glow. When the midge is caught on the sticky line, the glow-worm quickly hauls it up and sucks it to death. The female glow-worm has a special, soft light under her tail which only the male can see, to attract him. To shut off their glow, the glow-worms pull a piece of skin over it. The light takes two or three minutes to extinguish."

We drove along the Tasman Sea, camping within the sound of the waves, and the next morning at sunrise passed Mount Egmont, a massive, extinct volcano, just as fiery tongues of orange and gold were daubing the pale snow with hues of richest splendour. In the afternoon we reached Wellington again, and after bidding farewell to Mr Williams, I took the ferry to the South Island.

Some days later, on reaching Nelson, I realised that I still had thirteen days before my boat was due to sail for Peru, so I decided to get a job on a tobacco farm and earn a bit of money before returning returning to Wellington.

'Getting a job' simply entailed a ten-minute interview at the Nelson employment office, where I was given the name of a tobacco farm with instructions on how to find it. Labour was badly needed, it seemed. My farm was thirteen miles off the main Motueka–Nelson road, in the heart of the sheep and tobacco lands. The next morning at 8 a.m. I started work as a tobacco tyer.

"You'd better do a bit of passing first, until you get the hang of things," said my new boss, as I stood beside the kiln passing leaves from loaded carts to people who were stringing them on to long sticks, which were put up into the kiln to dry. Whole families worked beside me, and by 5 p.m., after a break for lunch, the kiln was full.

Those were happy, busy days. I loved the outdoor life,

working hard among pleasant company. Soon I was on the tying, and filling thirty sticks an hour — which was good for a beginner, people said. Slowly my hands became stained brown with the nicotine, and after working out in heavy rain, an irritating 'tobacco rash' covered my legs and arms. Getting to sleep at nights was no problem after eleven hours of work.

Five days after regretfully having to tell my boss that I should be moving on I found myself in a liner, crossing the Pacific Ocean. Ship life was full and interesting. I met an elderly English lady who gave me Spanish lessons; she had lived in Peru for twenty-two years and hated every minute of it. I swam in the pool, walked around the deck, and at night I read or attended film-shows. Soon I had made many friends on board and mealtimes were especially gay.

One evening a shout brought everyone running to the rails of the deck, and we saw the spouts of a school of whales moving along slowly through the water. Even whales are minnows in this vast ocean, I mused. "An extra day tomorrow!" I told my cabin steward when I went below, "we'll be crossing the International Date Line." "Don't talk to me about that," he replied grumpily, "I don't get paid for it."

Twelve days after we'd left New Zealand, the first stretches of the South American coastline loomed up out of the sea, shrouded in a morning mist. It turned out to be a large, rocky island, and beyond it was the harbour of Callao, backed by the dark shapes of the Andes Mountains. My Spanish teacher was at my side. "That island we just passed is a Peruvian prison," she said cheerlessly. "Really, my girl, I can't think why you want to disembark at a place like this."

Chapter 7

I took a bus to the Plaza San Martin in Lima and found the address of a colonel of the Peruvian army, which had been given to me by his brother in 1959. The brother, Ricardo, was a magician I had met with his wife on the Spanish frontier, when they were on a working tour of Europe. This led to my being introduced to a sister of the colonel's friend, who invited me to stay at her home during my stay in the capital.

Lima was hot and humid, and my host's daughter, Clarina, took me to many of the beaches and swimming pools around the city where we cooled off, swimming and eating the juicy, seed-filled fruits of a cactus, washed down with bottles of 'Incacola'. On the way to a beach one day, we passed some ruins of buildings made from mud bricks. "Those were the Inca holiday homes," explained Clarina. "It never rains here, so they are not built of granite like those of the sierra."

"And what about Lima?" I asked. "In 1535," said Clarina, "Francisco Pizarro, the Spanish conquistador, looked around for a suitable place to become the capital of this country, and chose this spot in the Rimac valley, near to the sea. He called it *'La ciudad de los Reyes'* – 'The city of the kings', but that title was dropped almost immediately and it has been called Lima ever since."

One morning I began to shiver, suddenly aware that I was extremely cold. With chattering teeth I called the Señora who said, *"Fièvre,"* quite calmly, and sent me to bed with some blankets and hot lemonade. I stayed there for ten days with a high temperature. The doctor advised me to leave Lima's humid climate as soon as possible, so I decided to move on to Arequipa, and, still feeling weak from my illness, I took a bus instead of hiking.

One of the people I met in this dazzling city was Don Jorge, a charming old gentleman who said that he wanted to help me as much as possible. He was often helping people, it seemed.

Before I left Arequipa, Don Jorge introduced me to one of the top railway officials who was a good friend of his. He offered me the possibility of travelling very cheaply on trains in Peru, and this helped me a lot during the next stage of my journey, to Cuzco and the Inca ruins.

Snow was falling as my train wound up into the sierras, past mud houses beside which sat Indians, cleaning sheep's wool and chewing coca leaves, with large herds of llamas grazing around them.

Don Jorge had arranged for someone to meet me from the train in Cuzco, and as we pulled into the station a girl came towards me and asked, "Are you Señorita Wendy?" She whisked me away, telling me that her name was Martha and that she worked for the tourist and Automobile Club of Peru.

On the following morning, Martha showed me around the ancient Inca capital. "We're 11,000 feet above sea level," she said. "A lot of visitors have trouble with their breathing up here." "My heart is strong enough!" I laughed, although I couldn't help noticing that I panted easily after little exertion.

"Peruvian Indians still speak Quechua, the language of the Incas," Martha informed me, "and in Quechua 'Cuzco' means 'navel'. We say that is because Cuzco was the birthplace of the Incas." First we visited the ruins of the Saccsahuaman fortress. The walls were made of enormous blocks of stone which had been ground and polished so well with sand and water by the Incas, that even a knife-blade could not have been slid between them. "That is typical of all Inca masonry," remarked my friend, "the Incas used neither cement nor mortar."

Martha arranged for me to visit Machu Picchu, 'the lost city of the Incas' and to stay with a friend of hers who ran the hotel there. So I was soon seated in a train which ran down into the valley of the Urubamba River, a tributary of the Amazon.

'The lost city' stood 2,000 feet above the river and I reached it by jeep along a winding track, with some other people who were bound for the hotel which stood beside the ruins. Orlando, one of the guides from the hotel, joined me for a walk around the next morning and explained to me something about them.

"These granite store-houses, temples, palaces and poor men's dwellings are set, as you see, between two hills – Huaynapicchu and Machu Picchu. See how the walls of the town were so cleverly put together: one of the stones has thirty-four sides on it, and look at these streets – made with thousands of steps. There were bathing pools also," said Orlando with a chuckle. "The Incas always washed facing the sun, they liked to be clean – unlike the Indians around here!"

That evening, I met Peru's Minister of War. He said that he knew my colonel friend in Lima very well, and was most impressed with some accounts of my travels. Two ladies were with him and before they whisked him away, he handed me his card with another name scribbled on the back of it. "This is for the Minister of Defence in La Paz," he said. "He is a good friend of mine and will help you in Bolivia."

The next morning, before dawn, I followed Orlando's suggestion and walked past a stone sundial to Huaynapicchu in the darkness. After climbing up numerous stone steps to its summit, I watched the sun rise over jagged mountain peaks, some of the highest ones glistening with snow. Far below me, the coffee-coloured river twisted through its lush, green valley. "You'll have six seconds in which to learn how to fly if you fall from the top!" Orlando had warned.

From Cuzco, I took a train to Pumo on Lake Titicaca, the highest of the great lakes of the world. I took a passenger boat across the 101-mile-long lake to Waiki harbour on the Bolivian side, from where I would take a small train to La Paz.

Thanks to more of Don Jorge's expert organisation, two gentlemen were at the station to meet me in La Paz. They had already arranged for me to stay with a certain Señora Lopez, so I moved in. However, during my stay in Bolivia's capital I was to spend most of my time with the Defence Minister's family, especially enjoying the company of his daughter, Maria Theresa.

We went out riding together. I was mounted on a sure-footed little mare and glad of it, as we set off at dawn one Sunday morning, trotting along a dirt track which led to the hills. The air was fresh and exhilarating, and I marvelled at the vivid colours of the rocks we passed, standing out red and purple against an azure sky. We rode down a steep ravine and across a wide, dried-up river bed, then up along a narrow ridge from where the view was extraordinary. Adobe farm-houses stood amidst cultivated fields and children in tiny ponchos guarded herds of goats and donkeys.

From the ridge, we rode down into another valley, which had a semi-tropical appearance, with giant cacti everywhere and a few six-inch-long centipedes creeping around. Dismounting, we flopped on to some long grass beside a gurgling river. After a picnic lunch we explored the river bank and found some Indians panning for gold, their mouths stuffed with coca.

Then Illimani's peaks loomed before us, the mountains around her base glowing blue in the twilight. Slowly she turned to silver, and then I stopped my pony and gazed in awe. I was seeing Illimani by the light of the moon.

In Oruro and Potosi I stayed with other kind people belonging to Don Jorge's long chain of friends. Potosi is one of the world's highest towns, perched 13,340 feet up, on the desolate, colourless antiplano of Bolivia.

Then on to Sucre, the legal capital of Bolivia, although far smaller than La Paz, nestling amidst the rugged hills beneath skies of deepest blue. A Belgian eye surgeon took me to the hospital while I was there and let me look on while he performed several eye operations.

A twenty-seven year old tin miner from Potosi was the first one on the table. He had been blinded by a blast of dynamite. "They come to me from all over Bolivia," said the doctor. "For him, I shall have to remove some of his iris and use it as a retina." The patient was given an injection to make him drowsy, and then a local anaesthetic, so that throughout the operation he could still speak to the doctor and answer his questions.

The operations for the removal of cataracts always fascinated me. The patient would arrive in the operating theatre blinded by grey lumps behind his cornea, and when these stone-like things were removed, he could usually see again quite well. I left a pint of my blood behind, in that hospital high in the Andes.

Soon I was sitting in the third-class compartment of a train bound for Antofagasta, the Chilean port, and from Antofagasta I travelled over the Atacama Desert to Copiapo, the central town of the Chilean copper, gold and silver mining region.

In Villemar, farther down the coast, I met a deputy of the Christian Democrat Party who took me to one of his political meetings. "There's just not enough water here," he told me as we walked through the rows of mud houses. "It hasn't rained for seven years." In a speech to the townsfolk, mostly iron and copper mining families, he told them that his party would help the people to make Chile into the land it could be. Finally he proclaimed, "We have a country which is rich in minerals and very fertile. Now we must work together and see that there is education for all who want it, that every home has electric light, and that there is enough milk for our children." Amidst the deafening applause he turned to me, "Now for a fried bat snack," he said.

As soon as I arrived in Santiago I went to find Ricardo and his wife, Maria. It would be our first meeting since Spain three years ago. At that time we had conversed in sign-language, as the magician and his wife spoke no more than a smattering of English. "I can speak to you now!" were my first words to Maria. "Querida . . . nuestra gringa!" she shrieked and embraced me joyfully. My friends were lodging in the tiniest of flats, but quickly arranged for me to stay at the house of another 'artista', a well-known Chilean singer. "Tonight you will come with us to a club and watch me do my magic," said Ricardo before he left me.

When my friend's exciting display of magic was finished, he whispered, "Stay here and watch the next act, he's a famous comedian." As I stood in the wings, a fellow kept trying to push past me. "Rude man," I muttered, and kicked him on the ankle. "Mier . . . coles!" swore the fellow under his breath. "I should let him get past, if I were you," said Ricardo, when he realised what was happening. "He's the comedian."

"I didn't know that 'miercoles', meaning Wednesday, was a swear-word in Castellano," I remarked to Ricardo after the show. "It isn't," he smiled. "Our friend had started to say another word – 'mierde', which in English means s-h-i-t, then he remembered that, however frustrating you were being, you were still a young lady, so he added 'coles' on to it to make the innocent word 'Wednesday'.

Ricardo's last words to me before I left Santiago held some psychological advice. "Don't be too direct here in South America, gringa, be 'flowery'; it goes a long way."

It was while I was in Conception that I started to get a soreness in my side, and upon reaching Temuco, I was in great pain and completely off my food, which for me is especially ominous.

63

"We'll soon have you better!" exclaimed Señor Vargas when I arrived at his house with a letter from a friend in Santiago and explained how I felt. "My wife will make a bed up for you immediately, with a nice hot-water-bottle."

The pain got much worse during that night, and the following afternoon, my host decided to call a doctor. When Dr Verdugo came into the room where I lay, he bounded up to my bedside and pressed me firmly in a spot where I supposed my appendix to be. "Does that hurt?" he asked, feeling around. "Ouch!" I replied dismally. "Never mind," said the doctor, "I'll have it out in twenty minutes, I have just one other operation to do first." At the clinic, the Vargas family left me with a comforting words. "Don't worry," they smiled, "he does numerous operations like this every day." "What does 'Verdugo' mean in English?" I suddenly asked Señor Vargas, "Ahem! executioner," he replied. But I saved my appendix.

Every day Dr Verdugo would come into my room and go straight to the window-sill upon which a urine specimen awaited him. He would shake it up carefully and study its dark sediment. "What is your diagnosis?" I asked him one morning. "Hepatitis," replied the doctor, "and as your tonsils, appendix and gall bladder are all in such a state, I suggest that you let me do one big operation and take everything out at once. Less anaesthetic would be needed," he added as if to tempt me. "Yes, but I'd have to be fitted with a zip fastener afterwards," I joked.

Looking back, I realise how fortunate I was to have escaped from that clinic complete with all my accessories. Rest, medicine and a strictly fat-free diet had dulled my pain, and I completed my convalescence at Señor Vargas's house. "We insist that you stay with us until you are quite better," the Señora told me kindly. "You must be well and strong to face the cold weather down south." That was where I spent my twenty-first birthday. On May 25th I sat up in bed devouring one of the only foods which had not been forbidden to me – a nice piece of cheese. A paragraph about me had appeared in the local newspaper, and the English community of Temuco came into my room singing 'Happy Birthday' and bringing me carefully chosen little gifts. It was a happy birthday.

I had been eating a normal diet for some time, with no complaints from my liver, when at last I packed my knapsack ready to travel on to Valdivia with a wine-merchant friend of the Vargas family. "Finished," I declared, and sat in the garden listening to a gramophone record. Suddenly the record began to bounce up and down. "Needle gone," I murmured, just as the Señora came rushing out of the house telling everyone to evacuate. "We're having an earthquake!" she called. A minor one, admittedly, but an earthquake it was, and I didn't forget to stand prudently beneath the threshold.

When my hostess in Conception had given me the address of her brother in Puerto Montt, I had taken it for granted that he was a family man, and was somewhat surprised to discover that the gentleman was a bachelor, living with another bachelor and a maidservant. "My house is large," said Eduardo when he had read my letter of introduction. "You will have a big room all to yourself overlooking the sea." That night after an enormous dinner of puchero – a sort of 'Lancashire hot-pot' affair containing choclo, I bathed in a bath which had seven taps but only two working, chuckled over an antique telephone which didn't work at all, and went to sleep on a straw mattress to the sound of waves crashing somewhere below the house.

When my ship for Punta Arenas arrived in the harbour I was allotted a pleasant cabin by the captain, who was a good friend of Eduardo's.

Eduardo had not exaggerated the beauty of the Archipelago. A mist had blotted out the view as we loaded potatoes from the island of Chiloe, and a thin drizzle fell all the time we were in Castro-port, but then the weather cleared, and with the sun came rainbows, standing out against the black hills and grey ocean on which bobbed white sea-gulls. We passed many green islands covered with lush vegetation, around which dolphins swam, and then glided through some narrow channels bounded by snow-capped mountains, from where waterfalls gushed into the restless sea. The most difficult channel to navigate was the 'Canal Inglesa', named after its awkwardness perhaps, for in it the ship had to make a difficult right-angled turn with no room for mistakes.

On the last night before we arrived in Punta Arenas I stood on the bridge looking at some gigantic glaciers which shone like silver in the moonlight. Thinking that the captain might be very busy the next morning, I decided to go and say goodbye to him that same night. I found him seated at a table in his cabin, guessing the number of spots on a row of dominoes. This fascinated me for the first half-hour. At last he said, "I have a small gift for you which I found in an oyster." It was a tiny pearl.

Radio interviews seemed unavoidable, especially in such a remote spot as Punta Arenas where news was rare, and it wasn't long before '*La voz del Sur*' 'The voice of the south' had me answering questions over the air, My Spanish was so fluent by this time that I quite enjoyed it, and anyway, I was only asked three questions. The first one was: "What was the nicest thing about your journey?" to which I replied, "Learning new facts and having new experiences." The second one was: "What was the saddest thing about your voyage so far?" and I said, "Meeting people who look down on other races and religions, customs and so on," and my third question was: "If you could choose anyone, who would you like as your travelling companion?" So I told them, "My husband, when I marry, for he will be somebody whom I will love very dearly."

A new voice always creates interest, and soon I was standing in a shoe-shop shouting enthusiastically into a microphone, "*Bonitas zapatillas! — por solamente 2.90 Escudos!*" The result of this advertising job was a new pair of shoes for me.

I had wanted very much to travel to the South Pole, while in such an austral spot, but the captain had informed me that expeditions were going there only once a year, and people had to have their appendix out before setting off—just in case. Having gone to such an effort to keep mine in Temuco, this news lowered my enthusiasm, especially as the next expedition wouldn't be leaving for several months, so I decided to travel over to Argentina and proceed southwards from there.

The pampas was turning to gold in the west, as I journeyed towards Argentina. At the frontier I put my watch one hour forward, and taking out a new diary, wrote on the fly-leaf:

> A book was opened for me
> by the hands of the Creator,
> and inside were stories of
> all the countries in the world.
> And I loved them and learned them
> and wanted to read more . . .

Chapter 8

August 1962–November 1962

The radio people in Rio Gallegos had been warned of my imminent arrival, and I moved straight into the house of Luisa Garcia, a radio announcer, and her brother, who read the news. Soon I had adapted myself to their topsy-turvy routine – having breakfast at 1 p.m., lunch at 4.30 in the afternoon, and dinner at about 3 o'clock in the morning after a long session at the radio. Friends would usually congregate at the house for tea or coffee and nobody would be in bed before dawn.

One afternoon I was introduced to the governor of the province, a charming gentleman who spoke fluent English, who invited me to see some films of Tierra del Fuego at his home.

"In southern Patagonia, on our section of Tierra del Fuego, we have the most austral town in the world," disclosed the governor before the films began. "It is called Ushuaia."

"I'd love to visit Ushuaia," I told Luisa when I got back to her house, and in her casual but efficient manner, she made a few phone calls and arranged for me to go there in an Argentine Air Force plane.

The plane was a Douglas DC3 with narrow, metal seats along its walls and a space for cargo down the middle. It wasn't long before I was permitted to go to my favourite place which was with the pilots in the cabin. We soared aloft through the cold air and into some thick cumulus clouds. "Got to get out of this porridge," muttered the pilot, and started to climb. Soon ice began to form on the windscreen and every so often we'd hear it cracking on the side of the plane. The pilots were just contemplating a landing in Rio Grande when they spotted a clear strip of sky ahead, and soon we were getting a fine view of the flat, marshy plains beneath us, unknown even to many

67

Argentinians. The jagged, snow-covered peaks of the cordillera dividing Argentine and Chile looked so beautiful from above, with fluffy-looking clouds drifting about them. Then in front of us spread the Atlantic Ocean, swelling around the hilly islands of Cape Horn.

Several days later, after a lively interview with *Impartial* – 'the most austral newspaper in the world', I boarded another DC3 to return to the mainland. First the pilots flew me over Cape Horn for a last look, and on the way we passed low over the Chilean settlement of Williams which was just a cluster of little houses around a green bay. Then northwards we flew, back over the ice-covered ponds and lakes of southern Patagonia to Rio Gallegos.

Owing to the waterlogged condition of the roads, no transport whatsoever had been leaving Rio Gallegos to travel across country for some time but my kind friends at the radio station quickly put me into contact with a group of semi-professional mountaineers, who would be flying right up to Bariloche that week after successfully climbing Mount Fitzroy. The 'Fitzroy Expedition' agreed to give me a free lift in their chartered plane, so my transport worries were over, for the time being.

When at last we were flying over the golden pampas to Bariloche, members of the Fitzroy Expedition began to shout and sing with pleasure, as well they might, for they were going home triumphant.

San Carlos de Bariloche stood on a lakeside in the Cordillera de los Andes. From there a kindly truck-driver took me to Bahia Blanca where I met an Italian driver making for the capital.

In Buenos Aires I stayed with a kind-hearted young girl, Celina, who taught democracy at a college there.

One morning over breakfast Celina told me gravely, "There was a movement last night." "A movement?" said I, still not quite awake. "Yes," she told me earnestly. "My friend, Chico, told me that he thinks that it may lead up to a revolution, although it was just a clash outside the city."

For the next few days, the radio blared announcements made by a division of the armed forces who wanted to overthrow the Argentinian president, Dr Arturo Frondizi, and replace him with another of their own choosing. Then buses stopped going into town, and the banks were surrounded by anxious people holding transistor radios to their ears, waiting to rush in and draw out their money if the worst happened.

We knew that things were really serious when on September 21st, Argentina's first day of spring, the usual parades were banned. However, many of the ladies staunchly wore flowers and Celina and I pinned white gardenia blossoms on to our blouses, in spite of the lack of festivities.

At 2.30 p.m. Celina and I were just finishing lunch. Suddenly bombers roared overhead and explosions were heard only a few blocks away. Then panic broke out. Women screamed, babies howled, and men shouted harshly, "Get into the houses and lock the doors, all of you!" I made for the roof in order to get a better view. After many flashes and loud explosions which sent pieces of shrapnel clattering on to the roof beside me, tanks began to rattle through the streets.

The next morning, things were back to normal again, with the sun shining down upon the grey rooftops, beneath which the pulse of the city throbbed at its usual rate. Unchanged, one might say, except for the grooves which the 'caterpillar tracks' of the tanks had made in the soft warm tar of the boulevards.

My journey from Buenos Aires to Asunción was marked by an unpleasant experience on the road from Salta.

Finding a vehicle which would be setting out to cross El Gran Chaco of the Argentine was even more difficult than I had anticipated. There had been no rain for many weeks and people feared getting stranded somewhere along the desolate, dusty road, where water and habitation were sparse. At last I was recommended by a lady to her brother-in-law, who would be taking an empty truck to collect some cattle in Taco Pozo. "That's about one-third of the way towards your destination," she informed me. "You might be able to pick up something else from there but I don't know — that part of the country is still unfamiliar to many of us Argentines."

Some days later found me wedged into the cattle truck cabin between the driver and Gonzales, his 'motor-boy'. Soon the tarred roads of Salta were far behind us, and we were moving through richly vegetated country with giant cacti here and there covered with delicate orange flowers, around which danced butterflies of brilliant hues. A few thirsty-looking cattle wandered beneath the trees in search of a drink, while sharp-eyed hawks

69

hovered high above them. "The area which we are approaching is full of jaguars, trunkless South American elephants, and poisonous snakes," said the driver grimly. "It wouldn't be a nice place to be left in by oneself." The significance of this remark escaped my attention at the time, and with a contented sigh, I went back to gazing out of the window with interest at the land around me.

Presently, the driver opened a small sack beside him, took out some coca leaves, and began to chew. Throughout the afternoon he chewed, until a dreamy expression filled his eyes. Later I asked him to stop the truck so that I could go behind a bush to answer the call of nature, and he came to meet me as I was returning. Grabbing my shoulders roughly, he tried to bring his mouth close to mine, but I pushed him away. He let go of me immediately. He can't be a man like that, I thought. After all, he was recommended to me by his sister-in-law. Climbing back into the truck, I still had a carefree heart.

At twilight we were driving along an open stretch of road, able to see quite clearly from one horizon to another. When darkness had enveloped us completely, the driver stopped the truck and sent Gonzalez underneath – 'to fix the engine'. Staring out of the window, I thought what a wonderful night it was. Suddenly the driver ordered, "Take off your trousers!" Thinking that it was some sort of joke which I hadn't quite understood, I smiled at him and continued to look out of the window. "Take off your trousers!" ordered the driver a second time and his tone of voice made me realise what his intentions were.

"No, I am not that kind of girl," I told him firmly. Edging towards me across the seat, the driver bellowed, "All girls are the same! Take off your trousers or I'll take them off for you!" Quickly I jumped out of the truck and looked underneath it, hoping that Gonzalez would come to my aid, but I couldn't see him at all. Meanwhile the driver had jumped out of the other side of the cabin and was running towards me. He caught the sleeve of my shirt, and when I resisted he hit me hard on the side of my head so that I fell on my back upon the hard surface of the road. Painfully, but rapidly struggling to my feet, I raised my foot in anger and kicked him viciously between the legs.

"Gonzalez! Gonzalez!" I called, in a voice that to me seemed no louder than the beating of my heart. "No use you calling him," said the driver with a sneer, "He's going to do the same thing with you that I'm going to do. Gonzalez, come and catch this girl!" When the motor-boy appeared his eyes were flashing rather wildly, and he looked quite a different person from the one I'd watched snoozing earlier that day. As he ran towards me, I set off as quickly as I could down the dark road. Right on the horizon I thought I saw a glow of headlights. "Oh God, I hope it's a car or a truck," I prayed as I sprinted along. I was far too fast for Gonzalez, who soon stood panting some distance behind me. However, when I stopped running and began to creep back gingerly towards him, he flashed the beam of a torch into my eyes so that I was temporarily blinded. I must get my passport from the truck, I thought, but how?

By this time the driver had started up the engine and leaning his head out of the window, he called, "All right, you can stay here alone with all the wild animals and without your luggage, if you don't want to come with us."

Running behind the vehicle, I managed to jump up and cling on to the back of it before it gained momentum. Suddenly Gonzalez, whom I had momentarily forgotten, was speedily chasing the truck on which I perilously hung. This part of the proceedings had obviously been pre-arranged by the two men, for the truck suddenly slowed down, allowing Gonzalez to grab my foot and pull me down on to the road.

"Come and help me!" he called to the driver, sitting heavily on one of my legs. When the driver appeared, I could see that he was still hobbling a little as a result of my kick. He held on to my beating arms, and when I saw the two grimy, sneering faces bending towards me I was filled with violent repulsion. Pulling back my free leg I shoved my foot into Gonzalez's half-open mouth . . .

"Oh, so you want to play like that again?" roared the driver, and hit me hard about the head with the back of his hand. Hundreds of tiny stars danced before me, and I felt my right eye go hot and begin to swell.

The motor-boy got up slowly from where he'd been sitting on my leg. It was quite numb and I could hardly walk. When I got to the truck, the men told me to climb up into the back.

Slowly I stood up and looked along the road ahead, thinking that I detected some lights twinkling not far away. They were real. If only I had known that we were so near to a hamlet, I groaned. At a cluster of mud buildings the truck rattled to a halt. When a man appeared from one of them, I jumped quickly to the ground. "Please, sir," I gabbled breathlessly, "where is your señora?" The man waved his hand vaguely to someone behind him. "Señora, may I please stay here for the night," I begged, "there is a serious reason why I should, please say yes, and I will explain everything to you inside?"

The woman looked surprised, but she nodded her head. Diving into the truck with renewed confidence now that I was among kind people, I rescued my belongings. The señora showed me into one of her mud rooms, and there in the light of a flickering candle, I recounted to her the whole of my terrifying experience. "You will sleep with my daughter tonight," said the woman gently when I had finished. "This place is a cattle ranch near to the village of Tolloche. Taco Pozo is just a few kilometres from here."

My bed was made from wooden poles with strips of cowhide stretched across them to make a mattress, and before sleeping I took out my diary to record the day's events. Something prompted me to write the last part of them in Spanish. I knew that my diary would reach home before I did. Just in case I don't make it, I don't want my parents to know about the bad things, I thought as I lay down.

Very much appreciative of being alive and well after the horrifying experience which had brought me there, I spent several days in Tolloche village during which not one vehicle passed along the main road. So when I noticed a cloud of dust on the horizon one morning, I called the farmer. "Let's stop them," I said, "they might be going to Formosa at least, and you can help me to judge if it would be safe for me to travel with them." The cloud of dust had been raised by a station-wagon, and the two men inside were on business from Buenos Aires. They said that they would be only too pleased to take me with them past Formosa to Clorinda if I wished, as that was their destination.

The road from Formosa to Clorinda was straight and fairly even and soon I was standing at the door of a house in that real frontier town, clutching a letter of recommendation for the lady doctor who lived there. I called goodbye and a special thank you to the businessmen in the station-wagon as they drove away, for each had given me 200 pesos (about four and twopence each) "to pay for your river crossing to Asunción."

I thoroughly enjoyed my stay with the doctor (who, incidentally, in her spare time swapped forceps for cleaver and worked in her husband's butcher shop), and then I was climbing into the muddy rowing-boat, which was crammed tightly with wet passengers bound for Asunción.

The port of the capital of Paraquay was bustling with people, all milling around the boats of various shapes and sizes. When I'd been through the customs I set off to find Delia, the doctor's niece, who was studying medicine at the University of Asunción. Delia turned out to be a most attractive and intelligent young lady who spoke good English and was glad of a chance to practise it.

"Come and see the university," said Delia when I'd showered and changed my clothes, so we walked along past the botanical gardens, where children played beneath trees heavy with blossoms, and then through the market, where bare-footed Indian women walked to and fro with babies on their backs and baskets on their heads. Suddenly I knew that I was going to like this cheerful, informal little capital.

The faculty of medicine interested me most, and as it was Delia's domain she showed it to me in detail. We even inspected the morgue, where she and the other students had their anatomy lectures. Bodies lay on most of the stone slabs and were in various stages of decay. They emitted an odour rather like that of bad meat and flies buzzed everywhere. "This one died today," disclosed Delia, leading me to where a young woman lay, naked and cold, her belly swollen as a result of the illness which had caused her premature death.

This was the first time that I had ever been so close to a lot of dead people, and I found that instead of experiencing fear or disgust, I felt as though I were looking at so much meat or so many machines – something which bore no relation to a living person at all.

Next day we went to see an Indian village. Borrowing bicycles we pedalled along in the hot sunshine until we came to a branch of the river. We left the bikes on the bank and paid an old man to paddle us over in a canoe. "There it is!" said my friend, pointing to a cluster of huts made from mud, reeds and branches of trees. Women sat outside their dwellings weaving belts and

73

other articles on hand-looms, usually with a baby dangling from their naked breasts. Children ran about or sat eating muddy shell-fish beside their mothers. "Where are all the men-folk?" I asked Delia. "I think I can guess," she smiled, and led the way to a sandy clearing beyond some bushes. There they were, all sitting cross-legged in a circle, holding wooden bowls. One of the men was pouring a soup-like liquid into each of the bowls, and by the shining eyes and loud laughter of his companions, I surmised that this wasn't the first round and that the liquid was quite potent. When somebody offered a bowl of it to me, I took it and sipped curiously. The liquid was warm and had a rather slimy consistency. "I shouldn't drink too much of it if I were you," whispered Delia. "They make it by chewing a special kind of leaf, spitting it out, and leaving the mixture to ferment."

On the following Sunday after attending a service at the Anglican church of Asunción, I was invited to lunch by the missionaries who ran it. "We shall not rest until as many people as possible have accepted Jesus as their saviour," they told me over the pudding. "And those who don't?" I asked. "Doomed," they replied. "'No man cometh unto the Father but by me', Jesus told us, and that's what we believe." "Yes, but there are millions of good moslems and Jews on this earth, not to mention the wonderful people of other religions and beliefs," I argued. "Surely God loves those people as well?"

"Of course," answered my host, "but He showed us His will in the Bible, and there is no other way to be saved but to follow it. No other religion or philosophy is quite the same as Christianity, you know."

"But what about those who have never had an opportunity to study the Bible?" I persisted. "Only God knows their fate," replied my host, "but it is the job of us Christians to deliver the message to as many people as possible. If you'd like to get a closer look at how we work, you may fly up to one of our Indian missions at Makthlawaiya – 'the place of the wire tree'. It is right up in the Chaco region of this country, which seems to alternate between floods and drought. They're having a drought there at the moment, so things are pretty grim."

I flew out to Makthlawaiya with a man who would be taking a census of the Indians there. As the little Cessna glided above the miles of parched grasslands, I found myself thinking back to my conversation with the missionaries over Sunday luncheon. I cannot believe that God will condemn people if they do not believe in Jesus' words, I thought. After all, I know so many fine people all over the world who are not Christians, but I'm sure that God loves them for what they are. And if I am wrong, I decided, then I would rather side with these people than with spiritual things which I don't really understand, at least until I discover more about the truth.

The mission house, surrounded by its flowering shrubs, stood out like an oasis in the desert. "It's so — so organised!" I exclaimed as I stepped off the plane. "It ought to be — it's been here for seventy years!" laughed Susan, one of the girls who worked there. "We run a school here, and a store. We are bang in the centre of the Indian village, you know. Unfortunately, as well as the drought, we now have a measles epidemic and some severe T.B. cases to contend with. I've got to visit one of the patients this evening, so you can join me."

That evening I followed Susan through the village to a smoky little hut, where an emaciated old woman lay dying of T.B. A nine year old girl crouched in a corner — too sick with measles to help her mother. Susan gave them both injections and some food, while I smiled and tried to cheer them up, but later, as I slept in my clean comfortable bed in a room well screened against insects, I had nightmares.

The next morning, the man who had come to take the census took me around with him, so that I could see a few more Indian homes. The dwellings we visited were all very similar, bare of any pictures or ornaments, except perhaps for a tattered calendar, usually some years old. Furniture consisted of wooden stools, skin mats, beds made from wooden poles and cowhide, and string hammocks for babies, slung from the roof. Often there would be a fire just outside the doorway, with a black pot bubbling over it.

"How do these Indians live?" I asked Susan at lunch. "Well, they still go hunting and eat what they catch," she replied, "and we are trying to interest them in gardening and animal husbandry, but patience is not one of their virtues, I'm afraid. For example, we presented an Indian couple with a cow last year. They had a lot of children who were all undernourished and we thought that if they grew healthy through having milk each day, it would encourage the efforts of the other villagers.

In a public lesson, we explained how the cow should be milked and looked after. Everything went splendidly until the next festival came along, then the couple killed their milk supply and ate it."

On most days I helped in the school during the mornings and in the clinic during the afternoons. Then, before supper, someone would usually join me for a ride. Away we would go, cantering past the swamps which were at their lowest because of the drought, where storks and herons stood silently, watching hopefully for fish.

One month after I had crossed over the river Paraguay to enter that country, I was once more on my way, travelling along a red dust road towards the river Parana. Soon I would be entering Brazil – the largest country of Latin America.

Chapter 9

The canoe glided lazily across the Parana River, and a mass of green jungle was my first impression of Brazil. Scrambling ashore, I wandered through the trees, into the village of Iguacu. This was the hottest period of the day, and the sandy, sun-baked streets were all but deserted. Wondering why the place had such a hastily put together appearance, I remembered the words of the canoe owner. "The Iguaçu region is going through a coffee boom at the moment," he had said. "This attracts the dregs of society from all over the country, coming here to try and make a bit of quick money."

After a visit to the falls of Iguacu, where the waters crash down from the jungles of Argentina on one side of the river, and of Brazil on the other, I set off on a bus to Montevideo. There, I met the daughter of an ex-president of Bolivia, with whom I had been horse-riding in La Paz. A friend of hers was a major in the Brazilian Air Force, who kindly offered to fly me to Rio de Janeiro, free of charge.

Some days later, I boarded a tiny looking DC3, which was waiting at the 'back door' of the airport. When we gained altitude, I took a last look at Uruguay and the river Plate, shining in the sunlight like a sheet of silver.

In Rio, I stayed with a doctor I had met on the plane and his wife. One night, I accompanied the doctor when he rushed to the hospital to perform a Caesarean section. Upon our arrival, we learned that the father wanted his baby to be born on Christmas Eve. This was eleven o'clock on the night of December 23rd, so we waited. On the stroke of midnight, I donned a mask and gown and followed the doctor into the theatre. I watched the whole operation, standing on a stool beside the table. It was the most thrilling event that I have ever witnessed.

At a New Year's party in São Paolo, I held hands with a group of young Brazilians, and we made sure of starting off the New Year on the right foot by holding it off the ground as the clock struck midnight. Then we started to discuss each other's ambitions, and when I told these city dwellers of my ambition at that time, to travel right up the river Amazon by boat, they were filled with horror. "But it's far too dangerous," they said, "there are wild animals, poisonous snakes, and flesh-eating piranya fish up river. Why, we are Brazilian, and we wouldn't even contemplate doing such a thing!" These are the sort of comments that spur me on, and I was soon travelling northwards, stopping off in Brazilia on the way.

At that time, this new capital of Brazil was only four years old and still being hurriedly built, on a cool, woody plain about 700 miles north of São Paolo. Very modern it was, too, with elevators in the huge bus station, the latest thing in schools and churches, and the enormous government buildings and offices standing like two matchboxes placed on end against the sky. Amongst all this ultra-modern architecture, I couldn't help noticing an 'English country cottage' style of place, and the roses and hollyhocks around the door left no doubt in my mind — I had found the British Embassy.

The air was hot and sultry as I boarded a tiny plane bound for Belém, on the mouth of the Amazon River. There I learned that a Brazilian passenger-cargo boat, for a very meagre sum, ferried people up-river as far as Manaus, taking its time. I was soon booked for Manaus, on the third-class deck of the *Lauro Sodré*. It was a sunny, stifling afternoon when I embarked, and I sat in a corner, watching passengers slinging their hammocks up across the deck, so that it was almost impossible to walk around. One woman set up a stove as soon as she got on board, brewing coffee and selling it to fellow passengers.

The *Lauro Sodré* stopped at all the tiny ports on the way to Manaus, which made the journey most interesting. Then came a morning when everybody was up at 4 a.m., to watch the boat pass from the Amazon to the 'rio negro' — 'black river'. We all leaned over the side of the boat, watching the brown waters mingling with the black. A couple of hours later, we reached Manaus.

While we were there, I stood on the deck of my boat in the cool of the evening, watching the 'rush hour' period on the river. Someone was in the process of punting his house and family to a new location. Another man paddled midstream wearing a pair of shorts, soaped himself, poured water over himself, bailed out his canoe, donned pajamas and paddled back home. Boats selling fruit and vegetables skimmed around, and others, full of fat, fresh fish, came ashore. On the way to the spare cabin which had been found for me, I watched as the crew fished, with a homemade wire harpoon from the stern. They soon ran out of their maize-flour bait, so they spat in the water to attract the fish, catching silvery, two-inch-long ones for their efforts.

Villages at which we stopped were always interesting. We arrived in Ipixuna one evening, and I went ashore to talk to the inhabitants. There were eighty children there, but with no school, and although the villagers said they were Catholics, they had no church or priest. The people understood my Spanish, thinking that it was an odd dialect of Portuguese. Horses, cows, pigs and other livestock wandered about the village, and exotic-looking fruits hung from the trees. I wandered around, and found some men making a boat. What a magnificent work of art it was! I gazed at the soft, elegant lines of the embryo vessel, each curve so smooth and so well proportioned. I was awed to think that this skill is hereditary, as these villagers have no charts and no mathematical knowledge, only their instinct to guide them.

I was sorry to leave my friends on the *Lauro Sodré*, when we finally reached Benjamin Constante, our destination.

With the help of the list of names which had been given in Manaus, I was soon able to find a friendly captain, who happily agreed to take me up the river as far as Iquitos, in his boat, the *El Caribe*.

The *El Caribe* was strictly a cargo vessel, and seemed to have more livestock on it than humans. Rows of parrots sat along the boat rails, gossiping all day long in Spanish, Portuguese, and Indian languages. Tame monkeys chattered in the corners, while munching steadily at rice and bananas. Crates full of hens and cocks contributed to the pandemonium. The only quiet creatures were the turtles, who wisely kept within their shells.

In Iquitos I met some friendly Americans, who were busy searching the jungles for rare orchids and ferns, making a fortune by selling them to collectors in the States. I enjoyed this interlude from life afloat, and then boarded the *Huallaga*, bound for Pucalpa up the Ucayali River.

The *Huallaga* chugged steadily nearer to Pucalpa, and my two-thousand-mile journey by river boat was almost at an end. I stood at the prow of the boat and watched an anteater swimming lazily across the river. His long snout was waving above the water, which the setting sun was transforming into a pathway of red and gold.

Upon my arrival in Pucalpa, I learned that over seventy-five trucks and buses were stuck on the pass over the Andes mountains, due to landslides caused by the rains. Several days later, news was brought to me that the Andean pass was open, and I was soon setting off in the first bus to brave the road since the landslides and consequent blockage.

We had almost reached the main road for Lima, when we turned a corner and came across a deep mass of mud and stones barring our way. We were now rather tired, dirty, and sick of the sight of mud. Only one passenger had decided to reach Lima in the condition in which he set out, and we had teased him unmercifully for not kipping in and working with the rest of us. As we stared gloomily out of the windows, the sky clouded over and a thin drizzle began to fall. Quietly, the driver passed around his hat, and with the soles he collected, paid some shepherds to clear the road for us.

When we rattled gaily into Lima we were all firm friends, climbing stiffly out of the old bus that for four days had been our home.

A week or so later I was sweltering in a cargo-cum-passenger truck on the border of Peru and Equador. For one and a half hours Peruvian officials searched the truck and its passengers, looking for smuggled goods. During this tedious inspection, some of the passengers started to grumble with impatience, but I noticed that the driver remained calm and polite throughout the whole procedure. At last we had satisfied the customs police, and were allowed to continue our journey to Equador. A short distance from the Peruvian customs we rounded a bend in the road and the driver stopped the truck. "Can they still see us?" he asked his mate. When the answer was no, the driver's mate

Taking the water-buffaloes for a soak on a Philippine ranch

I throw my instructor during a
judo lesson in Manila

Skiing in Australia's
Snowy Mountains

Making friends with
Paraguayan Indians

At the controls of a Chilean Air
Force Beechcraft

Dressed for an Alaskan winter

and another man sped off behind some bushes, and returned carrying a heavy-looking sack. Four more times the driver stopped the truck, and mysterious sacks were hastily loaded from various hiding places. The frontier was soon far behind us, the driver looked relieved, and I couldn't help chuckling with him and the other passengers as we drove on.

Chapter 10

April 1963–August 1963

"Come on, Señorita, it's too dangerous for you to sleep down there," said the firm but kindly voice which penetrated my dreams. Now where on earth can I be? I asked myself, when upon opening my eyes I saw a hammock swinging to and fro above my face. Of course – I was lying on a newspaper on the third-class deck of a boat which was rocking its way over the river Guaya towards Guayaquil. Thirteen sucres ... four shillings and tenpence ... not bad for an all-night voyage, I thought sleepily. "Come along now, follow me," said the voice above somewhat impatiently. So I got stiffly to my knees, crawled carefully from beneath the bulging hammocks, and stumbled along through the dark after what I recognised to be one of the ship's officers.

The man indicated an empty canvas bed in the women's dormitory of the second class, then he retired. "Kind people – all over," I sighed, and slept comfortably for the rest of the night. The next time I awoke was at 5 a.m. to find the boat docking at Guayaquil.

I found the Peruvian consul and, when we'd talked for a while, he sent me straight to his house in a chauffeur-driven car. It was a spacious building, overlooking a large rose garden. I spent the afternoon chatting to his wife and daughter, and that evening we all went for a drive around the city.

As we drove through one of the streets, a strong smell of chocolate pervaded the air. "A chocolate factory?" I asked, sniffing. "No, only the cocoa beans drying in the sun," said the señora. "Guayaquil is the economic centre of the country. A lot goes on here, it has a larger population than Quito, the capital, and incidentally, as you may have noticed, the inhabitants are very fond of statuary."

Some days later I was inhaling deep, delicious breaths of the fresh, clean air of Quito, high in the Andes. While travelling over the mountains on the way from Guayaquil, I had soon donned a thick sweater, for the coolness near the capital formed quite a contrast to the muggy heat of the tropical port. My hostess, for whom I brought a letter from her lawyer nephew in Guayaquil, turned out to be a corpulent lady known as Tina, who immediately invited me to call her Tia Tina.

"Such a brilliant blue sky," I remarked as I walked with Tia's nephew Felix among Quito's ancient, tiled houses, and then through the plaza where roses, palm trees and hollyhocks bloomed. "This is one of the most beautiful capital cities of South America that I've had the good fortune to visit." "Well, I'm not going to argue with you on that point, but then I'm rather biased!" laughed Felix. "I'm going to take you up to the top of the Panicillo hill now. The Indians made it themselves, so the superstition goes, and from there you will get a marvellous view."

Felix was right. From the summit of the hill we could see the whole of Quito spread out before us, and behind it two massive volcanoes towering into the clouds. "They are Pichincha and Cotopaxi," said my friend. Around us rolled black forests and green fields, through which peasants wearing brightly coloured ponchos drove their llamas.

"What else would you like to see while you're here, Wendy?" asked Felix. "Well," I replied, "Equador is on the equator, is it not? So I should like us to go to latitude nought degrees, just for the fun of it!" "Certainly," he chuckled. "Tomorrow morning your wish will be granted."

The equator was fifteen miles from Quito, so Felix borrowed a friend's car to take me there. We drove through rugged, undulating countryside, at last coming to a green valley in which stood a monument proclaiming the fact that through that spot ran the imaginary line which encircles the earth. It was so peaceful there in the valley, with no sounds other than the whistling of the wind and a distant baby's cry. I stood beside the monument for some time, reading the names of geographers who had proved that the equator was exactly there – and not another foot or two in either direction. Then, as I looked around, I saw a little shop. "It had to be – even out here!" I chuckled. "Come on, Felix – let's buy postcards."

A friend of Tia Tina's drove me to the Colombian frontier some days later, and there I picked up a bus, confident in the knowledge that in Colombia transport is extremely cheap. "Seven pesos to Pasto – which is as far as we're going," said the driver as I climbed aboard. "Seven pesos – two and sevenpence halfpenny," I calculated and took a seat. Very cheap for nearly 300 miles, I decided.

During the hot afternoon the air inside the bus became rancid and stifling, causing several of the passengers to vomit from the windows. Then thunder rumbled over the hills and, as rain began to pour down, the bus stopped. "Breakdown!" called the driver, and settling himself comfortably began to munch on a piece of bread, with obviously not the slightest intention of getting out and getting wet.

Grumbling, passengers made hasty decisions – whether they should wait in the bus with the driver, for a day or two perhaps, or try to complete the journey on foot. I decided on the latter course of action, which encouraged several other not too heavily burdened people to begin walking also, and it wasn't long before we were all lucky enough to get a lift in a private car going right to Pasto. "You'll be staying with Mrs Murray, I presume?" enquired the driver as we reached our destination. "Er, who's she?" I asked. "A Protestant missionary," he replied. "Well, I'll drop you off at her house, anyway."

"I'm not surprised that you were brought to me," smiled Mrs Murray as she opened the door, "I'm quite a legend around Pasto, I believe, having lived here for so long! Now you must be longing for a hot bath. They're rather scarce in this part of the world as I think you'll have found, so go and have a nice soak and then we'll talk over supper."

Refreshed in health and spirit from my short stay with Mrs Murray, I pushed on to Cali, where I had a letter of recommend-ation to Raul Jimenez, an American Field Service student. He strongly advised me to fly to Bogota because the bus route was subject to bandit raids. But the buses were so cheap that I ignored his kindly advice so as not to strain my budget. All the bandits must have been elsewhere that day. Nothing happened apart from the inevitable breakdown!

When we reached Girardot, a lot of people were getting on and off, so I dived into a café in search of a door marked '*Damas*' (Ladies). I found it, but the driver got there first, so I rushed

84

into the '*Caballeros*' which my bus-driver, in his hurry, had apparently overlooked. It was not surprising that the owner of the café raised his eyebrows when he caught sight of me emerging from the 'Gentlemen' and a dark, husky gentleman creeping out of the 'Ladies'.

In Bogota I was welcomed into the house of another American Field Service student, a girl called Ada Araujo. She took me to the museum, the market and the Great Falls of Tequendama, on the Rio Bogota. "They're four hundred and eighty-two feet high," she shouted above the roar. The falls crashed into a deep gorge, which she said was a favourite spot for suicides. When *I* fell into the river, it was by accident . . .

I continued my journey towards the Venezuelan frontier on another of the Colombian buses – forgetting all about bandits and political upheavals, until we passed through villages draped with red flags and crowded with tanks full of well-armed soldiers. Into a jungly valley we drove, where the road was bordered by swirling rivers, straw huts, and banana groves. Then we began to climb up into the sierra, mounting a narrow ridge between two deep ravines, and all along the edge of the road white crosses marked the places where vehicles had tumbled over into the brown rivers far below. The mountain-sides were stony and sparsely vegetated, leading up to summits which were sandy and bare, the snow-line being extremely high as we were still so near to the equator.

It wasn't long before I was discovering that the cost of living in Venezuela was six times higher than in Colombia. This was natural, I suppose, for her principle industry was petroleum, which drew in a lot of foreign capital.

Then – Caracas! – super motorways, the latest European fashions, flashing stream-lined cars. And also Caracas – the narrow, littered streets up which I was walking, houses made from mud and tin, emaciated children screaming in the gutters, and restless youths lurking in dark corners. I came to a grimy wooden door and knocked. A middle-aged woman opened it and drew me quickly inside. I produced a letter for her from a daughter in Cucuta. All was well. The woman smiled, embraced me, and seizing my knapsack, carried it into a room across a shady patio where gloomy-looking fish swam in green-glassed tanks, and lonely birds chirruped in small wicker cages beside some potted plants.

85

That night I heard gun shots – not far away. Then on the following morning, as I stepped out into the street, two men ran quickly past me, one of them carrying a rifle. A toy one, I thought, until several people came racing after the men, shouting, "They went that way!" and so on. Striding after the pursuers, I rounded a corner and found that they had caught up with the two men and were beating them. "Thieves and murderers!" somebody shrieked. Then a police car arrived and the men were pushed into it.

I don't think that I am lodging in a very select area, I reflected, as I walked through the centre of the city towards the 'Two Towers of Bolivar' the tallest buildings of Caracas. Beneath the offices contained in these massive structures were car parks, restaurants and shopping arcades.

I decided to phone a girl whose name had been given to me by someone in the Argentine. When I spoke to her, she invited me to her home for lunch, and then took me to meet some of her friends. Among them was a girl called Lucia and her brother, Pedro. Their father had worked for the United Nations and they had lived in many parts of the world. Accounts of my travels alone interested them enormously. "Do come and stay with us!" they implored at last. "Mama would love to meet you. Papa's away, but we have a dog, and a ginger kitten called 'Gringo'."

My second abode in Venezuela's capital was as sumptuous as the previous one had been squalid. I discovered that Pedro, although only seventeen years old, was already a keen politician. When I asked him about the shots I'd heard during the night, he nodded his head comprehendingly – "Ah yes," he said, "that would mean a minor manifestation in the 'red' section of our city, not far from where you were living. That's an area where the police daren't go."

"I'm getting quite used to fighting now," I said, and told him about the revolution I'd witnessed in Buenos Aires. "But, the difference between an Argentinian revolution and a Venezuelan revolution," Pedro said, "is that in Argentina the revolutions are military against military whereas here they are civilians or 'reds' against the soldiers and the police. And now let us listen to 'Hitler's Inferno'," and so saying, he opened the gramophone and played a long series of Nazi marching songs. "Tomorrow we'll show you the University of Caracas," promised Lucia,

86

"and then you will see why my brother and I don't wish to attend it."

As we drove through the university gates, Pedro whispered, "Ninety per cent of all the students here are 'red', and as the police aren't allowed on to the campus, they really 'let go' with their pro-communist propaganda." Then Pedro and his sister showed me a sort of 'museum' which the students ran, displaying many exhibits which mocked the government and Christianity. The one that I remember most clearly now was a stuffed effigy of Señor Betancourt – then the president – sleeping in a hammock, with a notice underneath it saying: 'This is your democracy' . . .

To approach Maracaibo, my next port of call, I crossed one of the longest bridges in the world, stretching eight and a half kilometres across the northern end of the Lago de Maracaibo, which, with an area exceeding 7,000 square miles, was the greatest of the South American lakes.

The small houses and bustling streets of the old port seemed quite confining after the modern spaciousness of the capital and I didn't see much more than that during my visit, for a sea mist descended upon the town and stayed there.

"Looking into that mist is like looking into the future," I soliloquised, "one knows that something exists within it, but one cannot make it out. Thank goodness for not knowing! I like to dream and how many of my dreams have come true." It was the morning of May 25th, 1963 – my birthday, and I was twenty-two years old. Flicking over the pages of my diary I wrote:

> I am one who lives my dreams,
> – and I dream my life away.

With a visit to the United States of America in my mind, I now had to get on to the isthmus of land which joined the two Americas – the North and South. That meant travelling back to Colombia, from where I could study the transport possibilities to Panama.

No cars or trucks had been leaving Maracaibo to cross the Colombian frontier for some days, so I got on to the cheapest bus which I could find, and that, I suppose quite naturally, was one of the most decrepit vehicles I have ever set my eyes on.

In Barranquilla I got my visa for the U.S.A. The consul there was extremely kind, trying to keep me waiting for as short a time as possible. In half an hour I managed to get a three-and-a-half-month permit, on a visa which extended over a period of four years.

Cartagena, I discovered, was the oldest town in South America and turned out to be one of my favourites. Situated on the Caribbean Sea, the ancient port was enclosed by a wall six yards thick in places. It was built by the Spanish to keep out invaders, I was told, along with the strong fortress.

One of the first things that Mrs Fowler, my hostess there, said to me when I arrived at her house was, "Here – chew some gum!" She and her children were all chewing gum rather frantically, as a pipe had burst just outside the back door. We all stuck our gum into the hole but it didn't work, so in the end Mr Fowler had to turn the water off altogether.

The Fowlers were North American missionaries who had lived in Cartagena for years, and loved it there. They liked people – and people liked them. Animals did also, and I was soon being introduced to a cat and a hen, just two of their many pets.

I had soon made many friends, including an American schoolteacher called Gay. It was with her and some other young people that I camped on one of the coral islands some distance from the coast. Skin-diving over the coloured coral was superb, I thought, just as if one were exploring another silent world. Not all of our party had simply come to look though and the men swam with harpoon guns, twisting swiftly along through the water, chasing fish. One evening the 'catch' was an enormous female turtle. When it was cut open we found about three hundred eggs inside its stomach, round and yellow, looking like hens' egg yolks. We fried them for supper. They tasted like roasted chestnuts to me. Later I lay in my hammock, swinging gently between two palm trees. Gazing up at the full moon, I wondered whether I should ever go there . . .

The Fowlers had a friend who worked in a travel agency, and I went along there one morning to discuss with him the next stage of my journey. "There is no road between here and Panama," said the man, and verified this statement with some up-to-date maps and air-photos. "My suggestion is that you go by boat."

When I went back to the travel agency to collect my ticket, I made another important decision. The agent told me all about a scheme wherein one could pay ninety-nine dollars and travel all over the United States during a period of ninety-nine days, using comfortable 'Greyhound' buses. "Only one dollar a day," he said. "Would I be able to make my own itinerary?" I enquired. "Of course!" he replied. "You could spend your ninety-nine days zigzagging backwards and forwards between Miami Beach and Hollywood if you wished. Remember, a normal bus fare from New York City to San Francisco would cost you eighty-eight dollars – one way!" That settled it. The United States of America was enormous, and prices there were high, I already knew. At least I would have a means of travelling all over the country, and I could easily live on dry bread and water. When I left the travel agency I was clutching a ticket which said, 'From anywhere to anywhere' on it.

Mrs Fowler was teaching on the morning of my departure, so her husband kindly took me to the ship. "Come back and see us again sometime!" he called as I walked up the gangway, sadder than usual, somehow, at saying 'goodbye'.

Three years later I was in Sierra Leone, when a paragraph in a newspaper told me that Mr Fowler had been shot by Colombian bandits in front of his fourteen year old daughter.

.   .   .

"Thank goodness for the Panama Canal!" said a ship's officer who was standing beside me, leaning against the rail. "We've come from Spain and are bound for Peru. Just imagine having to go all the way around the Horn."

It was dawn on the morning after my embarkation, and I was watching passengers get on and off at Port Cristobal, before we entered the canal.

Then we moved off, with the first lock, pulled by wire ropes attached to a tiny train, consisting of an engine with a cabin at each end of it, running along a track on the edge of the canal.

As soon as we were in the lock, water was added so that we rose up to the level of the next, then the enormous iron gates swung open and we passed through. It fascinated me how the ships which were coming in an opposite direction to us, from a higher level, always appeared to be floating in mid air. Glancing out over the brown waters I saw some forested 'islands'. They were the tops of hills which had been practically submerged when their valley had become the Panama Canal.

Almost eight hours after we had entered the canal we passed through the Miraflores Locks, and then slipped quietly into the port of Balboa.

A local bus took me to Panama City and after a few days, I moved on to Costa Rica where I helped in a hospital, at Somoto, on the border of Honduras, and spent a night in an orphanage run by nuns. Finally, a trip through Guatemala brought me to Mexico and my first bullfight, in the Plaza Mexico, the world's largest bullring. The 'Novilladas' which were taking place are fights between young bulls and inexperienced bullfighters; a sort of graduation ceremony before they become fully-fledged matadors.

Pedro Jimenez (nicknamed 'Pedrin'), Rafael Fernandez, and Alberto Bricio were on the bill for that afternoon, Pedrin being by far the favourite of the spectators, judging by their excitement at his appearance. During the fights which followed, it was sometimes difficult to decide who was the more afraid – the novillero or the bull. When a fight became too long and drawn-out, with the matador making bad passes or failing to kill his bull cleanly, the crowd let their opinion be known by sending a shower of cushions into the ring. Pedrin, however, gave us our money's worth.

His first bull came galloping into the sandy enclosure and immediately he began working close to it, linking his passes gracefully together and becoming as one with the bull when it wove past him after the blood-stained muleta. Sometimes he would go down on one knee, to offer the maximum of his agile body to the panting beast, who seemed slow to realise that the man was unattainable. Then Pedrin slipped during one of his passes and was tossed by the treacherous horns. The crowd groaned in helpless sympathy, but their favourite was not badly hurt and continued to fight – at last squaring his bull on all four feet for the kill. Remaining motionless as the bull made its last charge, he drove his sword deep between the animal's shoulder blades. Then speaking softly to it, Pedrin held up his hand, and as the bull tried to come forward once again its head sank down and it fell to its knees – to roll over, dead. It had been a good clean fight and the crowd cheered for Pedrin, who was later to tackle his second bull in the same skilful manner.

All too soon the day came when I was to leave Mexico, with a slow train bound for Laredo, on the frontier of the United

States of America. From there, my ninety-nine days 'anywhere to anywhere' travels would begin.

My last meal was substantial, delicious and typically Mexican. There were 'tamalles' – corn-paste and meat cooked in maize leaves and dipped into hot sauce, roast kid, avocado pears, black beans fried in pork fat, tuna and juicy green grapes. For many months afterwards I was to miss the biting flavour of the hot chillis which had been served with every Mexican meal, and that I had grown to love.

Then it was the railway station and 'goodbye'. *"Hasta siempre!"* called my Mexican friends as the train began to move. *"Hasta ... siempre,"* I replied, with a catch in my throat as I left Latin America, where I had spent one and a half years of my life.

Chapter 11

So this was Texas! I leaned back on the plush seat of my air-conditioned bus and gazed out of the windows at giant cacti, oil wells and wide open spaces. It was early morning and I was on my way towards Dallas, leaving Laredo and San Antonio far behind. Then there were sky-scrapers gleaming in the southern sun, and soon I was panting along the crowded city streets.

From Dallas, I headed westwards to Arizona, passing through Oklahoma and New Mexico on the way. As the bus sped by the petrified forest, the man at my side passed me what looked like a piece of wood, but was smooth and heavy like stone. "Here, you keep this as a souvenir of the forest," he drawled, "it's petrified wood, and very old. The wood atoms have combined with certain minerals during a long period of time and, hence, this petrified effect." I thanked him and then turned to enjoy the violent colours of the painted desert.

Then we came to that enormous gorge, two hundred and seventeen miles long, four to eighteen miles wide, and at places, a mile deep. I peered over the edge of the Grand Canyon. Yes, there she was – the Colorado River, winding her muddy course through a chasm which had become one of the wonders of the world. Oh, the colours of those rocks! – crimson, black, white, yellow and purple – gnawed into shapes which reminded me of abandoned old castles, pyramids, towers and sphinxes. "Geologists say that rocks at the bottom of the canyon date back millions of years," a sailor informed me. "They even found fossils of dynasaurs' eggs there, and beside them were possum fossils. Natural, I suppose, because possums used to eat the eggs." As the sun set, the Grand Canyon became such a wild and vivid mass of colour that I wanted to cry.

Pursuing my Greyhound gallop through the U.S.A., I called on a friend of my mother's in Long Beach, California, and after an afternoon in Disneyland, pushed on to Los Angeles where my hostess took me on the routine tour of the Hollywood sights. Here Lana Turner was 'discovered', there Jayne Mansfield was married, and in this very house lived Alfred Hitchcock. Then on by way of Las Vegas casinos and the Hoover Dam, near Boulder, which, in their very different ways, left me breathless with wonder, to San Francisco.

For a long time I just stood gazing at the Golden Gate bridge, stretching thinly above the harbour; the world's longest suspension bridge, it spanned the entrance to the Pacific Ocean. San Francisco was full of sharp hills, and I decided to ride on one of the old cable-cars which clattered up and down them. Before getting aboard at the terminus, I rolled up my sleeves with the other passengers and helped to turn the car around on a wooden disc which was laid into the road.

At the top of the hill I left the cable-car and walked along the sunny streets past a policeman on a corner who was standing beside a snoring drunk. Two blocks farther along a man with a bandage around his head fell down in front of me. Rushing back to the policeman I'd seen I told him about it. "Does he look drunk?" asked the policeman. "He looks as though he's dying," I replied dramatically. I left the policeman hovering between the two unfortunates.

That evening found me seated on a bus bound for Santa Rosa. Sitting beside me on the bus was a college student called Gail, who said that she and her sisters would love to have an English girl stay at their home. That was when I really fell in love with California! When I saw that rolling green countryside – and rode with Gail one morning in the Redwood Forest. The trees there were old and tall, stretching far into the blue Californian sky – gigantic – majestic – godly. The air around the trees was sweet smelling and balmy. Just to be among them was pure poetry.

"Where will you be going to from here, Wendy?" Gail's father enquired one day. "Salt Lake City," I replied. "Well," he said, "if you'd like to visit Sacramento, the capital city of our state, we can take you there on Saturday when we go to the trade fair, and it's on your way to Salt Lake."

I spent some hours at the Sacramento Trade Fair with Gail

and her family, before travelling onwards through the night. The bus drove right into Salt Lake City, capital of the state of Utah, and situated on the Jordan River. On my way to see the lake, I passed Temple Square, where the tall granite temple of the Mormons thrust six spires into a cloudless sky. The square is the centre of the Mormons' religious life, I was told, for it is where they perform the three most important ceremonies of their creed.

From Salt Lake I travelled eastwards, stopping at Denver and Kansas City, then proceeding southwards to New Orleans. I thoroughly enjoyed the days I spent in New Orleans, and especially liked to wander around the Vieux Carré quarter. As I walked along the narrow streets, past the laced iron balconies and red walls, I observed that every second house was some sort of dive, from which pure jazz would rip into an atmosphere already heavily laden with the odours of French cooking. Sometimes an open door would give me a glimpse into a shady patio, where palms, vines, banana trees and numerous tropical flowers grew with abandon.

Most of the passengers on my bus to Birmingham, Alabama, were negroes and they constituted forty-five per cent of that city's population. I was to learn. The countryside through which we travelled was beautiful, just acres of rolling pasture meadows where fat beef and dairy cattle grazed upon the succulent grass. The atmosphere, however, was not so beautiful. Waiting rooms at the Greyhound bus stations we stopped at were segregated. Here, a negro was really a negro, a word which to his white brothers obviously meant 'inferior', 'deficient', 'subordinate' – but never equal.

I arrived at Miami at noon one day, and stepping out of my air-conditioned bus, felt a great wave of heat. I explored Miami Beach, gaping at the ultra modern hotels, the millionaires' 'cabins', the private luxury yachts, and so forth. Fun there, maybe, with a nice partner and lots of money, I mused. That night I slept on the floor of a ladies' rest room.

The first place I visited in Washington was the Smithsonian Institute, which dealt with everything from space flights to natural history. Deciding to inspect the seat of the government, I walked along towards the white dome of the Capitol. With a special pass I was able to watch parliamentary debates, both in the Senate and in the House of Representatives. There wasn't much going on that day, but little page-boys still scurried around. Lads of fourteen to seventeen years old, they acted as messengers for the senators. They were well paid, I was told, attending their schools from 6.30 a.m. so as to fit everything in.

Before leaving the capital I climbed both the Lincoln and Washington memorials. Abraham Lincoln's larger-than-life statue sat overlooking a large stretch of water where goldfish swam to and fro, but the memorial to George Washington was a huge white marble obelisk, 555 feet high. From the top I gazed upon the whole city, the abundant trees, parks and wide avenues, immaculate beneath a brilliant blue sky. The capital of the United States seemed calmer and the pace of life slower than in the other cities I'd seen.

In Philadelphia I somehow got into the slums and might have stayed there all night, but for a kind lady in a car who offered me a lift. "If you are visiting our city for the first time, don't form your impressions from this area," she smiled. "How long do you intend to stay here?" "Oh, only a couple of days," I replied, explaining to her that I only had ninety-nine days of cheap Greyhound travel around the United States, and wished to see as much of it as possible. "Then come and stay with us," said the lady. "I'm Mrs Klein — we're Jewish. We will be celebrating Yum Kippur, our New Year feast, tomorrow. Would you like to join us?" This was a wonderful opportunity for me to learn something new and I gratefully accepted Mrs Klein's kind offer.

The next day at dinner I put a yarnalke on to my head like the rest of the family. Candles were lit and Hebrew prayers were chanted, then we dined on *'prociss'* — meat wrapped with cabbage leaves and cooked in a delicious tomato sauce. The rabbi had invited me to attend the actual Yum Kippur service at the synagogue and when we got there it was already crowded with people. Everyone wore yarnalkes and the men wore blue and white striped fringed shawls complying with a law in the Old Testament. The ark on the platform at one end of the synagogue was framed by a huge star of David and, within, when the curtain had been drawn back, the sacred scrolls of the Torah could be seen, decorated with silver and written out by hand.

"Our blood sacrifice was done away with in the year A.D. 70," Mrs Klein informed me as we all drove off to a friend's house

95

for the Yum Kippur feast. "All Kosher food," they told me as we sat down to eat. 'Kosher food', I gathered, was meat and dairy produce specially prepared or killed. The meat, for example, had been drained of blood. and only the front part of the animal was used. "We're 'stomach Jews' I'm afraid," smiled Mrs Klein later. "We eat all the right things, but don't make the effort to go to our synagogue very often. And, but don't tell the rabbi, for the children's sake, we have Christmas in our house."

Hustling, bustling New York at last! I was walking along Fifth Avenue, sweating with the weight of my knapsack beneath a vigorous autumn sun. In my pocket were several names and addresses, of friends of friends who lived way out in the suburbs of the city. However, I allowed myself to be pushed along by the 'rush-hour' crowd, not caring where they pushed me, but feeling that if I stood still or tried to turn around, I would be trampled over by the million hurrying feet.

When a girl beside me asked where I was from, I breathlessly answered her, as a familiar pain started to sear across my shoulder blades. She told me that she was training to become an actress, that she shared a flat with another girl, and that they had a settee . . .

Greenwich Village was crammed with dimly lit coffee bars, where long-haired poets wove impromptu ballads, negroes crooned endless blues, and beatniks plucked at their guitars and rendered folk songs. Into one of these places we went, to sit at a table among a mass of others, at which boys and girls were earnestly playing chess, studying books, or absorbing the entertainment.

The next morning found me walking beyond Times Square to Brooklyn, where I hopped on a boat which chugged around the Statue of Liberty. Then I made for the Empire State Building, the tallest sky-scraper of all. From its top story, I could feel it swaying in the wind, and, looking down, I really began to understand just how vast was New York City.

When I arrived at the United Nations headquarters a debate was in progress. I heard speeches given by Malian, Russian and Cuban representatives. The speeches were translated simultaneously into English, French, Spanish, Russian and Chinese, and with the use of headphones, all could get their own particular language. Mali, I remember, stressed most of all that

The end of a hunt for a Cambodian killer tiger

With Laotian press reporters

A Thai greeting

Glutinous rice
for a family
lunch in Laos

there should be no racial discrimination in her country. The representative of the U.S.S.R. expressed his country's hope that the signing of the anti-nuclear test treaty would cause a lessening of tensions between the nuclear powers. Then Cuba's voice was heard – blasting the United States with might and main, accusing them of warring in Cuba, Vietnam and Honduras and training men so that they could go and feed their imperialistic ideas along with 'Aid' to underdeveloped countries, so bribing them for their votes in the U.N. assembly. As soon as the Castroites had finished, the United States representative accused Cuba of being an obstacle to world peace for, with Communist China, they had refused to sign the treaty.

The days seemed to fly after that. There were all the museums to visit, the magnificent *La Boheme* at the Met. Opera, Central Park, the Stock Exchange; and, during the afternoons, I used to attend some of the city's interesting free lectures and TV shows.

Then at last I was sitting on a bus, leaving that unique city far behind. Looking back, I saw for a long time the dark skyscrapers which formed an unforgettable skyline. And to think, I mused, all that grew up from a jungly island, once owned by Red Indians and sold to explorers for twenty-four dollars' worth of goods.

The first Canadian city I went to was Montreal – the largest and most cosmopolitan, I was told. Informed that a newspaper there would appreciate an interview, I went straight to their office and, after supplying the information, met a journalist called Frank who invited me to spend my Montreal days at his home. When I accepted the first thing Frank did was to take me right up to the top of Mount Royal on the back of his motor scooter. On the summit, an icy wind blew around us from the North Pole, and dry leaves crackled beneath our feet. The view was striking: the busy port, the dark hills rising from the plain, and the immense Saint Lawrence River upon which the sun was sending a weak, silvery beam from a pile of cumulus clouds.

Before leaving Montreal I spent a day in Quebec City, a principal seaport, oozing with history. The countryside between Montreal and Quebec was all vast pine forests, clean-looking wooden houses and gurgling streams. Then came a long bridge, stretching over the Saint Lawrence River.

Quebec City, I discovered, could be roughly divided into two parts – new Quebec below, and old Quebec above, the two sections being connected by a funicular and a maze of alleys. Wandering through the narrow, slummy streets which had given the old part of the city rather a bad reputation, I observed pokey, French-looking tobacco shops, and mademoiselles exercising their poodles. When church bells pealed, whole families hurried to Mass. I watched them and sniffed the air which carried the unparalleled odour of newly baked croissants.

I had always hoped to see the Niagara Falls, and one afternoon found me dwarfed by the vastness and deafened by the perpetual roar of this marvel of nature. However, I could not help comparing these falls with those I'd seen in Brazil's Iguacu – and I preferred the wildness of the latter, in their jungle setting.

Soon I was travelling westwards through the United States again, to Detroit and then Chicago. The busy industrial section, the shopping centre, the white-domed B'hai Temple, one of the most beautiful of its kind in the world – the Natural History Museum, the Chicago Tribune building, the Civic Opera Building, the Art Institute, the airport and the slums – I was shown all over the gigantic city. Then we drove along the planetarium peninsular around which stretched the blue immensity of Lake Michigan, backed by Chicago's sky-scraper skyline.

It was in Minneapolis, Minnesota, that I was given the American Navy anorak, which I was to wear right until the end of my journey, three and a half years later. Upon hearing that I would be up in Alaska during the coldest months of the year, the lawyer's wife with whom I was staying searched her junk room and produced the faded anorak. She spent two days in shortening its thick sleeves, putting four inner (secret) pockets into the lining, and finishing it off with a waterproof hood – trimmed with a piece of her grandmother's mink.

Then I was travelling across the wide sheep and cattle plains of Montana, where cowboys, attired in tight blue jeans and high leather boots, lounged around Billings and other far-western towns. The old grandfathers in their battered felt hats looked to me as though they had just stepped out of a Western movie.

Snow covered the passes over the Rocky Mountains, and frosted firs glistened like tinselled Christmas trees in the sunshine. When the bus came to the last pass on the Rockies before descending to the coast, I made out some Swiss-type chalets and a ski-lift, through a sudden blizzard of snow. Then we plunged down into a green valley where rivers gushed and rain instead of snow beat against the windows. Pumpkins, left over from the festivities of Hallowe'en, still lay in the fields around the small-holding on which I stayed, before, on the ninety-ninth day of my ninety-nine dollar Greyhound bus ticket, I crossed the frontier into Canada again.

From now on, I should have to pay separately for each mode of transport I took, unless of course I managed to hitch-hike. However, I wasn't tied to time any more, so the first thing I did when I arrived in Vancouver was to get myself a job – this time as a 'mother's help'. I lived in with the family, learned (from scratch) how to change a baby's nappy, and booked my passage on a ship which would be sailing to New Zealand on February 9th, 1964. I had enquired at the travel agency if it were not possible to cross over the Bering Strait from Alaska to the Chukotski Peninsula of Eastern Siberia, now that the sea would be frozen over with winter ice. "Only Eskimoes take their dog sleighs over there," replied the travel agent flatly. "Some American whites went over once, but they never came back." So Australia would have to be the jumping-off place for my intended – and much hoped for – visit to China and other Asian Countries.

Then it was Edmonton for me, arriving in a blizzard with a temperature of eight degrees below zero. Staying with a kind family, I earned a few more dollars by shovelling snow, and baby-sitting for thirty-five cents an hour.

After spending one day in Grand Prairie, 600 miles farther north, I hitch-hiked on to Dawson Creek, situated at Mile Zero of the Alcan Highway, which continued right up to Fairbanks in Alaska. It was in Dawson Creek that I spent Christmas 1963, with yet another hospitable Canadian family, who stuffed me with turkey and cranberry jelly, sweet corn, stuffing, roast potatoes, mincemeat pies, and egg-nog ice-cream. It was cosy to be inside a warm house when the temperature outside was twenty-five degrees below zero, and wise too, when a chinook, or warm wind, had melted the snow which had then frozen again to make the streets of the town into a treacherous sheet of ice.

Soon I was travelling on to Fort Nelson and Whitehorse, •

where I spent New Year's festivities with some newspaper people, before proceeding to Fairbanks with a mail truck.

At the United States (Alaskan) frontier, we all got a good going-over by the stern immigration official, who gave me a lecture on the penalties of working in the States without a permit, the truck-drivers a lecture on giving me a lift, and then practically turned me upside down looking for smuggled heroin.

In Fairbanks a stranger, seeing me settling down for the night in an hotel lobby, made a quick phone call and then put me in a taxi. He said he was sending me to some people he knew. I wondered what sort of people would be ready to welcome a stranger at such an hour.

The driver stopped at a large wooden house and there on the doorstep stood what appeared to be a whole family – all in their dressing-gowns and pajamas. The father, I gathered, was a professor at the satellite tracking base.

"If you want to find a lift to Anchorage, phone the radio people," said the professor's wife one morning, "your message will be broadcast simultaneously. This is such a remote town, you see, that we all try to help each other." So that is what I did, and soon I was setting off towards Anchorage with the gentleman who had replied to my request, a Cherokee Indian called John.

"I'm a catskinner," disclosed John as we drove through dense ice fog, with a thermometer hovering around thirty-two degrees below zero. "You ... er ... skin cats?" I asked, somewhat dismayed. "Yeah, a bulldozer driver y'know," he smiled, taking a long pull at his enormous dollar cigar. "Durin' eight months of the year I'm a catskinner, an' durin' the other four months I come into town an' really live it up!" And with that he waved his cigar across the gleaming dashboard of his 1964 Cadillac. "Of course, I have another job as well. I'm a professional musician, actually – play the guitar and sing hilly-billy songs in an Anchorage night-club." Turning my head I observed several spangled cowboy costumes, along with hats, large boots and a guitar laid carefully over the back seat. "My ... this road's that slick ... !" cursed John savagely as we skidded across it over the grey ice. Then he patted a Bible which lay beside his windscreen. "I'm protected by the Lord," he muttered, and then said, "Yeah, doll, an eye for an eye, a tooth for a tooth! At school I fought my teachers cause I knew best, see? That's why I never made college. In this life, money's everythin', doll, the only means of happiness."

Upon our arrival in Anchorage, John took me to the house of Paddy McGill, an Irishman for whom I had a message from somebody in Whitehourse. It was Paddy who introduced me to a genial doctor and his wife. The doctor's house was situated on the edge of a bluff, and from it one could watch the blue, floating ice move slowly by all day long to form an ever-changing picture.

In that winter wonderland of the north I did some skiing — but on artificial snow. "It can only be made at below zero temperature," an Alaskan informed me as I watched the white powder shooting up into the air to fall on the mountainside. Another sport I practised up north was curling, but the one that gave me the biggest thrill was dog-sleigh racing, although then I went along with Paddy, merely as a spectator.

"The dogs have run over a fourteen-mile course today," Paddy explained, as we stood at the barrier of the snowy track waiting for the first team to appear. "There is a minimum of five dogs to a sleigh, huskies and other breeds. The most intelligent is the leader, and the two strongest are behind. For our annual fur rendezvous here, the competitors in the dog-sleigh races are mostly Eskimoes, who race their dogs until they drop — hoping for one of the money prizes." Just then the winning team came into sight, their driver scooting behind with one foot on the sleigh runner, his hands grasping the iron rail. People cheered, prizes were handed out and then it was over and the dogs were being loaded into the straw-filled backs of pick-ups to be taken home.

One evening Paddy took me to several honky-tonks where we listened to hilly-billy music; I was reminded of my redskin friend. At another dive the band were all Eskimoes. "I'd really love to meet an Eskimo family at home," I told Paddy. "I'll arrange that for you tomorrow," he said brightly.

The Eskimo family we visited lived in a wooden shack warmed by a wood stove, as did so many of their race nowadays, enjoying the benefits of white-man's civilisation, such as schools, hospitals, family allowances and so on. "Yes, we've certainly changed our way of life a lot during the past few years," said the Eskimo father of the family. "Not many of us live in igloos now except for our Canadian brothers. We still eat much of our own type of food though, mixed with white-man's food. Here, try some 'squaw's candy'!" This was dried, smoked salmon chopped into small pieces, and tasted like cold kippers to me.

"What I'd really like to try is raw seal blubber," I told him. "I believe that you eat it quite often." A rapid family conference in Eskimo followed, full of deep, guttural noises. "Yes, it is possible," the Eskimo father informed me at last, "we have some already in the house. Please join us for dinner." Some minutes later I was seated before a saucer on which lay the neatly chopped-up blubber, with some slices of toast. "I have left the door of the W.C. open – just in case!" said my Eskimo hostess with an understanding smile. The blubber tasted all right, but after having chewed the same piece for fifteen minutes, it had not got any smaller, so I swallowed it whole. A few pieces later, I raised my eyes to find that the whole Eskimo family were staring at me aghast. "What's the matter?" I whispered to Paddy. "You're only supposed to chew it, and when the juices have gone you spit it out," replied my friend with a grin. It was my hostess who clutched her mouth and ran to the W.C.

The days flew by, and I realised that I should soon have to be thinking about my return journey to Vancouver to board ship to recross the Pacific Ocean. The Alcan Highway was often impassable during spells of bad weather, and I couldn't afford to take chances.

On the night we left Anchorage there was a full moon, which rose above the mountains and caused the frosted trees to glisten around the Matanooska Glacier. After a meal in Whitehorse, we drove to a place called Takhini, where hot water bubbled out of the ground at 120 degrees, and that is where we bathed, in a hot pool with dazzling snow plopping regularly into the water, beneath an azure sky, where the temperature was minus twenty degrees.

I left it as late as possible before boarding a truck bound for Vancouver. I hated to go, to leave the spacious Yukon Territory, where babies sat in sleighs instead of prams, and where the 'Mounties' wore fur caps and long coats, instead of their familiar khaki hats and red jackets.

As the truck moved slowly southwards back along the Alcan Highway, I looked out of the window and saw a moon rise over the last of the deep northern snow.

Chapter 12

February 1964–July 1964

"Aloha!" is a greeting so familiar to anyone who has ever sailed to the Island of Hawai, and which I heard for the first time as my ship glided into Honolulu harbour. With only a few hours to spend on the island, I was determined not to miss even a minute of them, and rushed ashore. I made straight for Pearl Harbor and from the U.S. base there I took a boat out to the wreck of the *Arizona*. It was one of the American ships which had been bombed by the Japanese in 1941, and which now stood as a monument to the 1,550 men who had been killed aboard her, many of whom were still entombed within her rusting body. At every sunrise and sunset, I was told, the stars and stripes were raised and lowered above the wreck as a sign of respect to those who, because they had been pawns in the chess game played by world powers, would never enjoy the flowers and sunshine of the island again.

Four days later, just after 'missing a day' due to the International Date Line, we sighted Viti Levu, largest of the 322 Fijian islands. Only one day in which to explore Fiji, I sighed.

Rattling along on a bus through brilliant green rice paddies, we passed villages of grass houses and wooden stilted huts, a Hindu temple, and a moslem school. Then up through banana groves and sugar-cane plantations we climbed, until, twelve miles and a one and threepence bus-fare from Suva, later we crossed over a long bridge and stopped in Nausori – a riverside hill village.

I shall never forget the countryside I travelled through that afternoon. The emerald jungles, the masses of gorgeous flowers, the slender coconut palms, and the chattering mountain streams, wending their leisurely way towards the sea. Then as the sun set behind 'Joskai's Thumb' I climbed into one of the wooden buses, bound for Suva again.

"How quickly these two years have gone by since I was here last," I thought, as I set out from Auckland along one of New Zealand's leafy lanes, happy to sniff again the wild hyacinths and damp earth. "And now to the South Island," I told myself, "to work hard; apples this time, I think. Put the money into traveller's cheques, then Australia, more work, and after? With God's help, I shall go to China."

Some hours later found me standing at the rail of the *Aramoana*, crossing Cook Strait to Picton, on the South Island. There were white-crested waves, a howling wind in the rigging, and screaming gulls. Then it was the green fields of the land, snug-looking cottages, and two Maoris rubbing noses in their traditional form of greeting.

I had chosen apple-picking instead of tobacco-stringing in order to widen my experience, and on my first day in the orchard I suddenly realised that I much preferred working with apples; apples were edible. Apple-picking finished at 5 p.m. each day, and then I would trot down the hill to a tobacco farm and earn some extra money by lateraling for them. The tobacco crowd were gay and rough – and I enjoyed being among them again.

Some time before I left the apple farm, a *Teach Yourself Chinese* book arrived, from my ever-supporting mother. Immediately I settled down enthusiastically to learn at least one lesson each day, covering huge wads of paper with my sprawling characters, and filling the orchards with my earnest attempts at a genuine Mandarin pronunciation. The first time I started this "mun caw yu run? hao bu hao?" business, the farmer's wife came tearing along through the apple trees at top speed. After staring at me for some minutes, she gasped, "Oh, it's you! – I thought that one of our cows was in labour."

"Pan, nurse!" ". . . Pan!" came the familiar shout. I was back at work in my second Sydney geriatric hospital. There I was, rubbing alcohol on to bedsores, trying to press the lumps out of porridge, and scrubbing plastic sheets. One evening I was off duty and had gone into the TV lounge to watch a film about the funeral of Pandit Nehru. During the intermission the usual jingles came on, including an advertisement for B.P. "B.P. . . . bed-pan!" chuckled matron when she saw it. "You've got bed-pans on the brain, matron," I told her cheerfully. That was that. Sacked I was, and with only three weeks left before I would be sailing to Singapore. The only job I could get for such a short period was that of a 'mother's help', which I didn't mind in the least, having happy memories of the time when I did this kind of work in Vancouver.

Never had I appreciated a sea voyage so much as that particular one from Australia to Singapore. What a different atmosphere! The ship was Italian, with rows of washing hung, Neapolitan style, all along the lower decks. Even crossing the equator meant getting the 'spaghetti treatment' – to the accompaniment of Verdi's *Aida*, played by the ship's band.

Singapore – 'City of the Lion' – how pleased I was to be there once again, meeting Chi-Chin Chang and all my old friends. Sally and Sim Koo Liao, old friends with whom I was now staying, lived in an attractive bungalow in a smart suburb such as one could have found on the outskirts of any European city. To get to it we had crossed Singapore River, and the harbour where Indonesian boats and junks were moored, all immobile now, due to the current upheavals in their country.

Sim played the piano in a combo at nights, and during the day he was an assiduous business executive, so I didn't see much of him after the first evening. Sally, however, was tired of being alone in the bungalow all day and seemed only too delighted to take me around. When dusk fell, Sally suggested, "Let's go and visit my uncle. He's a nice fellow, but has one er . . . habit. He's a heavy smoker." "Oh, lots of people smoke," I remarked nonchalantly. "Does he spend all his money on cigarettes?" "Not on cigarettes," whispered my friend, "opium."

Uncle lived in China-town, down a narrow street where each family was squeezed into box-like apartments above the small shops that were their means of livelihood. Soon we were feeling our way up a dark, almost perpendicular staircase, to the top floor of one of these old wooden apartment buildings. The door upon which Sally tapped was opened by a sallow-complexioned woman in faded pajamas, who was followed by a string of children. She bowed and smilingly led us into the small room which was her home, along with ten other members of the family. I hardly needed to ask which of them was Sally's uncle. At one side of the room there was a raised wooden step covered with a rush mat, on which stood a table. Beside it lay the man whom I guessed to be uncle, an emaciated figure with mere slits for eyes, leaning back on a cushion. He seemed as pleased to see us as were the rest of the family, so, walking across to where he lay, I asked him if I might watch him smoke. "Yes, of course," he replied, displaying a row of black stumps that were beyond any dental care, "Come and smoke a pipe with me." So that was how I came to smoke opium – for the first and last time in my life.

Sitting on the mat beside uncle, I observed that on his table were some packets of what I took to be the opium, a long pipe, a small oil-lamp and various rags and pieces of wire. Taking one of the greaseproof paper packets, uncle opened it and heated its black, treacly-looking contents over the oil-lamp flame. Then, after rubbing it around the top of his pipe bowl, he pushed it inside. "Now first get into the right smoking position," said uncle, pushing a cushion beneath my elbow and passing me the pipe. "Hold the bowl over the flame and suck deeply." The opium had a sweet, sickly smell when burning, and after one pipe I suffered no ill effects. Then uncle smoked a pipeful, after which I smoked my second and last pipe. "Any more of it will make you drunk," said Sally, who had been keeping an eye on the proceeedings.

"Ah . . . wonderful!" murmured her uncle, as he settled down to yet another pipeful. "How many do you smoke a day?" came my question. "Four pipes," he smiled, "can't afford more; costs one Malayan dollar per packet. Expensive, but the trouble is that I've got into such a habit of smoking it now, that I shouldn't be able to work without it. It helps me to relax, and calms my nerves."

"I'd love to visit Sarawak to see the Dyaks, long-houses and so forth, but I'm not quite sure how much a return passage on one of the boats would cost me," I told Chi-Chin Chang one day. "Nothing," he grinned. "One of my business associates runs a shipping company and their boats go to Sarawak regularly. I'll arrange for you to go as 'the captain's niece' if you like!"

My Sarawak boat turned out to be a 5,000-ton cargo affair with Chinese sailors. The officers and captain were Malays. The following morning found us gliding between Indonesian jungle islands nearing Kuching, Sarawak's principal town, on the banks of the Sarawak River. The Malay kampongs, villages of thatched houses built high off the ground, became clearer as we approached.

In Kuching we learned that our cargo could not be unloaded until the following day as, in Sarawak, Mohammed's birthday was being celebrated one day later than in Singapore for some reason that nobody seemed to remember. "You can't win!" muttered the captain. "Come on, Wendy, my niece, let's go and see the town. I have three wives, who all live separately, and I'm keeping out of the way of wife number two on this voyage — she said something about her mother coming to stay . . ." "Hum, it must be thwarting, having three mothers-in-law to contend with!" I chuckled.

The next day I stayed on board and watched the work-gang in action. In the early afternoon we sailed through Amazonic type scenery — past fishermen in dugouts and thickly vegetated shores, towards Sarikai. A tiny port farther along the river, Sarikai was crowded with Dyaks, who, if it hadn't been for their mode of dress, I would have found hard to distinguish from the local Chinese. Their long-house stood side by side amongst orange groves and coconut palms, and their naked children ran to meet our boat.

The captain had a bicycle on board, and when we reached Sibu, he hired one for me. "Then we can get to my house and back quickly," was his explanation, "and cheap enough, at one hundred and fifty cents for twenty-four hours!" I worked this out at three and sixpence, and agreed.

Then we were off, cycling through the town and into the country, past pepper plants, orange groves and rubber plantations till we came to some tidy-looking, well-painted houses, one of which was the captain's. Soon I was seated at a table with the captain, his step-children and wife number three, enjoying a delicious lunch. Later, as we were relaxing over coffee, the quartermaster arrived and asked me if I'd care to attend a belated Mohammed's birthday feast at his house. "You can spend the night there," he said, "and we'll return to the ship tomorrow morning." "Go!" smiled the captain, "he lives in a long-house."

The quartermaster's home was in a Malay kampong, and no Chinese were permitted to live there, he told me. At the entrance to the kampong stood a mosque, from where the imam was calling the people to their five o'clock prayers.

"Welcome to my humble residence," said the quartermaster as we arrived at what certainly looked to be a very long house. His wife was quite beautiful and couldn't have been more than sixteen years old. "Fifteen and a half," she told me when I asked her. The house was already full of people. All the men were wearing small round hats, those of the hadjis being of pure white. Sitting down beside the quartermaster's young wife and baby girl, I drank the pink, syrupy liquid which somebody offered me – a non-alcoholic beverage which always seemed to be a firm favourite with female Malays. Later I was given a 'Bajukurong' – the Malay women's costume – to wear, "to make you feel at home," laughed the quartermaster.

My favourite dish that evening was the kebabs and I devoured twenty-four sticks of the delicious grilled meat, along with hot sauce, raw onions and cucumber. After the meal, the men retired to another room to chant prayers, while the womenfolk remained where they were, sitting cross-legged on a mat, so I stayed with them and played with their babies. Two hours later the prayers came to an end, and people began to settle for the night.

Breakfast the next morning was an omelette made with eggs, chillies and onions, after which the quartermaster and I repaired to our ship, sloshing through muddy streets, for it was raining heavily.

The next day the sun shone and we were soon at sea again, on our homeward voyage to Singapore, stopping at Binatang, Sarikai, and Kuching on the way. One afternoon, the captain was busy cleaning his bicycle, while I lay reading a book on the sofa in his cabin. Then I must have fallen asleep. When I awoke, it was to the Arabic strains of "Praise be to Allah . . . the beneficent and the merciful . . Lord of all worlds . . . Owner of the day of judgment." The captain had unrolled his prayer-mat and was praying on the cabin floor beside me. Shutting my eyes again, I also prayed that I, too, would always be as ready to evince my faith in God before strangers. It was a good lesson.

We arrived in Singapore after dark, and the first thing I heard was a voice over a loudspeaker, beseeching the people to live at peace with their neighbours.

Chapter 13

August 1964–November 1964

It was so kind of Chi-Chin Chang to send me to Bangkok on this train, I thought, as the locomotive sped smoothly on towards Thailand's capital. Hitch-hiking is not always easy. Then, glancing from the carriage window, I observed a long-tusked working elephant, a pond covered with floating masses of pink water-lilies, and some round-hatted farmers labouring in the rice paddies with their grey and fawny coloured water-buffaloes. This was Thailand! Filled with happy memories for me, a land of softly spoken, well-mannered people, whose musical language had no hard sounds at all yet contained more variations of voice tone than Chinese. Beautiful land of the Thais! land of the free people.

Mr Nai's friend, Xaloey Khoman, was in his Bangkok home when I arrived there, and, as Mr Nai had predicted on my previous visit, Mr Xaloey, his wife, and their three daughters welcomed me as a member of their family, to stay with them for as long as I wished.

How I enjoyed my first Thai meal for nearly four years! There was rice, mutton curry, octopus, sweet potatoes, and a dessert made from egg-yolks beaten with sugar. Then followed 'namyai' – a lichee-like fruit with sweet white flesh, and 'rambutans' – prickly round fruits with soft, juicy centres.

That night I slept on a settee and was glad of a rest the following morning when, as it was Friday, the moslem day of prayer was observed. In the evening we went to a restaurant for dinner and over whisky Mr Nai grew very pessimistic about the future. "Owing to the present communist activities in Burma, Laos and Cambodia, not to mention Vietnam, I think that we Thais have got cause for uneasiness – concerning the intentions of seven hundred million communist Chinese," he said.

Why didn't I stand up for all the wonderful Chinese I knew, when the Thais here were speaking against that race in general? A voice inside me warned that I shouldn't, and even without knowing why, I obeyed. Yes, upon thinking it over, I realised that from now on during my travels in this part of the world I must never become entangled with political discussions of any kind. Not if I still wished to achieve my ambition and go to China and the Vietnams and to get out of them again safely. I must learn to listen, but to keep my opinions to myself; for after all, I was travelling to learn, and not to judge.

Mr Xaloey had a friend who was a doctor in Nongkhai, so when I came to that northern town on the banks of the Makong River, from where I should be proceeding to Laos, I called at his home. The doctor's wife was a dentist so the couple were extremely busy but insisted that I stay with them and lent me a bicycle on which to explore alone. Nongkhai was a pleasant place, with flower beds, a fountain, a temple, some shops and a new hospital all set on the river bank.

"The Mae Nam Makong is the seventh largest river in the world," said the man beside me in the small motor boat which took us across to Thadua, a Laosian port just opposite to Nangkhai. Vientianne was some distance from Thadua, so to get there, I hopped on to a local bus. I think that I might have passed by that capital altogether, if the bus terminus hadn't been there. It may have been the earthen pavements where buffaloes wandered which made me think that it was just another village, or the small shops with tri-shaws moving slowly past them instead of the heavy flow of traffic which I had rather expected. At the top of what I guessed to be the main street stood a monument which closely resembled the Arc de Triomphe, and, like the Paris model, was also built over a tomb to the unknown soldier.

Well, at least, Vientianne has personality, I told myself as I searched for the home of the Laotian 'boy' — Vattha Sopsaisana — who had invited me to be his guest here. Upon arriving at his house, I was surprised to discover that he had five strapping children who were all seated on the floor beside him and his wife, eating lunch. When the introductions were over, Vattha indicated a vacant spot on the floor, and invited me to help myself to the food. "In this straw box there is glutinous rice," he informed me, "then here we have dried meat, green papaya curry and cabbage soup." Soon I was learning to eat as my Laotian friends – first squeezing the rice into balls in the palm of my hand, before dipping it into the various other dishes.

Breakfast the next morning was glutinous rice and dried meat left over from the night before, followed by pieces of sugar-cane and cold tea. Then the Sopsaisanas had to hurry away to their jobs – so I helped one of Vattha's pre-school-age sons to wipe the algae from the walls of the fish-tank. It was a spacious aquarium, set into the wall of the house – so that the people in the street could enjoy watching the fishes too. "What do you feed them on?" I asked my young friend. "Oh, bugs from the open sewers," he replied casually.

When I told Vattha of my intention to travel through Laos and into Cambodia, he advised me to take a boat as far as possible along the Makong River, as on the water there would be less danger of being blown up by the mines which were constantly being laid under roads and bridges by the Pathet Lao.

"There are some cargo vessels here which also carry paratroopers down the river," he said. "I'll get you on one of those. There won't be any charge." That evening Vattha announced that he had arranged for me to sail for Savannakhet on the following Monday morning.

My boat for Savannakhet was called *Viensavanne*. She was a small vessel, but quite conspicuous, with a brilliant blue prow. From prow to stern she could have been no more than twelve feet long, and I understood why the paratroopers on board looked so damp and dismal; they had been stuck there, waiting to leave Vientianne for the past two days.

For several days the boat moved slowly from tiny port to tiny port, Bungkarl and its woodmills, Ban Pang and its charcoal, Khammoune, and finally Savannakhet.

Here I stayed for a few days with a friend of Vattha's who had a pineapple and banana plantation. Then came the chance of a lift in a truck to Pakse which was too good to miss, despite the danger of mines. The road to Pakse was fairly good, and followed the banks of the Makong River through dense, soggy jungle. I had damaged a finger on a rusty door and when we reached Pakse my host took me to a doctor. When he had dressed my finger, the doctor turned to Mr Ouday and suggested, "Why don't you take our English visitor to see the

Filipino hospital at Paksong? I'm sure that any world traveller would find it interesting."

A small village up in the hills, Paksong had a cool, bracing climate, and abounded with flowers and clear streams. The many Filipinos there lived in Filipino-style grass huts, and I discovered that they had been sent by their government on a sort of medical mission to Laos.

The next morning I called at the clinic to tell the Filipino doctor how much I had enjoyed meeting his compatriots and seeing their fine work up-country. Just as I was leaving, into the clinic walked an American, who was also a doctor and a good friend of the Filipinos. Soon he was telling us all about his work in a leper colony not far from Pakse, and I expressed my eagerness to go there. "Yes, you should see it," said the young American, "but I would hate to let you run the risk of being captured by the Pathet Lao. The lepers live right away from the main road and you never know." Then he went on to relate how, not long ago, two English schoolteachers had been kidnapped by the communists and that the British consul, who had gone to rescue them, had been captured also.

The leper colony was divided into two parts by a river, and I couldn't help a chuckle when my American friend informed me that the lepers on one side of it were Protestant, and on the other were Roman Catholics. "A French padre lives permanently with the Catholic ones," he added, in a voice full of unconcealed admiration.

During the course of that afternoon we visited practically every house in the colony, crossing the river by means of a tree-trunk bridge. It was stimulating to see the expressions of hope and confidence in the eyes of the lepers that I realised were often lacking in Buddhist villages, even though the people were healthy. Here, the lepers were being encouraged to live normal, active lives, bringing up their children, going to church, weaving baskets, and so forth. With the use of modern drugs, their flesh wasted away far more slowly than would have normally been the case, and in some circumstances the patient was cured. As we took our leave of those fine people, I saw what I shall never forget as long as I live – a bouncing healthy baby boy, being lifted on to the shoulders of his handless father.

I spent many happy days in Pakse with Mr Ouday and his

family, but when his wife had to leave suddenly one day to visit a sick relative I decided I must move on.

The next day I leaned out of the truck that was giving me a lift to watch the last of the Laotian jungles and paddy-fields rolling behind me. Then we stopped at a bridge which had been blown to smithereens by the Pathet Lao. "Thank goodness we shan't have them to worry about, once we get across the border into Cambodia," muttered the driver, somewhat nervously.

The last thing I saw as we crossed the frontier were three proud elephants wandering through the forest. A fitting last impression, I decided, of the country which used to be called 'Lang Xang', or 'Country of a thousand elephants.'

. . .

The man whose name was written on the envelope of a letter of recommendation which I had for Stung Treng turned out to be the governor of the province. A good-natured, hospitable person, he welcomed me into his magnificent home, and there I spent many happy days playing badminton with his children or going for walks along the bamboo bordered river which gives its name to Stung Treng – 'Treng' being a special type of bamboo which grows near the water.

One evening the governor said that he had to go to the capital on the following day and offered to give me a lift there. "Only don't talk to anyone about our journey," he warned. "I want it to be a secret, because I have just heard that the United States are encouraging Laos to come and make aggressions here and I shall be wearing my uniform." "But surely you don't believe what you heard?" I exclaimed. "Why not?" my host continued, "they're helping South Vietnam, who are fighting our friends the Chinese. We prefer to accept our 'aid from the Chinese because they give us machines, not just food and we're not afraid of them at all. Cambodia wouldn't be as valuable to them as Singapore, and what's more, it would be bad propaganda for them to take us over. Anyway, your country is friendly with Russia, what's wrong with us being friendly with the Chinese?"

The next morning, after a breakfast of rice soup, steam-cakes, fried bread and coffee, the governor sent one of his servants to put my luggage into his black car. We both sat on the back seat, the governor remarking that it was more comfortable than sitting up beside the chauffeur. That day, there could be no doubt at all as to his military rank or importance. He wore his full dress uniform complete with five stars proving that he had won fifteen battles. The governor was also a commander.

As we sped southwards, groups of men and women attired in black trouser-suits with rifles slung over their shoulders stood on the roadside and saluted my host as we passed. "These are our rural volunteers," he explained, "they assist our regular soldiers in guarding the country against capitalists, communists and anyone else who threatens Cambodia's freedom. We are a neutral country and will always be ready to fight for our rights."

From Pnom Penh I travelled to Siem Reap. There, among the governor's friends in the ancient capital, I found a man who helped to run the tourist office, and it was with him and his wife I stayed. The governor's other notes had all been for army people, and between them these kind Cambodians helped to make my stay in Siem Reap quite wonderful.

We managed to visit Angkor Wat, Angkor Them, the Pnom of Bakkong, Pre Rup, and a simply fantastic temple of red sandstone with two hundred stone faces staring from its walls called Bayon. After a wonderful few days I returned to Pnom Penh to deliver a letter to a doctor, and it was at his house that I stayed for the rest of my time there.

During the first week I called at the Japanese Embassy, which, since relations had been severed between Cambodia and South Vietnam because of the war, was now controlling the latter's affairs in Pnom Penh. The Japanese ambassador told me that although he wouldn't be happy at the thought of my travelling to Saigon by road, he would grant me a visa on condition that I had a letter of permission from my own embassy. This I procured, from a solemn British consul, whose only demand was a signed statement from me to say that I accepted entire responsibility if I should be killed or captured – or worse – in South Vietnam.

My main ambition was to go to China, and upon calling at their bustling embassy, I was informed that my application would have to take the form of a letter which would be sent off to some excellency or other in Peking.

The Chinese visa – if granted – would take at least six weeks to come through the 'red' red-tape, I was told, so I decided to go along to the North Vietnamese embassy and apply for a visa to visit that country; although I had little hope of getting in, once they discovered that I'd mingled with their enemy in the south. The Embassy for North Vietnam turned out to be my favourite, actually. It had comfortable chairs, interesting works of art in glass cases, and hot green tea being served continuously. The people there were charming and told me that if I'd care to write out a letter of application – similar to the one I had prepared for the Chinese – they would send it off to Hanoi immediately.

Now all I had to do was to wait for the visas to come through and, during the days which followed, I not only endeavoured to become as physically fit as possible but I also had a good look around Pnom Penh.

One day the Vietnamese doctor and his wife with whom I was staying proposed a trip to his pineapple plantation situated 100 kilometres east of Pnom Penh, right in the heart of tiger, bear and wild elephant country. For seventy-eight kilometres we drove along a good road, through villages and cultivated lands, eventually turning off on to the dirt track which led to the plantation. The track was so waterlogged in places that we had to make several detours and, before we came to our destination, the moon rose, making the surrounding forest mysterious and beautiful. A river ran in front of the doctor's plantation home, so there we abandoned our vehicle and took to a canoe. We were just transferring our paraphernalia into the two-storied wooden house, when a man from the village near by ran up to the doctor and proceeded to pour out a rapid stream of Cambodian, his eyes bulging with fright. "He says that a tiger has wounded two of his friends," said the doctor curtly and, seizing his box of medical supplies, he disappeared into the night. I tagged on to the line of people who followed him and, upon our arrival at one of the stilted village dwellings, I pushed up the steps until I was standing beside the doctor, so that I could hold the lamp for him as he examined the first patient. The man had a fractured thigh, some enormous gashes and was suffering from acute shock. Quickly the doctor injected anti-tetanus into the leg, then bathed the wounds with alcohol before fashioning a bamboo splint. Giving the man a large gulp of brandy and some dates from his medical kit, the doctor turned to me. "Pull the leg," he instructed. "I want to tighten the splint." The man's face screwed up in agony as I firmly straightened the battered limb but soon the neat brandy had its merciful effect, and his eyes closed.

The second victim had no bones broken but, judging by the size of the holes made by the tiger's teeth in the flesh of his thighs, the beast must have been really huge. "May have to come off," muttered the doctor as we taped up the wounds, " — look at those claw marks!"

Back at the doctor's house, he related to us all the full story of how the men had been attacked. "The tiger was first seen by the two villagers as it lay in a forest clearing, devouring a newly killed wild boar," the doctor began. "Wishing to get not only the wild boar for themselves but the tiger as well, they clapped their hands and drove the beast away. Then, grabbing the boar, they left its entrails in the clearing to entice the tiger back to the spot, and then returned to the village to arm themselves. Sixteen men came back to face that tiger, armed with nothing but one rifle which proved to be rusty and unreliable!" the doctor groaned. "They shot him and he fell — dead they thought. But he was only wounded in the paw. He leapt up on to the first man who ran to inspect him and cracked his thighbone. Luckily, the man fell backwards into some water, which saved his life. The tiger's nostrils became full of the stuff and he had to open his mouth. Then, the man who had come to drag his friend to safety was also mauled, before he managed to shove a thick stick down the tiger's throat. So they both escaped with their lives, leaving a wounded tiger on the prowl which had tasted human blood and must be got rid of. I shall send my nephew Khim and some of the men back to Pnom Penh tonight to fetch my carbines and to take the two injured to hospital."

On the following morning the weapons arrived and, after an early breakfast, the doctor 'dosed' his dog handler with half a bottle of whisky, for the old fellow was trembling with fear. "They're all nervous," my host informed me. "This tiger's the biggest they've seen in these parts. You'd better not come; stay here with my wife." "Oh no!" I exclaimed, "this will be my first tiger shoot — one of the most exciting experiences of my life! You can't deny me that."

Once over the river, we climbed aboard the jeep, driving off the trail into thick undergrowth, not following any tracks at all. The dogs, who were scampering on ahead, suddenly picked up the tiger's scent and bounded off into bamboo so thick that we had to abandon our vehicle and continue on foot. As we stalked along, there was a loud hiss and a long, black king-cobra raised its head above the grass. The doctor shot at it with his revolver, missed, and it disappeared. After that the men really did begin to lag behind. "It's a sign of bad luck here to see a snake on a tiger shoot," the doctor whispered. "I'm afraid that these chaps are becoming rather uncontrollable now, in spite of the whisky."

When we set off again, the doctor had almost to pull the dog handler along, and his dogs didn't prove much braver either, for as soon as they realised that the tiger was very close, they refused to proceed any farther. Almost bent double, I followed the doctor through the dense bamboo until we came to a shallow stream. Imprinted in the mud of the bank were fresh paw marks. "Now," whispered the doctor, "did he go across it or up-stream, or down?" We listened . . . Plop! . . . Our eyes followed the sound and there he was, a big male tiger standing in the water near a bend in the stream. Raising his carbine, the doctor shot the tiger dead – right through the heart. Meanwhile, the villagers were standing on each other's heads, struggling to get up into the bamboo trees. They were taking no more chances with the beast!

The doctor went cautiously up to the tiger and shot him through the head with his revolver. Then the men came crowding around the animal, giggling with relief and plucking out its whiskers, which were supposed to bring them luck. Tying the tiger to a pole, we hoisted it on to our shoulders and trudged triumphantly back to the jeep, the men's excited laughter ringing through the forest.

At last my visa was granted for South Vietnam and one morning found me travelling towards the frontier, having to stop at about twelve checkpoints on the way. "Well, that's as far as we go," said the driver of the motor-cycle, pointing to some barbed wire which lay stretched across the road and I gathered that on the other side of it was South Vietnam. Squeezing my-self between the strands of wire, I trotted up to the frontier office to show my papers. The only official in sight was sound asleep on the top of the desk. When he awoke he stamped my passport and, as we stood exchanging news, two jeep-loads of American and Vietnamese soldiers came along and greeted us cheerfully.

They told me that they'd come to check up on some shooting which had been heard on the Cambodian side of the frontier the night before. "Maybe some folks are not so neutral as they try to make out," muttered one of the Americans. "Say, would you like a lift to Go Dau Ha, the nearest village? It's nine miles from here and there's no public transport. From there you can easily catch a bus to Saigon."

So off we went, and later, as I sat in a bus bound for Saigon and watched the sun go down, one of the Americans came panting up to me. "Our major suggests that you spend the night here," he said. "To travel anywhere after dark in this country is dangerous nowadays – with the Viet-Cong so active."

Before we retired that night I met the Dai Uy of the South Vietnamese troops, who were based next door to the three Americans. The latter (in those days) were only there to advise, I was told, and not to fight unless asked by the South Vietnamese in charge.

At 2.15 a.m., I was sleeping peacefully beneath a jungle-green mosquito-net, when the American major called to me to dress quickly and come outside. I did so, to find the others slinging rifles over their shoulders. "The Viet-Cong are bombarding the next village, only three kilometres away," said the Dai Uy, poring over a map. "Listen, you can hear the artillery – machine-guns and eighty-one mortars!" Gradually the shooting became very close to Go Dau Ha until it was actually on the outskirts of the village. Then a flare-ship arrived from Saigon and dropped flares over the battlefield to illuminate it, which quietened things down somewhat, although the mortars continued until 6 a.m. Later, a radio from the attacked village told us that thirty Viet-Cong had been killed and fifteen weapons taken. That morning a helicopter carrying press people from the capital whirred above rice-paddies which were strewn with mangled dead and weeping survivors.

The road to Saigon being blocked, I stayed in Go Dau Ha all that day and the next night, the only shots being those fired at somebody breaking the curfew. On the morning of my departure the Dai Uy came on the bus with me as far as the first road-block, a great mound of earth on top of which a skull and cross-bones was drawn on a piece of cardboard. "There's a mine underneath," disclosed my Vietnamese friend. "Well, goodbye and safe journey to Saigon!"

One hour later I was wandering up Hai Ba Trung — one of Saigon's busiest streets, in search of an address there. It was that of a kindly young radio announcer named Vo and his large family and, the next day, Vo showed me around the city. To the port, the Nhu's old house, General Khan's residence, and the zoo. Saigon was an old city with few large buildings and shops, but with some wide boulevards and spacious parks which were now marred with trenches. "No, we can never forget our war," sighed Vo, waving his hand towards a trench. "See, this is the junction where the first buddhist monk burned himself alive, and this hotel had the whole of its fifth floor destroyed by a bomb."

Around the busy market we walked, and then crossed the river and gazed at the dilapidated houseboats and shacks of the poor. Rotting fruit and vegetables made the turbid waters stink, yet I couldn't help but see beauty in the scene before me — of so many slim, round-hatted men and women bustling to and fro over the narrow bridge. "Let's go," muttered my friend, "it wouldn't be prudent for us to stay here too long. A lot of V.C.s live in these slums and operate from here. A fire razed many of them, that's why you see those large blocks of new flats, but this is still a very doubtful area. See those cops over there — busy searching cars?"

My visa for South Vietnam had only been issued for two weeks, so after five days in Saigon I caught a bus for Dalat. Vo had furnished me with a letter of introduction to someone working at the radio station there.

Vo's friend at the Dalat radio station passed me on to another in the radio station in the lovely seaside resort of Nha Trang. One afternoon the announcer with whom I stayed, Ngoo, and his brother took me to a football match, which I enjoyed hugely. But the evening which followed was one that I shall never forget. The director of the radio came to inform me that he had just received a telegram from my embassy in Saigon, then mumbled something about my mother being seriously ill and my father wishing me to return home immediately. I was stunned. "What did the telegram actually say?" I asked the director. "That your ambassador wishes to see you right away," he replied. "The other news came from your radio friends in Saigon."

The journey back to the capital early on the following day was a nightmare. Wanting to know the worst as quickly as possible, I went straight to the British Embassy.

"Well, we really wanted to know whether you were still alive!" boomed the vice-consul. "A Laotian newspaper has worried us all by publishing an article to the effect that you have been tortured to death in Cambodia. Even reached the Foreign Office in London — who phoned your father. He told them that the article couldn't possibly be true, for as you write home every three days, your letters from Vietnam have already arrived there proving that you left Cambodia safe and sound. The reason for that article we don't yet know, but, combined with the dangers of the war here, it disquieted your parents so much that they have asked me to tell you that if you wish to return home now, they will gladly pay for your air fare."

So nobody was sick! — only anxious. "Please wire to say that I am safe and determined to finish what I started," I told the vice-consul. "In the meantime I shall write them a long, comforting letter."

Soon I was on my way up to Nha Trang again, and then on a cheap and ancient bus to Quinhon, where it was suggested that I stay at the house of some of the Vietnamese who interpreted for the Americans. "No use you coming to our base here!" laughed the major. "We've all got to be inside our compound like good boys, at 8 p.m. and I suppose you'll want to see the town. Tomorrow if the roads are clear we'll give you a lift up north with us."

On the following morning, the American major was a little dubious about his promise of the evening before. "See those sand-bags on the floor of our jeeps?" he asked. "They're to stop us getting our legs blown off when we go over mines. But they don't always work, and there is a constant danger of ambushes." "Oh, please," I urged, "I shall be entirely responsible for myself." "Then sit in the middle of us," ordered the major, "and, here, use this if you see us using ours." He handed me a thirty-eight revolver. "It's all ready to shoot with," he said. "You just pull the trigger. Trouble is, in this damn war both sides are dressed the same, look the same, and speak the same. If a man in black pajamas shoots at us he's a V.C., if he doesn't he's our friend. They don't bother to smile or salute, so your eyes must stay on their weapons."

A thin drizzle was falling as we passed Furmi and came to a great hole in the road, filled with muddy water. "Into the hole!" shouted the major, and into the water we jumped, just as artillery and mortars started to back up the machine-guns.

The fighting that morning was heavy and seemed to be going on all around us. At least two Viet-Cong were shot dead before our eyes, and several others were taken prisoner. When things quietened down, we climbed out of the hole and into the jeep, hoping that the planks we put over the hole wouldn't give way. They didn't, and soon we were winding over a pass through some mountains, all alerted and ready for trouble. At the other side of the pass we came to where a bridge had been destroyed, but the Dai Uy was waiting with planks for us to cross, and soon we were safely in his house, swapping news. "The road is blocked a little farther north from here also," the Dai Uy informed us, "so for some days it will be impossible to go either north or south by road. The dangers of ambush are exceedingly great." So that is how I came to spend five days with the allies in Bonson village.

Never have I seen such rain in all my life as fell in South Vietnam when I was there, during the monsoon in October 1964. Nobody ever had a chance to dry off at all, wet fatigues hung about all over the place, and everything we touched seemed damp and soggy.

One day, two suspected Viet-Cong spies were brought before the lieutenant, and he invited us to go with him down the hill to his abandoned headquarters where the men would be interrogated. One of the captives was a dirty, undernourished-looking fellow attired in black pajamas; the other wore a neat grey suit. They were led into a small room by an Intelligence officer, who carried a metal box from which wire protruded. "Electrical torture equipment," disclosed the major; "they shove those live wires into the sides of the victim's faces and other spots. It makes 'em talk. Come and play ping-pong, there's an old table here!" Try as I would to adopt a sang-froid attitude, telling myself that this was war and that information from the enemy could save lives, I found it exceedingly difficult to concentrate on ping-pong that afternoon.

Back in Bonson two mornings later, the American major

decided to go with the Dai Uy to inspect the pass on the Quinhon road. "Right," he said on his return that evening, "the road's still dangerous but we'll make up a huge convoy and go to Quinhon tomorrow."

Even the convoy was ambushed, and again we were crouching under heavy machine-gun fire. I remember thinking how strange it was that a man whom I had never seen in my life before was at that moment endeavouring to shoot me dead. When at last we were safely in Quinhon, the major suggested to me with a smile, "Go camp on the doorstep of the seventeenth regiment and simply thumb a lift with the first plane flying north." That's just what I did, and soon I was seated in the belly of a fat cargo plane bound for Danang.

My stay in Danang was rather marred by an attack of dengue fever. When I was on my feet again I visited the Danang hospital, and the sight of the numerous and appalling war casualties there made me forget my own grogginess. It was so crowded that often there were three in a bed, most of them limbless children.

I made my flight to Hue in rain so heavy that the plane had to land at Fubai airstrip, fifteen kilometres from the town, instead of the regular Citadel airfield.

The flooding had brought canoes and sampans on to the streets, and I managed to visit the ancient royal palace with its magnificent throne room, tall red pillars, enormous vases of Chinese design, and vast gardens. The royal tombs were equally of interest, each guarded by stone statues of elephants, soldiers, horses, and so forth.

My visa had almost expired by the time I got back to Danang, so I went hopefully to the airfield. A C47 was just about to take off. Sticking his head out of the cockpit, the pilot called, "Going to Saigon?" "Yes!" I shouted. "O.K., jump in then," he told me with a grin, and sent somebody to open the door for me. The big plane was empty, except for one or two Vietnamese soldiers who were being sick.

On the day after my arrival back in Cambodia, I received word that the political investigation people wished to see me. I had no doubts at all as to why, and only hoped that they would believe what I had to say. "Why did you tell people that you had been imprisoned and tortured here?" were their first words. So I explained the whole story – how I had known nothing about the newspaper article until I had spoken to my embassy in Saigon, and how I had not met anyone from Laos since I had left that country.

To my relief the Cambodian authorities believed my innocence in the case and demanded only that I write out a couple of declarations – one to be sent to Laos, stating that I was alive and well and had been kindly treated in Cambodia. This I was glad to do – as it was the truth.

Suddenly I was a heroine! My picture appeared once again in the Cambodian newspapers. I received invitations to attend the prince's inauguration ceremony of the new football stadium, and then to sit in the royal barge at the water festival.

I was greatly excited when the Chinese Embassy informed me that my visa had come through, and waited impatiently while an official there went through my passport for what must have been the twentieth time. Once again the austere eyes were examining every character on my stamps for Taiwan.

"Now how do you know that I'm not a spy?" I joked. There was an awkward silence. At last the official looked me straight – and hopefully – in the eye, and asked, "Well, you're not, are you?"

Other V.I.P. treatment which I received from the Cambodians, as a result of clearing their name, was a ninety per cent reduction on the price of a ticket to Hong Kong with Royal Air Cambodge. Ten dollars was little to pay for a flight to the island, especially at a time when there were no ships in port bound for that destination.

A Cambodian tourist official drove me to the airport and saw me safely on to the plane. It could be that he's been sent along to witness that I really get out of this country alive, I thought. But in my hand I clutched a beautiful silver brooch that he had given to me as a souvenir of Cambodia.

Chapter 14

November 1964–January 1965

On the eve of my departure for the People's Republic of China, I had a scrumptious dinner with my old friend Brian Wong in Hong Kong. The next morning I was seated in a train, speeding past mountains, lakes, paddy-fields and tiny villages towards Canton.

The train chugged into Canton station at dusk, and I went to 'The People's Mass' (some said 'Mess') Hotel. I showed the interpreter there the address of a Mrs Sung, for whom I had a woollen suit which a friend in Hong Kong had asked me to give her, which I had written out in Chinese characters. "You'll need a guide and a taxi," he told me quickly. "Not at all," I said. "Which bus do I catch to go there?" "Er . . . number one, stops just outside the hotel," and before he had had time to reconsider the matter of a strange English girl wandering around the town alone after dark, I was gone.

The bus conductor was most helpful, not only putting me off at the correct stop, but indicating, with a series of signs and grunts, which road I should take. Down a narrow street I went, past silent market stalls and shuttered shops, until I came to a dark alley. "Third Road . . . Guei Gan . . ." I muttered, and came to a tall building. "Mrs Sung should be living at the bottom of it."

Mrs Sung was delighted with the woollen suit, telling me that her coupons were never sufficient to clothe her and her daughters warmly for the winter. "We have to use coupons with which to buy flour, rice and all woollen goods here," she explained. "Something like in your country just after the war. Now do join us for dinner."

While Mrs Sung was preparing the meal I looked around her home. There was a sitting-cum-dining room, a bedroom, a kitchen, a w.c., and an extra room where a lodger stayed. The house was dim, light coming into it from small windows high in the walls by day, and weak electric light bulbs by night. There were no pictures on the walls, and no books or ornaments anywhere, although Mrs Sung was an educated woman. On the inside of her door I noticed a red sticker. "To show that my house has been proved clean upon inspection," disclosed my Chinese friend flatly. Then entering her kitchen she went to a bucket and lifted up a hen which had been sitting inside it. Beneath the hen was a small egg. "Good," she said, and breaking the hen's egg with a duck's egg into a basin, she added water, whipped them up, and steamed the mixture which, with rice, salt fish and soy sauce, constituted our meal.

"I'd keep you here to sleep with us in our home," smiled Mrs Sung as I took my leave, "but we should all have to go through so many tiresome formalities first." My small room (the cheapest, costing seven yuan — one pound) in the People's Mass Hotel overlooked the Pearl River, and at sunrise the following morning I watched the little boats which moved silently to and fro on the rose-coloured water.

During a sight-seeing tour with Mrs Sung which took in the zoo and the Botanical Gardens, I booked a third-class ticket to Peking for that evening.

The train was extremely crowded, but being huddled up together kept everyone warm. As soon as we began to move, a man came around putting pot mugs with lids on to the small tables shared by each group of passengers. Then another man followed selling tiny packets of tea. There was black and green tea, and I bought a packet of each, just for curiosity. They were very cheap. When the other passengers poured tea from one of the packets into their mugs I did likewise. Some minutes later a man came along carrying an enormous kettle of boiling water, and poured some into everyone's mug, to make the tea. No sugar or milk was provided but the drink was warm and soothing. The boiling water was brought around about every twenty minutes, so one had a permanent hot drink.

As we sped onwards through the night, the moonlit country-side became bleak and arid, and each time the doors were opened, we were pinched by frost and lashed with a biting wind. The last thing I recollect before drifting off to sleep among my new friends, were some ruddy peasants who came into the compartment clutching their small bundles.

At 6 a.m. the air was filled with the strains of Chinese and Russian revolutionary songs. They were stirring, with catchy tunes, and I found myself enjoying them until I found that most of them gibed at the capitalists, the imperialists, the royalists. A young man who, I was told, was our voluntary leader, put in charge of the compartment until we arrived at our destination, jumped on to one of the seats and began to lead the singing. Everyone, including some toddlers, joined in. So did I, until a neighbour grinned and whispered, "Know what the words mean? — Down with Britain and the United States of America!"

Gazing out of the windows, I watched as the brown countryside moved slowly by; the villages of mud huts, the dirt tracks criss-crossing the enormous fields, and the rattling donkey carts. Then, inside the compartments, everyone stood up. "Exercises!" explained my neighbour cheerfully, "do as we do." I guessed that the exercises were all part of China's 'great leap forward' physically as well as economically, and soon we were vigorously touching our toes, swinging our arms, and executing various movements which suggested a form of shadow boxing keeping time with a voice which called, "I ... erh ... san ... ssu ... " and so forth, over a loudspeaker.

In Peking station, an interpreter who happened to be meeting somebody else took me to the Shin Chow Hotel. I could not afford the thirty shillings a night for the cheapest room, and said so. The interpreter regarded me thoughtfully for several minutes. "Go and sit down," she said at last, "and I'll make some telephone calls." Then, after an interval, she called me over. "There is a small hotel just around the corner from here," she said. "It will cost you only three yuan fifty per night — which is ten shillings. No foreigners have ever stayed there before, and there are no tourist facilities, of course. Do you speak any Chinese?" "A little, with the help of my book," I replied. "Well, you will find the hotel people very friendly and ready to help you and, of course, you can come back here if you need something."

The following morning I left my snug little hotel and rushed past the park, which was full of people doing morning exercises, to the security office where I deposited my passport, as was the rule. Then I went to the Shin Chow Hotel to meet some French people who had offered to take me with them to see the Great Wall of China.

We set off, first passing between flat, frosted fields, then climbing some rocky hills, through which a caravan of shaggy camels was wending its way. Then, there she was, winding over the sparsely vegetated hills like a grey stone serpent. Abandoning the car, we climbed up to one of the wall's watchtowers, shivering with the bite of the wind. "This Great Wall was built by the first ruler of unified China, Shih Huang Ti, over twenty-two centuries ago," one of my French companions said. "He built the wall as a defence from the nomadic Huns, who had been raiding the farms of Northern China for many years. More than three million soldiers and conscripts are said to have been employed in building the wall, which is fifteen thousand miles long and forms a boundary between Inner Mongolia and China proper."

On the following morning I went to Tien An Men Square, to find it surging with a mass of people. Inspection left no doubt that they were demonstrating against United States paratroopers being in the Congo. They were marching along like a great army, some brandishing weapons, some carrying red flags, and some waving posters on which cartoons and slogans degrading President Johnson and the United States of America were daubed. As long files of them set out to march through all the streets of Peking, those left in the square acted little charades, some dressed as negroes, others as soldiers, and several paraded as grotesquely made-up American women. They all sang revolutionary songs, chanted their war-cries, and shook their fists for three whole days.

Later that morning I called at the security office, where I arranged to leave China for North Vietnam, calling at Nanking and other cities on the way. The opportunity to see Hanoi should really not be missed, I decided, especially as I had a valid visa in my passport.

I travelled to Nanking by way of the industrial port of Tientsin, on a long, slow train. Unable to get into an economical Chinese hotel there, I was taken to the enormous Nanking Hotel, where my room was big enough for at least four people, and cost me ten yan (nearly thirty shillings) per night.

In Shanghai, my next stop, I spent only a few hours, during

127

which I sat in a worker's waterfront restaurant and devoured a steaming bowlful of noodle soup.

Then, after Hangchow, I was again seated in a Chinese train, which two days later brought me to the town of Henyang, in the Hunan province. Henyang was not one of the Chinese towns which were said to have facilities for tourists, and I was curious to get a look behind the scenes, as it were. I did. The streets were muddy and full of holes, a pane in my bedroom window was smashed, bathing facilities were a jug of cold water and a pot basin, and the toilets had no walls.

Not many people were bound for Hanoi, it seemed, for upon upon reaching Nanning, everyone descended from the train, and I spent the night with the compartment to myself. The following morning I awoke stiff with cold, just as the train was chugging on towards the Chinese frontier.

Glancing from the window, I watched the sub-tropical landscape slide slowly past . . . the wooden shack villages, banana groves, and emerald paddy-fields. In Hanoi, the British had a sort of unofficial embassy called 'La maison Anglaise' where I was greeted by a tall, moustached compatriot, whose first shattering words were, "Now, my girl, the first thing that we must do is to try to get you out of here!" Inwardly annoyed as, after all, I had entered the country quite legally on a tourist visa, I asked, "Why, are things that bad?" "Hummm . . . we're expecting big trouble at any moment," was the reply. "Anyway, go off now with our interpreter, who will lead you to Hanoi's cheapest hotel, and come and have lunch with us tomorrow."

Hanoi's cheapest hotel delighted me, costing only two dong (four shillings) per night for a single room. The toilets, however, were . . . well, I was pleased that my room was well away from them. My joy at finding such a place was short-lived. At one o'clock I was shaken awake and told to go and get my passport stamped. Off I went to face an accusation that this formality had not been observed when I crossed the frontier — which it had. At half past two I was woken again. The police said that no foreigner was allowed to stay at a North Vietnamese hotel without first handing their passport over to the Ministry of Foreign Affairs. "Go and stay at our Hotel Metropole!" they ordered. "That is where our *genuine* tourists inevitably reside." After an argument with the manager of the Hotel Metropole,

Just off a train
in North
Vietnam . . .

. . and with a
friend in the
South

A brief stop
on the way to
Hanoi

Re-enacting Mongolian battles on the Great Wall of China

In Tien an Min Square in Peking,
outside the main gate of the
Forbidden City

A visit to Peking Zoo with
Japanese friends

I was forced to take a suite there at the rate of three pounds ten shillings for the one night. The next morning, after another row with the manager, this time about the lack of hot water, I went back to the Ministry of Foreign Affairs, where I finally managed to persuade them to allow me to return to the Hotel Hanoi — at one pound per night.

Compared to Peking, Hanoi had quite a country village look about it, though food prices there were twice as high as in China's capital. I was taken to a congested workers' restaurant, where we squeezed on to a wobbly bench to eat Chinese soup and fried noodles. Our black-pajamaed fellow diners took no notice of us whatsoever. Their 'Ho Chi Minh sandals' (made from strips of abandoned motor car tyres) were plastered with mud; they were famished and weary, after a hard morning's digging of air-raid trenches along the streets of the town.

When I strolled back towards my hotel that evening, it was late. The narrow dimly-lit streets were quite deserted, except for an old woman crouching beside a dusty green glass case, from whom I bought some maize and rice cooked in a leaf for supper.

During my stay in Hanoi, the occupants of La maison Anglaise greatly assisted me in procuring visas for Mongolia and Russia, and another visa for China, seeming only disappointed that I would not allow them to book my passage straight to London.

When the day came for me to return to China, my North Vietnamese visa was checked quite thoroughly.

As the train sped north-eastwards, a harsh voice croaked over the loudspeaker. "He says please jump into the trenches beside the railway line if the Americans start to bomb this train," disclosed the man beside me as though he were expecting such a crisis at any moment. We arrived at Dong-Dang sometime during the night, and it was then that my troubles began. Upon entering the train, the customs officer came straight to me with a look in his eyes which said: I have been tipped off — you are a number one spy! Slowly and systematically he took every one of my possessions and examined them thoroughly before a fascinated audience. Labels were read for the benefit of all to hear, toothpaste was squeezed into a worm and inspected, undergarments were held aloft with pleasure, soiled by searching, unwashed hands. Then the official started on me.

Ripping open the hem of my skirt, he delved within. Finding nothing, he gave my waist-band the same treatment, and, pulling out the paper stiffening, held it to the light, no doubt looking for a secret message. Although there was no writing on it, he carefully folded it and tucked it triumphantly into his pocket.

This continued for over an hour, until another beaming official came into the compartment to inform his leader that I could not possibly leave the country by train, as on my visa was written Gialam — the Hanoi airport. "But both Dong-Dang and Gialam were written on the visa," I exclaimed, "so that I could choose my mode of transport." "It says Gialam!" bellowed the customs official impatiently. "Get off this train!" Tremblingly piling my belongings, which were scattered all over the floor, back into my knapsack, I stepped out on to the freezing platform just as the train gave a whistle and began to move.

Leading me into an empty room, the customs official motioned towards a narrow wooden bench, and left. I peeped from the door and, observing the broad shoulders of an armed guard, I told myself, This is it. They know that I've been in the south, living alongside the troops who were shooting the Viet-Cong there. After all, they *are* the Viet-Cong. My teeth chattered, with fright or cold; the hours dragged by. Then I heard a jeep pull up close to the railway station. The driver came and signalled me to enter it, evidently not speaking a word of French. I wasn't sorry that the customs officials now seemed to have disappeared.

After driving some distance through the dark countryside, the jeep stopped at a large house. Striking a match, the driver lit a candle and called someone whom I guessed to be the caretaker of the place. An old man appeared, and taking the candle, led me to a small room at the top of the house which contained a dusty bed. Then everyone disappeared, until, a little later, the caretaker brought me a bowl of rice. I didn't see him again.

Feeling for my bed in the darkness, I curled up on it fully dressed until dawn and then tried the handle of my door. To my surprise, it opened to reveal no lurking guards and, upon creeping downstairs, I found that the house was completely deserted. I must get back to Hanoi, and to La maison Anglaise, I decided. I persuaded a man to indicate the direction for me, and when I arrived at the station was overjoyed to find somebody who spoke French, but not so overjoyed when they handed me a bill which I was told I would have to pay before I boarded the Hanoi train. The bed I had slept in at the house, the rice I had eaten there, the petrol for the jeep which had been used to transport me from the station to the house, and the fee of the man in the street who had simply pointed out the station to me – all were listed.

Once on the train I felt uneasy again for the guard had put me into a compartment full of soldiers, who neither spoke nor smiled, but regarded me somewhat disdainfully. I must take precautions, for this day I could well end up in prison, I thought, so, using the toilet as an excuse, I walked slowly along the corridor. To my joy, an Indian member of the International Control was seated in one of the compartments. Quickly I told him in English. "Please keep an eye on me when we descend at Hanoi station. If you see me disappearing with some guards, inform the English here. They . . ." "Come along you! You have no business in speaking to the other passengers!" growled one of the soldiers, waving me along the corridor, which didn't help my nerves.

At Hanoi station I took a pedicab to the Hanoi Hotel, wondering whether my second Chinese visa would now have to be altered so as to include Canton. I sped off to La maison Anglaise. My unexpected return caused my compatriot's moustache to quiver a little, but he quickly observed my haggard face, and any rebukes were left unsaid. "Well, you were due for a good going over!" was his only remark when I'd explained.

Then I was in Canton airport, and suddenly it seemed to be the safest, most friendly place in the world. "I'm so happy to be back in China!" I shouted to the nearest official, who smiled at me warmly. The following day I spent with Mrs Sun Sung, before boarding a train for my second journey to the capital.

During my second visit to Peking I more or less knew my way around, and found myself acting as a guide to new arrivals from overseas on several occasions. One evening I was buying postcards at the Shin Chow, when a smartly dressed Japanese came to me and asked, "I wonder if you could tell me whether there is a Japanese restaurant in the city, my companions and I are simply gasping for some seaweed soup!" "Yes I can, actually," I smiled, "I remember seeing one in the bazaar." My offer to take him there resulted in an invitation to dine with the Japanese, who introduced themselves as Zenko, Soko and Kato.

The dinner was a great success and the following day we had lunch together at the Moscow Fountain. "It will be Christmas Eve tomorrow," I told my friends, "and I shall be setting off for Europe on the trans-Siberian railway."

All three of them came to see me off on the train, and pushed a bag of fruit into my hands for the journey. Then Zenko gave me a beautiful model Japanese treasure ship. Soko gave me some Japanese coffee-flavoured chewing-gum, and a bottle of cold mixture, and Kato gave me some seasoning, "To flavour the Mongolian cooking! — Happy Christmas!"

I travelled third class on the trans-Siberian train, and slept comfortably in a bunk for each of the six nights that I was on it, for the Chinese had decided that nobody should travel for such a long distance without a bed.

On Christmas morning we crossed the frontier into Outer Mongolia. One banana and a half a sandwich was my self allotted portion of food for that day, but I told myself firmly that there were more important things to think about at Christmas-time than roast turkey and plum pudding.

When we came to Suke Bator, on the Mongolian frontier, some customs officials leapt on to the train and soon had the contents of my knapsack strewn all over the compartment. Without a word, they confiscated my diary, my maps and a small packet of sand that I had purloined from the Gobi Desert (which I had rashly presumed that they would never miss, but later thought how catastrophic it would be for me if that bit were to be found radioactive). Then they left the train and, just before it pulled out of the station, returned my maps — but not the diary or the sand.

At Naushki, on the Siberian side, a hard-faced efficient-looking Russian woman went through my belongings. "Any Russian money?" she asked. "Only ten roubles (four pounds) which I bought at a bank in Hanoi," I replied, showing them to her. "Against our rules!" snapped the uniformed woman, and seizing my bag of oranges, she enquired, "And where have these come from?" "Peking," I mumbled. "Then they cannot enter the Soviet Union!" she barked, adding something about hygiene. Just as she was about to leave the compartment, I burst into tears. "Oh, what a horrible day it has been for me!" I gulped, "first my sand and diary were taken from me, and now my money and fruit! All right," I sniffed, "take the money to buy vodka with if you want!" A sudden conference took place between the woman and her entourage of uniformed men, accompanied by sympathetic noises from my fellow passengers. Then she turned to me, and the hard look softened for an instant as she silently handed back my money and oranges.

As the train wound through the last of the Urals and Siberia, I sat with a young Russian named Ivan in the dining car, having lunch. "Nowhere on earth could hold as much for me," he declaimed, "I am proud to be a Siberian – I love my vast, rugged country." For some time we gazed in silence at the glistening snow, then another Siberian joined us – a handsome fellow who had always seemed to be involved in long games of chess whenever I saw him. "He doesn't speak a word of English," said Ivan. The Siberian was staring at me with the same look which Ivan had given to the majestic Ural mountains. Then he spoke. "He says that he would like to marry you," interpreted Ivan. Trying not to laugh, I said, "Please remind him that I live in England, while he resides in Siberia – and therefore such a marriage would be . . . err . . . awkward." There followed a lengthy discourse between the two men. "He says that he would be quite willing to live in England," disclosed Ivan gaily.

The next day found me walking through the streets of Moscow.

"Well, darling, you came in through our back door, you know," said an In-Tourist official. "Anyway, we can arrange for your transit visa to be extended, and we shall put you into the Berlin Hotel. Now how long will you be staying here? That will mean three meal coupons for each day. Which class? First, darling? Third, Fifth? Oh, sixth class, darling! Why? – because there isn't a seventh? Oh, you English!"

That night I donned a skirt and sped off to the Bolshoi Theatre, where I was lucky enough to get a seat not far from the stage for the ballet's performance of *Giselle*, starring the famous twenty-two year old ballerina, Byestnevtova, and her young partner, Liepa. The couple took ten curtain calls after

133

the performance, the Russians around me shouting "Bravo! bravo!" and swarming towards the stage. When the lights went up I had a good look at the theatre. It was a strange mixture of past and present, with its boxes edged in red and gold, enormous crystal chandeliers, and the walls and ceiling covered with painted scenes from the revolution. Just like the audience, whose attire ranged from furs, jewels and satins, to the coarse loosely fitting apparel of the workers.

The morning after my arrival in the Russian capital I sloshed through the snowy streets, amidst Moscovites, many of them clothed in the very latest European fashions, hurrying to Gums department store, which displayed quantities of Santa Clauses and 'Christmas' trees; for the New Year's celebrations, of course. In the grounds of the Kremlin, I visited the sixteenth-century cathedral of Saint Basil, which had been constructed by Ivan the Terrible. Its onion-shaped towers, typical of Russian architecture, were asymmetrically placed and covered with a light powdering of snow, which glittered even in the weak, winter sunshine. Inside the cathedral, wooden staircases led up to the dome-ceilinged towers, which were connected by narrow passages.

Wandering into the In-Tourist office at the hotel, I decided to treat myself to the New Year's Eve performance of the Moscow State Circus, and approached the woman at the desk, who was endeavouring to answer three telephones simultaneously in three different languages. Also trying to attract her attention was an English gentleman and his son. The gentleman turned out to be an author named Eric Newby who was discovering Moscow and writing an article for *The Observer* at the same time. Supplied with his first-class, all-in-ticket was a beautiful Russian guide, and he kindly invited me to go along that afternoon when she would be taking them to see Lenin's tomb.

An hour later we joined a serpentine queue of loyal Russians, and slowly moved across Red Square, at last to gaze down at the embalmed and wax-like Lenin. Stalin had begun to smell, we gathered, and was now buried around the back, along with other heroes.

The Moscow State Circus turned out to be somewhat smaller than I had expected, but the acts were excellent and, of course, included Popof – the celebrated clown. On New Year's Day I took one of my excursions — thrown in with the meal coupons — around Moscow, returning to the hotel by way of the university, past an outdoor heated swimming pool and numerous yellow blocks of flats.

Then I left for Leningrad, after giving Eric Newby some Gobi Desert sand and a diary to take back to England — both of which had escaped the eyes of suspicious Mongolians. Saint Petersburg, Petrograd, and now, Leningrad, most northern of the world's great cities. I was walking across an expanse of blue ice, beneath which was the Gulf of Finland. "Careful!" called a distant voice, " — it's cracking!" Back on firm ground I found that the warning had been delivered by a young Russia girl. "Lucky you speak good English," I told her. "Well, I should do!" she laughed. "I'm training to be an interpreter and hope to go to England soon, using the excuse to polish my pronunciation as a means to travel a little!"

On my last evening in Leningrad, I went walking through a blizzard past Falconet's enormous statue of Peter the Great on horseback on the River Neva for a final look at Gclot's equestrian statues on the Anitchkov Bridge, the illuminated Saint Andrew's Square, and the Saint Peter-Paul Fortress. Suddenly there was a ferocious bark, and through the dusk bounded a massive Alsatian. He was muzzled, but jumped up and knocked me into a snow-drift. A man who was obviously his owner came running up to me, and, fastening a leash on to the dog, bowed very low. Then came a gesture of bygone days, when that tall, rosy-cheeked Russian, attired in a fur hat, thick great-coat and top-boots, smiled through the snow-flakes and gently kissed my hand.

Chapter 15

January 1965–April 1965

I arrived in Warsaw tired, cold and hungry, but a chance encounter with two Polish journalists soon put everything right. Over an enormous meal, one of them interviewed me and the other took photographs. Then, in the short time available, I was whisked off to the Basilica of Saint John where the photographer had to take pictures of the famous Cardinal Wyszynsky and after that on a sight-seeing tour of the tortured city, ending up in a jazz-club.

At one point on the tour I was standing looking up at a statue when a man who had been staring for some minutes at the Union Jack on my sleeve (sewn on for identification in Vietnam) ran up to me. After glancing furtively around, he seized my hand, shook it firmly and whispered "God Save the Queen!"

My train fare from Warsaw to East Berlin was paid for by the press in return for the interview. On arrival, I wandered among the drab streets and crumbling buildings for some time. Then I jumped on to one of the odd, yellow double-decker buses going to 'Checkpoint-Charlie' – the gap in the Berlin wall. As I walked through it East Berliners behind me were standing in silence, looking wistfully towards a part of their city that perhaps they would never see again. Then I was in the West, a few feet away, where eyes shone brighter somehow and heads were held higher. Before leaving the wall I climbed up on to a raised platform and had a last look at the searchlights, barbed wire and armoured cars on its east side, and the armed guards from the United States on the west, waiting to mow down any East Germans who overstepped the line when pursuing their escaping compatriots. What an odd situation, I thought, fleeing from one's own people.

Then taking the U-Bahn (underground train) to the centre

of the city, I called on some press people who interviewed me about my journey 'from the Great Wall of China to the great wall of Berlin', took a photo of me thumbing through the snow, and gave me some Deutsch Marks which were to come in useful for train fares.

That night I slept in the Jugendherbergen, and before I left for Prague the warden proudly showed me my press photo which he had pinned to the hostel notice board.

I saw little of Prague, but have a happy memory of two young Indian engineers with whom I climbed to a hill-top to view this beautiful city nestling in a countryside that had donned the mellow colours of winter.

Breakfast the next morning was dark brown bread, cheese, poppy-seed strudel and coffee. Then, Vienna. The Danube was grey that day but no less beautiful than I had imagined it to be. Home of so many artists, poets and musicians, the balconied houses where they had lived, the churches where they had worshipped, and the statues in the parks which would impress their features for ever in the hearts of those who loved the art they had created; all were so alive, so cherished in that city.

Always a lover of horses, I made straight for the Spanish Riding School, a part of the Imperial Palace of old Vienna. Inside the building, all was white and gold and crystal glass, the walls covered with pictures. Coming to the State Ballroom, I sat on one of the red plush seats in the gallery, beside one of the gleaming white columns which rose to the decorated ceiling. Below me, the floor was not that of a ballroom, how-ever, being covered with soft, brown earth. As I watched, the first of the world-famous Lippizaner stallions was brought in for his morning exercise. Others followed, their riders clothed in elegant, eighteenth-century Spanish costumes, as befitted their mounts – who were all of Spanish origin. Passes, caprioles, levades; the schooling was so intensive, I learned, calling for so much mental and physical concentration that the stallions worked for only forty-five minutes each day, after which rugs were flung over their sweating bodies by grooms who led them back to the Imperial Mews.

The snow fell thickly as I travelled eastwards again, to Budapest. There, people hurried through the blizzard in gaily coloured Hungarian national costumes, side by side with the latest fashions. Glittering cinemas and night-clubs caught my eye, and advertisements, usually lacking in the communist world. But the other signs were there; the high prices in the shops, the empty churches, and the grey-coated Russian soldiers who marched officiously along the streets.

I had not done any hitch-hiking during my travels through the communist bloc, partly due to the lack of private cars. Yugoslavia, however, was different, I decided, surveying the station at Sabotica. At three o'clock in the morning it was like a dosshouse, the floor covered with snoring people. Joining them, I slept happily until daylight.

Soon I was on my way to Belgrade with two Yugoslavian businessmen in their gleaming new car. "We're capitalists!" one of them told me with a grin.

By dusk the following day I had got as far as Nis, and was wandering along a rocky road when several farm carts came clattering past, loaded with gaily dressed people who sang and played musical instruments. I was so captivated with this jolly scene from what I took to be a rural Yugoslav wedding, that I jumped with surprise as a car crunched to a halt beside me. "Would you like a lift?" enquired the driver. "Yes, please!" I replied, "how far are you going?" "To Baghdad," he called.

My transport problems solved for some time, I relaxed and chatted to Hamad, my new friend, who spoke English well. Every so often he would stick his head out of the car window and call in Arabic to someone who was driving behind us. "My brother, Hussein," he explained. "We have bought these two new cars in Germany and are taking them home to sell for a good price."

On the Turkish frontier Hamad presented a packet of Indian tea to one of the guards. "I give him one each time I come here," smiled my friend, "he believes that it will take his soul to Heaven – and forgets about my suitcases." In Istanbul we booked into a cheap hotel which Hamad knew, in Stambul, the old part of the city. Then we went for a stroll and I noticed that all the restaurants were quiet and empty. "They'd refuse to sell us even one cup of coffee before sunset," said Hamad. "It's Ramadan month, you know, when we moslems should fast. Moslems who are travelling, however, are allowed to eat, but should do so discreetly. At home I never fast anyway, it's only the old-fashioned people who do. I'm not at all religious. Come, we'll buy some oranges and hide somewhere to eat them!"

So we climbed a grassy hillock overlooking the Bosporus, with the Black Sea to our left and somewhere to the right a glimmer of blueness that was the Sea of Marmara.

Then we cut through some back alleys, ducking beneath lines of washing and peeping into 'kaffanas' which were just coming to life, their clients sucking at hubble-bubble pipes and sipping sherbet or coffee. Next day our two cars moved on relentlessly to Ankara where there was a little trouble at the Iraqui Embassy, over my visa for their country.

"All right," said the consul at last, "I shall give you a visa. Only, I tell you this; if you turn out to be Jewish I shall lose my job. And what is more, if you so much as set one foot in Israel, we will know, and then you may never come into Arabia again. And, do not think that you can be clever by getting a separate passport for your Israeli visa. We have our spies everywhere."

I believed him, and although to me the Israelis were like any other people and I would have been most interested to see their country, I realised that by so doing I might ruin my chances of visiting all the Arab countries. So I nodded my head and kept quiet.

Aleppo was my first introduction to Syria, an ancient town with a beautiful castle and bustling bazaar-like streets. From there we drove through snow-covered desert land, dotted with the black tents of nomadic Bedouins. With the darkness a thick mist descended, and in a mud village we pulled the cars to a halt and slept with the ease of weary travellers. The roar of camels awakened us the next morning, and soon we were approaching the East Syrian border, munching a breakfast of bread and oranges.

"Now soon you will see the sun!" smiled Hamad as, shivering, we got into his car again to cover the nine miles of no-man's desert between the Syrian and Iraqi borders. At the Iraqi frontier Hamad lost no more time, simply presenting the various officials with some shirts which he had brought from Germany. The cars and cases remained unsearched.

All through that afternoon we drove steadily eastwards, the land becoming a desert of stones and deep water-filled holes keeping our progress painfully slow. It was nightfall before, in a heavy mist, we reached the main Damascus–Baghdad highway. How welcome were the lights of Baghdad as we drove through that silent city towards the flat-roofed white houses of the sandy suburb where Hamad lived.

"Yumi! yumi!" called Hamad when we arrived at his house, and out to greet us ran a little old lady, her head covered with a traditional black fringed shawl. She knew no English, but welcomed me with silent kisses, and soon I was sleeping on the carpeted stone floor with the other members of the family.

"Land of the Arabian Nights," I whispered the following morning, standing at the front door of Hamad's house. "What's that white flag for, outside your house?" "My yumi put it there," said Hamad, "to thank Allah that her sons have returned home safely."

Breakfast was typical of many more that I was to enjoy at Hamad's house. Sitting on the floor of the lounge, we ate fresh cream, bread, sheep's liver, boiled eggs, goat's cheese and oranges. To drink there were curds mixed with water and passed round in a bowl, followed by strong, sweet tea.

Later that day Hamad, Kiddish, another brother, and I were standing in the muddiest part of Baghdad, where sheep were being bought and sold, trying to select one for the coming feast. Then Kiddish went off on a hunt of his own, returning with a struggling animal in his arms. For a moment I was sure that Hamad would kill his brother. The words were in Arabic but the gestures were plain enough. "Bloody fool!" growled Hamad when Kiddish and the sheep had made a hasty departure. "Imagine him thinking that he can choose — when I am his older brother! Bil Koran, I'll teach him to act without my permission!" Then, still seething, Hamad quickly chose a sheep and we brought the shepherd home with us, so that he would know where to come and kill it some days later. "He'll get the skin and the head as payment," Hamad informed me as we drove back to town.

Some mornings later the man came to kill the sheep, and Hamad told me that the Aïd feast would be starting if we could see the full moon that night. It is as though the whole of Baghdad is out looking for the Aïd moon, I thought, when, some time after sunset, I stood beside Hamad on the bridge with hundreds of others, hopefully scanning the dark sky. Then she rose, peeping coyly from behind a curtain of cloud and from the crowd issued a hushed roar of delight. The feasting could begin.

Late that night the sheep appeared, stuffed with rice and raisins for the whole family to eat their fill. Then the following morning we went visiting, to wish everyone 'happy days' and 'happy feasting'. "We're going to collect my brother, Jaleel, from Musayab," said Hamad later. "He's a schoolmaster, but on holiday at the moment, so we shall go and eat fish at the Hindya Barage and return via Hilla."

As Hamad, Kiddish and Hussein were tall, with honey-coloured skin and sharp Arab features, I was surprised to see that Jaleel was short and stocky, with a round face and fair skin. "Same father – different mothers," explained Hamad, reading my thoughts. "Father had four wives."

After stopping to buy some oranges in the market place, we had driven some distance outside Hilla to relax and eat them under a palm tree, when all of a sudden a baby's cry tore into the peace of the afternoon. Standing up, I began to look about me, and another wail brought me to the foot of a date-palm where a wicker basket lay. Inside the basket was a baby, not long born, I guessed, for its cheeeks were still smeared with the blood of birth. Lifting it carefully from the basket, I called to Hamad and Jaleel. "Look what I've found!" Emerging from the car, they stood at the top of the bank, and, when they saw the baby, shrugged their shoulders and looked at each other as if to say, "So what?"

"It's a live baby!" I shrieked, thinking that may be they hadn't realised. "I know," shouted Hamad. "Now put it down and let's be getting home." "But we can't just leave it here," I gasped, "it will die." "So do hundreds of others that are abandoned each day," called Jaleel. "In some Iraqi families if an unmarried girl has a baby, her father or brothers have the right to kill her to save the honour of the family. So the girl has her baby in secret and . . . er . . . disposes of it. What were you thinking of doing with this one?" "Well, we must get it to a hospital or it will starve," I replied, trying to keep my temper. "It will have to go to the police station first," growled Hamad, "this isn't like England, you know. I don't want to spend all the rest of the day signing forms to say that it isn't mine. Supposing they think it's yours?" "Well, you go on home and I'll take this baby to the police myself," I snapped. "If I leave the helpless creature here I shall feel responsible for its death." The brothers argued for a while. "Come on then," said Hamad at last. "I should never allow an Iraqi girl to boss me around as you do!"

The chief inspector at the Hilla Police Station was quite obviously surprised that we had interrupted our drive to bring the baby in, but carefully made out his report, believing Hamad and Jaleel when they described how I'd found the baby. "Don't you want to keep it?" was his first, hopeful question. Then putting down his pen wearily at last, he enquired, "What sex?" I was nursing the squawking infant and quickly unwound its swaddles to discover with relief that it was a boy. Immediately the expressions in the room became more tolerant. The navel was smeared with some black, tarry-looking stuff, to stop the bleeding, I guessed. "Now if you don't want to take it with you, could you please put it back in its basket," came the voice of the inspector, "and thank you very much for . . . er . . . helping us."

By this time, however, the baby's hunger cries had become most urgent, and impatiently I thrust it into the arms of a young policeman. The last I saw of the baby was it disappearing in a cloud of dust along the road to the hospital, in a jeep with four burly policemen.

One Sunday morning found us bumping along a desert track which followed the Euphrates, with Hamad's dentist who was taking us to visit his friends in the country. At last we came to a cluster of mud houses rising from the sand. "These belong to a Bedouin sheikh and his family," the dentist said. "They have stopped roaming now and are farming, having good herds of camels and horses."

Inside one of the mud houses, brightly coloured hand-woven rugs covered the sandy floor, on which Hamad, the dentist and I lounged with the sheikh and the men of his family – our elbows resting on silk cushions – while the women-folk prepared lunch. I had brought a pair of slacks with me in the hope of a chance to ride, and was soon galloping across the sand on a saddleless Arab mare, guiding her with nothing but a rope halter.

When we got back to the others, Hamad said, "The sheikh says that you ride so well you may keep this mare as a gift!" How I wish I could have accepted it!

Hamad's father had also been a country sheikh, it seemed, and on several occasions we visited his old mud castle which which was now inhabited by three of Hamad's brothers and their families.

The mud castle was a mixture of old and new, with its tall pillars, stately archways, thick hand-woven carpets in all rooms, electric lights and a large smoky kitchen where whenever I entered, the women would beckon me to sit down and pass me a huge bowl of warm whey to drink.

Bread was baked in round brick ovens outside the castle, and the women-folk tried to teach me how to make their flat, local variety — by sticking the wet dough on to the sides of the oven, and peeling it off when it was cooked — but I lacked their skill and only succeeded in burning my hands.

A typical meal would consist of freshly shot marsh birds, new bread, rice and soup, which I would eat with the men, for the women of the castle and the children would eat what was left over, much later, and certainly not in the presence of males.

Hamad's mother and the other women of his family did not often come out with us, for in Iraq it is not the usual custom for women to gad about — though the modern ones have started to, a little. One day, however, yumi wanted to go and pray at the sacred mosque in Karbala. "You can wear a habya like a moslem girl and come inside with us," said Hamad.

Inside the mosque I pulled my habya about me and stood admiring the polychrome tiles, and gold and silver ornamentations of the mosque's interior. An elderly imam whispered something in Hamad's ear. "He says that as we're here, we should pray," disclosed my friend — so once again, my knowledge of Arabic prayers came in useful.

We had camel cabobs for lunch, in one of the balconied restaurants of Karbala bazaar, and afterwards we drove through Hindya to Babylon.

Standing in what used to be Nebuchadnezzar's main procession street of Babylon, I tried to imagine what the ancient city used to be like. The Ishtar Gate with its bas-relief animals was surely as lovely as it had ever been, and the stone lion of Babylon still stood over a woman as a sign of the king's ponderous strength over all things.

So, winter turned to spring, in the land between two rivers.

The air was fresh, the fields shone emerald in the sunshine, and dates began to pinken in the palms. Baghdadis joyfully munched the first freshly picked lettuces as Londoners do apples, crowds of would-be hadjis left for Mecca in flag-decked buses every day, and Hamad dismissed his nephew from the house, as I gathered he did annually, for getting a bad school report. That was one of the happiest springs that I have ever spent. As well as exploring the country I had had a wonderful opportunity of absorbing a little of the Iraqi way of life, tucked away in that sandy suburb of Baghdad.

"I must be on my way now," I sighed, "westwards to visit the Holy Lands and Egypt, and then to return again, to travel through Kuwait and Saudi Arabia." It was decided that I should get a lift with Hamad as far as Damascus, from where he would be travelling north.

The days that followed were spent in getting necessary visas and paying last visits to an Iraqi girlfriend of whom I should see more upon my return to Baghdad, and by Hamad in purchasing foreign currency in the bazaar — to smuggle out of the country.

A fertile oasis in the desert, my first sight of Syria's capital, Damascus, was minarets rising from among date-palms. Then I was wandering with Hamad through its two-thousand-year-old bazaar.

Our last meal together was the local 'sahaleb' — a sweet, milky dish containing nuts and eaten with seed-covered bread rings. My heart felt somewhere around my feet as I looked across the table at the Arab who had been my constant friend for over two months. "Goodbye, peace be with you," I told him, staring down at the table and biting desperately at my upper lip. When I glanced back at Hamad, tears were streaming down his cheeks.

In front of St. Basil's Cathedral in Moscow's Red Square with a
Russian Interpreter

In a wintery Warsaw

Chapter 16

The taxi-bus from Damascus sped through rolling green hills to Amman, the capital of Jordan, where I stayed with a young Christian Arab called Eli who had extended the invitation to me when we had met on a boat on the Java Sea. The following morning found us bowling along the road to Jericho, past poppy-filled fields dotted with clusters of black Bedouin tents. Standing beside the river Jordan, a sluggish, yellow stream winding its way between green banks, we looked across at the ageless rugged hills, and, for me at any rate, it was not hard to imagine Jesus Christ walking down to the very spot where we were standing to be baptised.

Overlooking the fallen walls of Jericho towered the Temptation Mountain. We climbed up the steep mountainside to the Greek orthodox monastery near the summit. From there the view was unforgettable – the river Jordan, the 'wilderness', the Mount Nebu, where Moses was said to be buried. One of the old monks showed us round the church and the place where Jesus was said to have been tempted – on the edge of a sheer drop down the mountain.

The following morning Eli, most of his brothers and sisters and I squashed into his car and set off for Jerusalem which, as we approached, stood out conspicuously on a range of grey limestone hills beneath a pure blue sky. Not unlike Berlin, Jerusalem, the half Arab-half Jewish city, displayed U.N. fortresses, barbed wire, and signs such as 'No Photos' along a well-guarded wall.

Parking the car at the foot of the Mount of Olives, we first visited the garden of Gethsemane, where all kinds of flowers made the air smell sweet, and olive trees which had witnessed Christ's betrayal spread their shady branches. Near by stood a little church which enclosed the flat rock on which Jesus had knelt to say his pre-crucifixion prayer. Usually a scorner of such things, I suddenly felt the urge to stoop and kiss the place that His knees had touched.

Some days later found me travelling past the old Roman temples of Jerash and up into the Lebanon Range which overlooks Beirut, the wealthy capital on the Phoenician coast. There I was welcomed into the home of Eli's friends, a family called Warwar who were refugees from Palestine.

On Sunday morning the Warwar family closed their tailoring shop and turned out *en masse* for a drive into the mountains, where we enjoyed a delicious lunch and a view of the glistening 9,000-foot Gebel Sannin. In the afternoon we drove around the campus of the American University, where later I gave a donation of blood – and earned forty Lebanese pounds (about £4 12s. od.) which practically paid for my boat passage to Egypt.

The following week I sailed for Port Said, sleeping in one of the vacant dog kennels on the poop deck of the boat – good protection from a biting wind.

From Port Said I went on to Cairo, travelling in the third class of a train which ran along the edge of the Suez Canal.

My first night in Cairo was spent in the Y.W.C.A., but the next day, on my way to the Coptic Museum, I encountered an Egyptian family who kindly took me under their wing. With Gabi, a son, I visited an alley where wealthy hashish smokers indulged their forbidden habit, Maxion's night-club, Saladin's Citadel, Mount Mokaltam and, finally, the Pyramids.

Set on the bank of the river Nile, these tombs of the Pharaohs loomed large and imposing. Gabi took me right into the centre of the Cheops Pyramid – said to be vast enough to contain St Paul's Cathedral – which entailed a long climb up to the dark, smelly hole, whence a Pharaoh had been sent to eternity. Out in the glaring sunshine again, we smiled at the gaily decked camels who knelt obediently for tourists to be 'snapped' upon them, and marvelled at how the pyramid's stones had been fitted together so tightly.

I had decided to return to Beirut via Cyprus, taking a boat from Alexandria, and travelled there from Cairo over the 'Sahara route' – through marshlands and around rushy lakes, eventually arriving at a river across which the tall buildings of

Alexandria could be seen. My hosts there were Coptic friends of Gabi's family in Cairo, but it was Faizal, a pleasant young moslem with a degree in commerce and a job in the tourist department of the Montazah Hotel, who became my most frequent companion.

With him I had a pleasant stay in Alexandria, swimming often in the blue bay of the yacht club, and watching several operations performed by a doctor friend at the hospital.

When the time came for me to sail for Cyprus, Faizal accompanied me to the port. Then it was the dog kennel again. On the following evening, when we docked in Limassol harbour, two American boys with stomach trouble, a Canadian boy – who had been immersed in the Bible for most of the voyage – and I were pounced upon by a Cypriot who offered us two rooms in his hotel for only six shillings each. As that included being driven there in his car, and as we were all weary and about to look for a place anyway, we jumped at the offer. I shared a room with the Canadian boy, who still clutched his Bible. That reassured me.

The countryside on the way to the inland capital next day was superb, with fields of golden corn bounded by wild flowers of brilliant hues, shady lanes, and green, wooded hills. One could sympathise with the Cypriots who wished to remain Cypriots. In Nicosia I asked some Greeks to direct me to the address of my letter, a house on Victoria Road. Rather amazedly they informed me that it was in the Turkish section of the town, which had been blockaded for the past sixteen days, and that they couldn't accompany me there. I got past the checkposts with no trouble at all, however, and returning my 'salaamuel-aikum' ('peace be with you') the Turkish guards smilingly led me to the house of Mr Topaloglu, whose address had been given to me in Alexandria by a Turkish girl who was his niece. The door was like any other door in the wall of the old street, but when it opened and I was drawn into the house, I observed that the Topaloglus' residence was quite palatial – with gilded chairs imported from Paris, hand-woven carpets from Iran, and walls panelled with wood shipped specially from Malaya.

"Oh thank God that you have brought news of our niece," exclaimed Mr Topaloglu in exquisite 'Oxford' English. "We haven't had any mail for two weeks now, the phone's cut off and our food supplies are inadequate. We Turks are going to

147

stay in Cyprus, though, for what we lack in numbers, we make up for in the property we own, and our land. Makarios wants Cyprus to become part of Greece because he thinks that we Turks have no right in ruling the country. To him we're just a useless minority. Oh yes, the U.N. are here – to sit and sunbathe, most of us think. Funnily enough, that's the only point on which both the Greeks and the Turks agree!"

Some days later I was on my way to Paphos, where Aphrodite was born, swinging around a coast where the azure sea mingled with the sky. I had a letter for one of Mr Topaloglu's friends, but when some Greek police saw me making for the Turkish quarter they went through my luggage and papers. When they at last suggested that I give up the idea of visting Turks I reluctantly heeded the warning note in their voices and spent the night in a five-shilling room of a near-by hotel carefully destroying the undelivered letter.

Then it was Limassol again and a last lunch, with a Cypriot goldsmith and his family to whom Mr Topaloglu had sent me with the message "Your mother's chickens are all right." After the meal, my host placed a gold pendant around my neck, from which hung the symbols of Turkey – a star and crescent. I didn't remove it, not even on the Greek ship which took me back to Beirut. My second journey to Baghdad was made in an ancient bus which stopped continually.

Now the summer had come to Iraq, the warm wind brought with it a choking dust from southern deserts. People slept on their roofs, and in the sandy street below an imam tearfully retold the sad story of the fate of Hassan and Hussein to a crowd of mournful people. Men beat their breasts and chanted "Allaaaah" at various intervals, and their women-folk, swathed in black habyas, clustered together in the background, trying to keep their babies from howling too often.

Then I was on my way to Kuwait, squashed into a ramshackle bus between two prisoners tied together with an *ishmok* and a man with two wives. He had to get off at the frontier, for having a visa for only one of them. When I arrived, I mentioned to a kind gentleman at the Kuwait Information Centre that I should like to have the opportunity of spending a few days with a Kuwaiti family. He obliged by putting me in touch with a girl called Miriam who worked at the Foreign Office, who said that she would be delighted to take me home.

'Home' turned out to be a residence so enormous that the family of four employed a lift to get from one part of it to another. "Father's a millionaire merchant," Miriam informed me casually. "We often entertain the sheikhs here, so the extra space is useful."

To get my visa for Saudi Arabia, Miriam whisked me straight off to the Ambassador himself. Although my host's position helped enormously, His Excellency was still reluctant to give me permission to travel overland through his country, where the movements of all girls — whether Saudi Arabian or foreign, were restricted. "Fly over it," he suggested with a smile. I persisted, however, and was at last given permission to travel to Jeddah from Dammam by road.

One day, Miriam drove me to see the oil-drilling site at Ahmadi. How easily the Kuwaitis were able to exploit their oil! It flowed down a natural slope to the tankers in the port, each taking roughly seventeen hours to load up. The drilling site was well equipped, with swimming pools, a cricket pitch, a football ground — but no bars, of course.

I often went out with Lotifa, another Kuwaiti, who also worked for the Foreign Office, and whom I had previously encountered in Beirut. Like most of his compatriots, he sat at the wheel of a gleaming new car. "Kuwait is now the richest oil-producing country in the Middle East," he informed me. "There is no need for a bus service here; our cars and taxis are enough. Many of us have television sets, numerous servants, and a holiday in Europe each year. There is a liquor ban here now, though, and since people have started making 'moon-shine' in their homes, yeast is no longer allowed into the country."

My parents had sent me a cheque to Baghdad, but I wasn't sorry to learn that ten pounds was handed out to blood donors in Kuwait. Trotting along to the Amiri Hospital, I had my blood taken by a jolly Egyptian doctor, who spent some time in telling me how wonderful Egypt, Nasser, and money all were — in Kuwait.

Between Kuwait and Saudi Arabia lay a neutral zone, shared by both countries, and I got a lift in an oil company bus, along with a host of Arab workers and some Japanese. My hosts there in the neutral zone were Japanese. I hardly thought that I would be seeing the Japanese tea-drinking ceremony performed again so soon, in the Arabian desert.

Chapter 17

June 1965–October 1965

The kingdom of Saudi Arabia! I gazed up at the green oblong flag with the white scimitar across its centre and above it the white Arabic device, "There is no God but God, Mohammed is the Prophet of God". As did the Japanese who had kindly given me a lift, I paid five pounds for the privilege of entering the country.

I stayed in Damman with two English teachers, one of whom, Mike, gave Engish lessons to a wealthy Saudi Arabian merchant called Farid. I called at the immigration office almost daily, hoping to find that my visa extension had been granted. Some days my passport would be lost, then it would reappear; promises would be made only to be broken. At last, however, the day came when the immigration authorities seemed eager to attend to my case if only to be rid of Wendy Myers's nagging for ever. I was sent straight to the office of the director who turned out to be quite an amicable fellow, and told me in excellent English that all would be well if I could produce Farid to confirm everything. Having done this, I had to spend a couple of hours running up and down stairs, standing in queues, and collecting forms, stamps, and at least seventeen signatures. Then, when we seemed to have sailed through all with flying colours, right to the desk of the Director of Residence whose pen would have to put the final signature on my passport, he looked me straight in the eye, and said conclusively, "One week is enough." "One week?" I shrieked, "only one week in which to explore and form an opinion of such a vast and intriguing country as the Kingdom of Saudi Arabia? Why, if you came to little England saying that one week was enough in which to see everything, I should be most insulted!" I won my case, obtaining permission to stay in the country for a period of one month.

All the Saudis I spoke to about my proposed journey to Jeddah by road seemed most apprehensive about it, and could offer little information; most of them travelled by air. However, somebody told me to consult a fellow called Shafik, who ran a car auction. "I'll fix everything," Shafik assured me. "I run a bus service myself as far as Taif, and from there you can easily get to Jeddah."

It was Shafik who came to see me off on his crowded old bus. "No charge for you!" he smiled as the bus began to move, "and don't worry about anything, the other passengers have assured me that they have no objection to you travelling with them!"

At sunrise we arrived in a village of mud houses called Afif. The inhabitants were just waking up, and I sat with the driver and my fellow passengers on the thick carpet of a café, sipping hot tea.

A few miles from Afif the asphalt road ended and we bumped along over a dust track through the desert, everyone hanging on to the luggage racks and singing. Before noon we came to the village of Muwai Hakran. "We'll be staying here for five hours," the driver told me, "I don't move during the heat of the day." As I was wondering what to do during that time, a young man offered to show me around. I enjoyed Muwai Hakran, with its mud castle, tiny butcher's shop, and streets of low houses from which veiled women called to us. When we returned to the main street we found the male passengers from the bus and a group of villagers seated on the carpet of a *kaffana*. "I'd love to ask them all sorts of questions," I told my guide Omar. "Well, do," he urged. "They won't mind. Allow me to act as your interpreter." The questions and answers went something like this:

Wendy: "What do you people think of a European girl coming and sitting with you, unveiled, wearing trousers, and so forth?"

Villagers: "If you are honest, you are welcome. We know that your customs are different from ours, and we are happy to meet a new type of person."

Wendy (feeling surprised and pleased): "Thank you!"

Villagers: "What do you think of our moslem religion?"

Wendy: "I think that it teaches many good things, such as monotheism, cleanliness, charity, and self-control, but I don't approve of this business of having four wives! A man can't possibly be really in love with each of them." (Here I deliver a lecture on falling in love.)

Villagers (nodding their heads understandingly): "How old are you?"

They all gasped in astonishment when I replied that I was twenty-four, unmarried, and would not be considering matrimony until I was at least thirty years old.

Soon we got on to discussing village life, and I was relieved and happy to learn that there was both a girls' school and a boys' school in Muwai Hakran – although only the boys could go to Ryadh or Jeddah for higher studies – and that by law, circumcision was now being done at infancy. "What about slaves?" I asked Omar. "That custom is finished here now," he replied.

"And hand chopping?" I inquired. "Yes, that's still practised here – on thieves," admitted Omar, "but only after they've had many chances, and it's done by a specially trained man."

Then the shadows lengthened and we were on our way once more, following a tyre-mark track over the desert. And then there was desert no more, for we were climbing into a spine of hills which arched through the Yemen, its streams watering Aden's crops. Taif air was fresh and invigorating, vegetation was lush and like no other in that vast country. An English couple were expecting me there, and they introduced me to Jamil and his family, who owned the best hotel. During my stay in Taif, I spent many hours with this delightful family, and one evening Jamil and I joined a party of King Faisal's ministers who were staying at the hotel.

Tall, dark and handsome they were, with flowing garments which added to their charm. Conversation ranged from the Ryadh university, which now allowed girls to attend lectures (though separately from the boys), to whether or not syphilis could be caught from camels. Suddenly a man rushed into the lounge, opened a black bag, and asked us all to roll up our sleeves. "The king's doctor," Jamil explained. "There's a smallpox epidemic in town."

I had to be thinking about transport to Jeddah. Although there was a road around Mecca for non-moslems to take, vehicles did not use it regularly. "Don't worry about that," Jamil assured me when I broached the subject. "I'll have a chat to my friend in the airlines department." The chat produced a free ticket to Jeddah, and, as I thanked him profusely, Jamil enquired "Have you arranged your lodging there?" "Well, no," I replied. "Leave it to me," said Jamil, and when we met the following morning he was smiling. "Something you'd never dream of, Wendy!" I was going to stay with a Saudi family, the father of which was the brother-in-law of the king.

The taxi brought me scrunching to the door of a massive house on the edge of Jeddah, set in a even vaster garden. "Ah, you must be the English teacher we sent for!" beamed His Excellency's wife, waving me to a chair. "Er . . . well no, but I will give you any amount of lessons if you wish," I stammered. "You see . . . Jamil . . ." "Oh – Jamil!" she exclaimed. "Yes, he's an old friend of ours. If he sent you, my husband knows about it and everything will be all right." Thus I was installed, and showered with the most unforgettable kindness and hospitality during my sojourn in Jeddah.

As soon as I entered that house my onward journey to Aden was taken care of by one of the secretaries. Although I had longed to travel overland through the Yemen, owing to recent outbreaks of trouble this was well nigh impossible.

The plan was that I should go to Kamaran Island by ship, and from there take a small boat to my destination.

Having said my goodbyes, I arrived on board the ship to find myself quickly given one of the spare cabins set aside for the crew. I discovered the reason for this later, when I came up and stood on the bridge with the captain. There were over a thousand Yemenese pushing for places on the deck. All clothed in brilliant colours, they wore their hair long and curling about their shoulders, dragged their women and children behind them, and carried armfuls of bedding and baggage – which, without exception, included a transistor radio covered in some glittering material.

On the morning when Kamaran Island loomed from the mist, the Yemenese became quite excited and several fights took place. "Better let them get off first," advised the captain. "Then you can disembark." But I never did. For although Kamaran Island is British and I am British, there are apparently some British territories where even the holder of a British passport cannot go without a special permit – and that was one of them. That meant that I would have to stay on the ship for its round trip to Somalia and then back to Jeddah, for which I had no guarantee of re-entry. I became a member of the crew, and was put to work mending a pile of tattered flags.

When we tied up at Berbera, Samel, the ship's radio officer, took me ashore to show me around and have lunch at his house there. Returning to the ship that afternoon we found the captain and officers lowering one of the lifeboats, and a few minutes later we were all chugging across the bay to go skin-diving. "Follow close behind me," said the captain, before he disappeared beneath the water with a harpoon gun. We saw sharks, but eventually emerged from the depths with two fish, a lobster for the pot — and all our limbs. In all the excitement we hadn't noticed the tide go out, and our lifeboat was now high and dry on the beach. We had to wait three hours for the high tide, and finally got back to the ship too tired and dirty to think of anything but bed.

The following morning hundreds of animals were being slung into the hatches — the sheep in crates, and the camels separately, with ropes. It hurt me to see those proud 'ships of the desert' vomiting with fear and stretching their long necks in helpless humiliation. Like the sheep, they too were being exported for meat.

Four days later we were weaving our way between wrecks and rocks into Jeddah port. Due to the unfailing kindness of my Saudi Arabia friends, instant visas were organised, and I was saved from a monotonous future life at sea. Apart from other concerns, His Excellency owned some aeroplanes. That finally solved my problem of transport to Aden; I flew.

An Indian who worked with one of the airline companies at Aden airport advised me of a cheap hotel and promised to collect me from it the following morning.

The next morning when Lal, my Indian friend, came, he said, "You'll be staying at my house tonight. I live in Crater, the hindu quarter of Aden. As you probably know, the state of Aden was formed by the twin volcanic peninsulas of Aden and Little Aden — hence, the crater."

As we strolled along the dusty streets below bare, rocky cliffs, a noise which sounded like Chinese fire-crackers broke the stillness of the early morning. Lal's house was in a block, and he shared two rooms with his wife and brother. The basement was occupied by a family of goats. It was just as we'd finished a substantial vegetarian lunch, sitting on the floor of the kitchen, that we received the news. The 'fire-crackers' that morning had been caused by a revolver. "The English chief of police was shot down outside the bank by terrorists," a friend of Lal's informed us quietly.

That afternoon, Lal's brother kindly took us for a drive. First we went to Steamship Point where the port was now quiescent, owing to a strike, and then on to Elephant Bay, where white-crested waves crisped over golden beaches. I had a swim there, and smiled to myself as I heard familiar dialects; at that time, Aden was full of British servicemen's families.

Returning via the modern shopping centre, we then drove out to a beautiful garden at the base of the rocky cliffs. In it there were some dried up water-tanks. "No rain here since nineteen twenty-two," said Lal. Before entering Crater we were stopped by British soldiers and the car was thoroughly searched. Sentries stood on top of the bank building. "Not only are they alerted because of this morning's murder, but Parliament is sitting over there, in that abandoned church on the rocks," whispered Lal.

Lal knew that, being interested in the ways and customs of all peoples, I was eager to meet some of the Aden Arabs, and one day he came to me with the news that somebody important in the company for which he worked had invited me to spend a few days with his family.

That evening I was installed in Abdelaziz's cliff-top residence, and introduced to his charming young wife, teenage niece, and enormous dogs.

The following day I spent in town with Abdelaziz. Driving through Crater, we turned down a street where a sign said "No whites here". "This is where the trouble started," muttered Abdelaziz and we were so harassed by British soldiers there that as we left, I exploded. "There's always another side to everything! I was on a bus with Lal two evenings ago, when a very drunken British soldier who was one of the passengers started to be most rude to the conductor, using filthy language and shaking his fist for no reason at all. When the conductor told the soldier politely that he was only doing his job and would have to report him if he didn't cease making a disturbance, the drunkard swore even more obscenely and patting his gun, shouted, "You can't touch me — see what I've got here!"

The next morning we were all up at five-thirty — to go to the

Sultan's palace in Lahej. "What an odd time to meet royalty!" I chuckled. "Over breakfast!"

When we arrived at Lahej palace the Amir greeted us warmly and although he understood not one word of English, he was able to use one of his young, sharp-witted sons as an interpreter. We breakfasted in a room near to where the harem lived, and as we sat shoeless on a thick carpet they set trays of pillaw, rhoti, lamb, eggs, curry, bread, curds and honey before us.

Although conversation was limited, it was a lively meal. "He flies with me to the U.K. each year – likes shopping in Harrods," disclosed Abdelaziz when the Amir had left the room. "Ah, I think he's gone to get some sort of a gift for you." The gift turned out to be a solid gold watch, and a wad of notes worth thirty pounds.

That was the first of several visits to Lahej and the Sultan's palace, visits which helped me to 'discover' and grow deeply attached to Aden which, as tourists usually see it from the port, seems stifling, barren, and perhaps rather dull.

To fly across the Gulf of Aden to Djibouti, the 'jumping-off point' for my African safari, was as cheap as sailing, I discovered, and the morning came when Abdelaziz drove me through Aden for the last time. The troubles were worse. A strict curfew had been imposed the night before and now British helicopters were causing quite a sensation by hovering low and noisily over the rooftops. The car checks and searches were more ferocious than ever and, as there was a road-block on the Crater side of the airport road, Abdelaziz took me around 'a back way'. "Those b—— soldiers!" he chuckled as we sped along unhindered, "any fool can bluff them!"

· · · ·

The afternoon was stifling and I was surprised at the bustle of the docks. "Busy, mademoiselle, because of the harbour strike in Aden," disclosed Monsieur Pouget, a bank manager. After flying from Aden, I had taken Monsieur Pouget a letter from Lal, and now he was showing me round Djibouti. "Djibouti is now full of the English, for one always knows them by their ridiculous hats!"

During the whole of the twelve-hour train journey from Djibouti to Diredawa, I stayed in the luggage-wagon, the only place on the locomotive which wasn't overflowing, though a selection of tribesmen, soldiers, guards, women, children, and goats came and went all day long. There were Somalis, Ethiopians, and some of each crossed with Sudanese – all most polite and friendly. The Ethiopian tribesmen interested me greatly. They wore their hair long, kept in place by long toothed wooden combs, and feathers lent that added fascination. Also of interest were their necklets, ceremonial staffs, home-made leather sandals, and the daggers which were strapped to their waists. The women, attired in brightly coloured cloths, were unveiled, and carried their babies on their backs. Their hairstyles were not half so lavish as those of the menfolk, consisting simply of a lot of tiny plaits sticking out from all over the head.

I didn't spend long in Diredawa, but made for Addis Ababa, where I discovered that all the cheap hotels were very full. "You see, tomorrow is our New Year's Day," explained an Ethiopian who had been listening to my conversation with the desk clerk in what must have been the tenth hotel I'd tried. "We go by the Coptic calendar, and for us today is the last day of nineteen fifty-seven. My name is Messele, by the way, and I'm just up from Gughe for the New Year. I'm also looking for a room here. They only seem to have either a room with three beds in it – one of which is already occupied, or a single room – which I have already taken. However, if you trust my integrity you are quite welcome to share it."

It was close to midnight, and thanking Messele for his kindness I wearily followed him. "I was just about to eat," he smiled, waving towards a table in his small room on which lay some thin, brown, spongy bread with hot chillies and meat inside. We shared this repast, and Messele stood up. "You take the bed, Wendy," he said, "I'll sleep on the floor as if I were your bodyguard!" "Oh come on," I told him, "this bed's big enough for two but we'd better sleep top to tail!" The next morning I opened my eyes to see a pair of black feet on my pillow. "You see – we're not all savages here!" said Messele with a grin.

The scenery on the way to Dessie was quite absorbing. There were green hills dotted with sheep and round thatched wooden houses, tiny uneven fields being tilled by peasants with oxen ploughs, men rolling water-filled oil-drums to their villages, women and children carting faggots in dried goat-skins, others working in the rice and sugar-cane plantations, and baby

157

donkeys everywhere rolling and then scurrying after their mothers as our noisy bus rattled past them.

We stayed the night in Dessie then went on through Macalle and Asmara to Tessenei, my stepping stones to the Sudan. At Tessenei, as I stood in the office of the District Officer there, he sighed and told me: "The road from here to Kassala is temporarily closed, owing to rebels, I'm afraid. They wish to make Eritrea independent of Ethiopia (which used to be Abyssinia)."

It was other people's financial difficulties which eventually helped me to get to Kassala along the blocked road. I was seated in a *tukul* (a round, grass-roofed mud hut) one evening, watching white Ibis flying around the tree-tops outside, appearing luminous in the moonlight and squawking like ducks, when a message was delivered to me from the District Officer. It said that on the following afternoon a special bus was to be allowed to go through the road-blocks as far as the Ethiopian frontier with a group of Sudanese.

The next day, after thanking the District Officer for all his trouble, I climbed aboard the special bus. At the Ethiopian border, soldiers ran in front of our vehicle and, waving machine-guns, ordered us all to stay seated. Very gingerly, one of the officers inspected our clothes and luggage. Then, we were permitted to descend, the soldiers explaining that their precautions had been taken because earlier a bus had been stolen by the rebels, who had driven it to the frontier and killed all the nationalist soldiers on guard there.

When we were ready to leave a collection was taken, and the sum of one pound was presented to an old man on a camel who then went galloping over the sand in front of us as far as the next village, where his job was to find a Sudanese bus which would take us farther. The Sudanese bus was a converted truck, the sides of which were wooden bars.

I stayed in Kassala that night, in one of the large, mud residences that were by now so familiar to me, with tiny windows, doorless gaps to encourage welcome draughts of air, and a palmy patio full of beds.

From there I travelled fourth class in the crowded Khartoum train, feasting my eyes on the ever-changing scenes we passed. During the afternoon some ladies beside me uncovered a bowl of hot sauce made from potatoes and chicken, and invited me to dip pieces of bread into it with them. When night fell the ladies got out, and in their places came a group of local tribesmen, with dark skins and flat, hole-punched noses. Daggers were strapped to their left arms, and from their waists hung long swords. The other more urbanised passengers motioned to me to change my place, hinting that the tribesmen might rob me during the night but, not wanting to hurt my neighbour's feelings, I stayed where I was, and all went well.

I spent twelve happy days in Khartoum and Omdurman, and although most of my time was filled with looking and learning, I also had the important task of visiting certain officials to ask permission to travel southwards through their country, which was at that time being torn apart by political strife. Then one day I learned that I could make that journey to the south, travelling for ten days by boat along the White Nile.

In Kosti the boat was waiting. Wearily I found the women's dormitory on one of the third-class decks, and climbed on to a bare, iron bunk. At dawn the next morning I was seated on a pile of onion sacks writing my notes, and every so often gazing at the Nile. Wide, smooth and brown it was, its purple hyacinths swishing and smashing beneath our prow as we proceeded up-river. Feeling hungry, I devoured some of the bread and sardines which I had brought along, as food wasn't provided for third-class passengers. Munching contentedly I watched cunning crocodiles swim to and fro across the river with only their nostrils showing, and the pink backsides of hippopotami disappearing into the papyrus. The other passengers seemed friendly but didn't speak, weighing me up, perhaps, until a very dark-skinned Sudanese came and sat down beside me. "Enjoying your trip?" he enquired somewhat cautiously. "Oh yes!" I replied. "How far are you going?" "Right to Juba – my home's there," said the man. "I'm Richard, by the way – I'm a tailor and a member of the Moro tribe. Tribesmen all over our country have got problems nowadays," he sighed, "and especially us down in the south. We southerners are pure African negro, you see, with no Arab blood at all. We don't speak Arabic usually; next to our tribal tongues English is our second language, brought to us by missionaries with lessons on how to say our prayers, of course. What a mistake the English made in suppressing us and keeping us different from our northern compatriots, so that now we feel very alien to each other in blood and language. There is no doubt at all that the northerners now feel superior to us. All the big-shots down in South Sudan are Arabs, and it's they who always get the scholarships to go abroad and study. That is partly due to the fact that all our best schools and the university are up in the Arabic-speaking north, where, language-wise, we are at a tremendous disadvantage. However, some of my friends have even managed to overcome that hurdle, and are now holding professional jobs. I can tell you one thing, though; many of the southerners who are on this boat and normally work up north will never return there. Like me, they are going to join the rebels, to fight for our freedom!"

The following morning when I went on deck Richard handed me a wooden bowl. "I think you'll like this," he said. "It's our gruel, made from corn, milk and sugar." I did, and Richard seemed to have been so impressed by the fact that I could drink from the same bowl as he and his southern friends that he insisted I take all my future meals on board with them. "No trouble at all!" he assured me. "Most times our women-folk cook it all together on the charcoal fires you see around the deck."

There were some interesting menus: boiled crocodile, for example, or dried fish boiled with onions, scooped up with a brown cereal which we moulded with our hands.

One morning, having volunteered to prepare the breakfast, Richard hopped up on to the roof of the boat where he'd left some strips of fish to dry in the sun. "Bother!" he muttered when he came down. "It rained in the night – and now look!" I looked, and the fish he was holding was crawling with maggots. "Oh dear!" I sighed. "Now we can't eat it." Richard, however, was sloshing the fish about in the brown river. "Have to wash it, that's all," he called, and a few minutes later he was cooking it. The remainder of the maggots were boiled to death and, if anything, added to the flavour.

Thus I had joined the South Sudanese community, and couldn't help but notice small things which understandably aggravated their grievances, such as when the soldiers on board turned them off the onion sacks, while I or any of the northerners could sit on them all day long without being disturbed. "We're just that much heavier, I suppose," murmured Richard ruefully.

The following day the Nile became twisty, and with great

difficulty we manœuvred alongside the bank at a place called Adok—just three wooden sheds and a lot of mud. At the sound of our whistle an excited host of naked men, women and children came scurrying towards the boats, carrying rush mats they'd made with which to barter with the people on board. The sole attire of the assemblage before us were the string aprons of the women and the bead bangles on the wrists and ankles of the men. They were relaxed and uninhibited and moved with silent grace, complementing and complemented by the unspoiled landscape which was their home.

Then came the final evening of our voyage up the White Nile. As I sat chatting to my southern friends, one of the sheep on board broke loose from its tether. Getting up, I was in the process of tying the animal back to its post when a young northern soldier who was passing kicked it in the face. Furious, I kicked the soldier on the ankle and then went back to sit beside Richard. Following me, the soldier shook his fist in front of my nose, spat at me, and hit my cheek. Still seething more about his cruelty to the poor sheep than anything else, I cursed him and all his ancestors in Arabic. The other passengers, meanwhile, had been watching all this with great consternation, and somebody rushed off to fetch the soldier's immediate superior. When the superior told the soldier to behave himself with the passengers, he growled, "Even if I had beaten her they shouldn't have interfered. After all, she is only a bloody foreigner!"

Some time later we arrived in Juba and I went straight to the house of the chief of police, who was expecting me, and with whom I stayed. The overland route to Uganda had been cut completely owing to the recent attack of one of the border villages, so it was decided that I leave for Uganda's capital, Kampala, by air.

Then it was unfamiliar territory for me once again, as the Sudan Airways plane winged her way across a turbulent, cloud-filled sky towards Lake Victoria. Not all, however, was unfamiliar. "'Ello, luv!" called the radio officer from the pilot's cabin. "I cum from Yorkshire too!"

Chapter 18

While wandering around Kampala on a chilly afternoon in a thin grey drizzle, I was given a lift by a young English teacher named George. He quickly organised some sight-seeing for me and that week-end I saw Lake Victoria, the largest lake in Africa, the palace of King Kabaca Mutesi, and the great white building that houses the Parliament of Uganda.

On making enquiries at some of the embassies of other African countries about the possibilities of travelling from them to the Congo, Rhodesia, South Africa and so forth, I arrived at the conclusion that nobody seemed to know or particularly want to know about what was going on in other countries.

I hitch-hiked to Nairobi, through forests of wattle trees, coffee plantations, fields of cattle, and highlands dotted with sheep. At the Nukuru Lake bird sanctuary, I had the unforgettable sight of thousands of pink flamingos. As I stood on the lakeside, captivated by the scene before me, the waters were suddenly whipped up to fury by an approaching storm, which sent the birds squawking and huddling together in flocks like rosy clouds. A pungent, salty odour filled the air, from the bird's droppings mixed with mud, I guessed. The wind moaned against the cackling, and their feathers became luminous against the darkness of the hills behind.

In Nairobi I spotted a newspaper with a baby rhinoceros taking up most of its front page. Its name was Caesar. There was an interesting story connected with Caesar and with amazing good fortune I happened to meet an English couple who were friends of the baby rhino's foster parents and took me to visit them.

Mr Carr Hartley, Caesar's foster-father, was introduced to me as one of the world's best hunters and trappers of big game, with a grown-up son who followed closely behind. "My boy was rounding up a herd of rhinos three hundred miles south of the capital," explained the brawny hunter, "and didn't notice that one of the females was pregnant. She fell dead, and, going to her side, my son observed that the beast must have been in labour, so he decided to perform a Caesarean section operation on the spot. He cut out the baby rhino but it was still-born. Then he gave it the 'kiss of life' — mouth to nostril, as the baby rhino's mouth was too big — and the animal at last began to breathe! Appropriately, it was christened Caesar there and then, and I sent a plane down to collect it. Drinks three pint bottles of milk five times a day now, little blighter! House-trained though, at the moment. Last one we had ate all the living room curtains!

Pens in the garden contained some of the adult rhinos brought back from the safari; they were waiting to be shipped off to zoos. One enormous male kept charging at the side of his wooden pen, so that the whole fragile affair shook violently. "Ever escape?" I asked, my eyes never leaving that rhino for even a second. "Sometimes; then we run!" came the reply. "Those horns are damn dangerous. See the sides of our safari trucks." The thick metal was bent and battered as if it had been Plasticine.

A local bus took me from Cairo to Mombasa, and then on to Tanga, where I stayed with an Indian family. I reached Tanzania's capital, and 'Harbour of Peace' Dar-es-Salaam, by another bus from Tanga, an eight-hour journey along a rain-slippery road, past kapoc trees, sisal plantations and chattering groups of black-faced monkeys.

The bus bound for Mbeya, in West Tanzania, was full to overflowing and I found myself squashed firmly between an African and an Arab, trying not to breathe in and out too deeply. Day after day we sped through the countryside, stopping each night at rest-houses or small villages. On we went, harassed by tax-inspectors in Tanzania and by officious 'young pioneers' in red shorts in Malawi. Then, rounding some fresh, green hills in that country which is one-fifth taken up by water, we arrived in Blantyre. I spent the night there with American Peace Corps volunteers, and decided the next day to hitch-hike straight off in the direction of Salisbury, for at that time Rhodesia had lived through only one week of her Unilateral Independence and I wasn't sure how a Britisher would be received there. An Indian gave me a lift to Dedza and a South

African another to Tete in Mozambique. I had no trouble at all in entering Rhodesia on the following day.

My hostess, Mrs Ross, whose husband was a business associate of a friend of mine in Baghdad, took me out to her beautiful home in one of Salisbury's 'swimming-pool suburbs', and on the next morning drove me around town, a mass of smooth new buildings gleaming in the sun, with avenues bordered by mauve-blossomed jacaranda trees that scattered their colour everywhere. "A truly beautiful capital – and so peaceful!" I remarked, leaning out of the car window. "Well, what did you expect to find when you got here, a revolution?" asked Mrs Ross with a chuckle. "If you did, you're not the only one. Our hotels are packed with newspaper reporters from all over the world, waiting for the riots that will never take place. You ask a black African what he really thinks about the U.D.I. and he'll undoubtedly tell you that he's glad that we whites are in power because the black Africans are always disagreeing with each other and they don't yet have anyone suitable to take the place of Ian Smith."

Mrs Ross was wonderful as any hostess could be, but there was always a barrier between us, a barrier that was never so clearly defined as on the last morning of my stay. We were seated together on the stoep watching her youngest son toddle aimlessly about the garden. "He gets so lonely when the others are at school," remarked my hostess. "But I've often heard the voice of a child next door," I told her. "He sounds just about your son's age." "Oh, he is," said Mrs Ross. "Then why can't they play together?" I asked. "He's black," was the conclusive reply.

The following day I travelled to Bulawayo, past Gwelo, the 'garden city' of Rhodesia, and Que Que, sight of an ex-gold mine, now in use as a prison.

Johannesburg was the first city I stopped at in the Republick van Suid-Afrika, and amidst its towering, modern buildings I wandered for hours, getting sweaty and rather lost. A girl, with a look which said that she understood just how wearisome walking around a hot, dusty city with a knapsack on one's shoulders could be, introduced herself as Marilyn and invited me to go to her flat for coffee.

After a look round the University of Witwatersrand, where she was a student, she took me to the cellar of a friend of hers called Colin Bunbury. Cosy and interesting, its doors and windows were draped with sacking, and all around the walls were books, musical instruments and works of art. Colin, another boy, and a girl lived there, all 'varsity students and all anti-apartheid. After supper when we got on to that subject, Colin warned me, "Be very careful who hears you give your opinions on discrimination here. A lot of us students have spent ninety days in jail already, only because we had certain books in our possession. The censors even banned *Black Beauty* until they got beyond the title!"

To get to Laurenco Marques, the capital of Mozambique, I had to travel through Pretoria, a modern city built by the Boers, and the administrative headquarters for the South African Republic. On a hill-top there stood a huge monument to commemorate a Dutch victory over the Africans. An elaborate affair, it had cost over one million pounds to build, and on one day of each year, I was told, the sun shone through a hole in the roof on to a stone engraved with the words: 'We are for South Africa.' The 'lantern of civilisation' stood in the wall behind it.

I was cheered by the fact that Mozambique did not practise apartheid and the Africans mingled everywhere with the Portuguese, went to white schools, and were often extremely well dressed. The palmy beaches were quite magnificent, I thought, and for a long time I stood watching the sail boats made from palm wood strung together, the fishermen on board working very hard indeed when they wished to haul them from the rough breakers on to the sand.

I loved Swaziland with its green hills, dales, chattering stream and 'liquorice allsort' people. There was no colour bar there at all, and all races could live and work together as equals, the Africans, if they were qualified, being able to obtain executive posts which were even denied to them in Mozambique. In M'babane, its capital, 4,000 feet up in the knolls, I stayed with a Portuguese–Bantu couple, and from there got a lift straight to Durban.

It was a sweltering afternoon when I arrived at that coastal town, so I took one of the surprisingly unsegregated Natal buses to a safe area of the beach, where the surf, I was told, was less treacherous than elsewhere along that section of South Africa's coast. I enjoyed swimming and watching the odd dolphin or two playing beyond the surf, and then strolled along the shelly sand, where bronzed 'beach-boys' with peroxided hair ran with surfboards of foam-rubber-filled plastic. Sand, sky and sea! For a minute I could have been anywhere: for a minute. A woman smiled at me as I walked by, so cheerily I called, "Good day for sunbathing!" "Sunbathing?" she shrieked, "Personally, I think it's quite degrading of them to try to get like the blacks!"

Pietermaritzburg, Natal's small capital, was my next destination, and I hitch-hiked there, past Zulu kraals, grassy veld over which weaver birds and egrets swooped, and through 'the valley of a thousand hills'.

From Pietermaritzburg I travelled to East London, and then all around the coast to Capetown, a cosmopolitan place, with English, Afrikaans, Bantus, Hottentots, Cape Malays, Cape coloureds, and Indians walking between Dutch colonial style buildings spread out over the lower slopes of Table Mountain.

In Capetown I stayed with an actor, Archie Nolan, and his family, who had given me a lift when they'd found me, on my first night there, struggling through the darkness towards the Youth Hostel.

Wandering along through the botanical gardens to the Houses of Parliament one day, I was shown around by an officious Afrikaans guide. It was when we arrived at the Chamber of Representatives that Wendy Myers dropped the clanger. "This is where the nationalists sit, and here is where the opposition are seated," chanted the guide. "Oh, you mean the black people?" I blurted out. The expression on the Afrikaaner's face became one of contempt. "No! No! No!" he corrected, "they have their own place."

Then it was Christmas 1965, and that's when I met Bengt Hanovitch, a Lithuanian–Jewish potter and a friend of Archie's. Bengt's pottery was a converted hen-house on a Constantia hillside, from where the view was all mountains hugged by dark green firs, jagged grey rocks, and white homesteads in lush valleys.

Christmas Eve found me with Bengt at the house of an abstract painter and his wife, who were Christians. As we sprawled over cushions in candlelight, I suggested that we commemorate the feast with a Hebrew prayer from Bengt. After this I thought about all my moslem friends and treated

166

everyone to some verses from the Koran in Arabic, then we all rounded things off with our favourite Christmas carols. The next day I went with Bengt to give sweets to the African labourers' children from all the near-by farms, and that night there was much revelry, resulting in groups of Africans swaying drunkenly through the streets of Capetown. One of them came boldly up to me, asking, "Will you shake this little black hand?"

'Rusty', an old friend of Bengt's, was a celebrated cartoonist. He, Bengt and others of their group took me to Citrusdal, 100 miles from Cape Town, to see the bushmen's cave-paintings. It was there I spent New Year's Day 1966.

Rusty, Archie and Bengt had already had one book published which they had prepared on bushman's cave-paintings, and Rusty would lead us on many expeditions to search for unexplored caves in the bushlands around Citrusdal, so that I had the opportunity of seeing some works of art which no white man had ever seen before. Sometimes we found numerous handprints made by bushmen who couldn't paint. Their pigments were ochres, oxides, and wood or bone charcoals, and there were some interesting effects. The figures of men and women were astoundingly well drawn, as were the animals. All were full of life, and the painted lions, rhinos, giraffes and so forth, which had disappeared from that region of Africa many years ago, reminded us that we were seeing the work of South Africa's earliest known native race. We traced many of the scenes before us, and with the use of a colour chart and a camera Rusty and Bengt got them all recorded correctly for their next book. Evenings around the campfire were the perfect ending for days of rock climbing and exploring. It was then that we heard tales which were only safe to be told far from the ears of Capetown. Of interrogations by the Afrikaaner police. . . . "And then he asked me, 'Would you marry a kaffir girl?' and owing to my sexual preferences, I replied, 'No, I'd have no desire to' – so he shouted, 'But you would, man, you would, if it weren't for your sexual preferences?'" And their policy. "Just because they aren't trading with China, the Chinese are considered coloured, but because they are trading with Japan, the Japanese are as white as we are!"

After Capetown, I travelled through the Bechuanaland Protectorate – now Botswana – and on the way there I stopped for a brief look at Kimberly's 'Big Hole', an old diamond mine abandoned in 1914.

Then on to Vryburg and Mafeking. I had no difficulty whatsoever in hitch-hiking through that country. Cars were few and far between, but when they came, the occupants were only too glad of fresh company with which to cover the vast stretches of desert. Instead of being called 'tukuls' the round mud houses were called 'randeveles' and in Mahalapye I stayed in one of them with an English Voluntary Service Overseas farmer and his wife, who found it a cool and comfortable abode.

Petrol rationing in Rhodesia was severe when I returned and I was grateful for anything at all that would take me northwards along the two parallel concrete strips, so typical of a Rhodesian highway.

Before leaving, I visited the famous Victoria Falls, which cascaded noisily down into the heart of a lush rain forest. There is so much beauty in this part of Africa, I thought, watching as sunbeams made dancing rainbows in the spray; if only it weren't for the 'toothache', that constant, nagging pain one feels in one's heart when something is wrong. Then I thought back, to a conversation I had had with Annie, the Bantu maid at a house I had stayed at in Worcester, Cape Province. She had told me that nowadays Africans have to have permits to travel anywhere at all, and that she and her husband, who belonged to another tribe, were now forbidden to reside in the same town. "And this U.D.I. business, do you think it will last?" I asked her. The eyes were sad, the voice was perhaps a wee bit hopeful. "We'll just have to wait and see," said Annie.

Chapter 19

January 1966–April 1966

Lusaka, capital of the Zambian Republic, is a modern little town containing even a Chinese restaurant to provide 'your oriental adventure in Africa'. I stayed there with an 'anti' South African couple in their enormous house, the garden of which included a reservoir, ideal for swimming. "All bought with insurance money?" smiled my host. "Both broke our legs in a car accident two years ago. Have to break them again if we want a gardener though!"

Some days later I was speeding through North Zambia's copper-belt towards the Congolese Republic. Police with tear-gas bombs fixed to their belts were waiting at Elizabethville station. I stayed with a tall young woman named Josephine Ndanu to whom I had an introduction.

I loved my days in Josephine's household. It had a casual, friendly atmosphere. In some things rich; good food, radios, expensive clothes, servants: in others poor; old furniture, a wrecked bathroom, no books or pictures. It was a place where friends came and went at leisure, to eat, do their ironing, or sometimes just to sit around and talk to me.

Josephine always accompanied me on my excursions to the 'Immigration Ville', to request an extension of my fifteen-day visa, and maybe because they knew that I was happily installed in the home of one of their compatriots, the immigration people readily gave me a three-month visa stamped into my passport. Then one day I booked a third-class passage on a train bound for Port Francqui on the Kasai River, from where I would be able to catch a connecting boat to Leopoldville – now Kinshasa.

Even the third-class compartments of the train were provided with wash-basins. On my first morning on board I climbed down from my top bunk to wash. The bunks were in tiers of

169

three. The other five, I observed, were occupied by men. I remembered that white people to whom I had mentioned my forthcoming overland trip across the Congo had told me quite frankly that it would be suicide. They were remembering the recent riots, no doubt.

However, the men in my compartment all seemed to be most polite and friendly, so I relaxed and enjoyed the Congolese countryside, getting off at each station we came to, for fresh air and exercise. The train sped on smuttily over lush, green grasslands, through dense jungle, and past tiny villages. At each station we stopped at women sold fried ants, sweet corns, manioc, bananas, and boiled peanuts, through the open windows of the train.

At Port Francqui mosquitoes whined in the chilly morning air. We had arrived at our destination. There would be a long wait at the station before the boat came into port just a few metres away, so we Leopoldville passengers huddled together, shivering and swatting alternately. Then at 7.30 a.m. we were summoned to check our tickets: and mine was wrong. "Not my fault!" I shouted impatiently. "If the E'ville people make a mistake, why should I pay?" I demanded to see the chief. He turned out to be an anaemic-looking Belgian in a faded topee and dazzling shirt. Upon hearing my lament, he suggested that I rest, and, looking at me closely, added that I might repair to his house and take a bath. "Leave the ticket business to me," he instructed with a smile, "come on."

B.C.K. (Bas Congo Katanga) transport took us up the hill upon which Port Francqui nestled amongst green jungle, the wide, brown, Congo River winding below. "That's it," said the Belgian, pointing to a white bungalow which stood back from the sandy road, banked by dense foliage and wild flowers. "Not a bad little place, Port Francqui; comes to life once a week when the train and the boat arrive. *Voilà!* Bienvenu to the house of Monsieur Jean Brouhon, despised by a wife in Brussels, adored by a Congolese mistress in Part Francqui!"

I should have boarded my boat bound for the capital that evening, but Monsieur Brouhon persuaded me that a week's experience of Congolese village life would be all to my benefit, so I stayed. That evening we went visiting, first of all to the house of another Belgian. He had lived in the Congo for thirty years and had a magnificent collection of ancient and modern hand-made African articles, such as carved wooden stools, beautifully patterned bark-cloth mats used for the wrapping of the dead, painted masks, raffia mats, carved ivory tusks, old maps.

On another evening we went to a bar and dance-hall owned by a Monsieur Kishwe, a friend of Monsieur Brouhon. One side of the dance-hall was raised, and crowded with chairs and tables, and on the opposite side sat the band. The concrete dancing-floor in the centre was on a lower level, and the whole place was roomy and well-lit. The band was good, and I was most impressed.

Monsieur Kishwe came, sat us down, and ordered beers, orange squash and saucers full of boiled groundnuts to munch. Then Monsieur Brouhon and I rose, and, much to the pleasure of the villagers, danced the first dance, which was a nice, easy foxtrot. The floor was filled for successive dances, with smiling, swaying Congolese, who vibrated with an inborn sense of rhythm to the resonant music. It was fun to watch them gather in circles and little groups to dance together, or to see several men get up and step around the floor in a long line, as if in a trance. The women would do likewise and they looked so picturesque in their flowing, multi-coloured clothes. As the night wore on, the dance-hall and bar became glutted with people, laughter and conversation flowing loud and long, oiled with beer and wine. The scene made me imagine an Africanised version of a Toulouse Lautrec canvas, with voluptuous prostitutes everywhere – throwing back beer straight from the bottle while being pawed by over-ardent clients.

Just as Monsieur Brouhon and I stood up to leave, a man dressed in navy blue shorts and a shirt to match entered the bar carrying a torch. "Odd uniform to come dancing in," I remarked to Monsieur Kishwe, for most people wore casual, everyday clothes, and open sandals or no shoes at all. "You mean him? Well, he's a big business man here, but now he's in prison for political reasons," disclosed our friend. "He's only got two more months to go, and each evening he gives the prison warder some money so that he can come out for a few hours. When he's had enough dancing and drinking he goes back and locks himself up again."

Monsieur Kishwe and other friends of Monsieur Brouhon filled my days with interesting experiences and when they learned that I had intended to travel to Leopoldville in the third class of the boat, they presented me with a first-class ticket and ordered me to use it.

As I sat in the dining room of the *Commissaire van den Bogaerde* at the beginning of my three-day voyage to Leopoldville, I looked through the porthole at Port Francqui disappearing, and felt a pang of fondness for that tiny hill village all lost in green jungle, with its smoky station and busy port below, alive with their weekly bustle. Then I settled down to my meal of cabbage soup, boiled potatoes, beans and meat loaf, followed by a warm soggy bun.

Much of the voyage I spent in hanging over the rails, watching the Congo slip by. At Seko port I was reminded of Venice, when hundreds of tiny dugouts were paddled and punted around the ship, their owners selling sweet potatoes, sugar-canes, peanuts, peppers, bananas, fish, chickens, pineapples, lemons and other local produce, and doing a roaring trade.

In Leopoldville I stayed with friends of my Lusaka hosts, a Belgian family called Dehousse with whom I went riding in the undulating green countryside around the Congolese capital.

The *Baron Leibrecht*, which would take me up the Congo River as far as Coquilhatville, was full to overflowing, and as many as three passengers were finding themselves holding the same cabin number. People got themselves all sorted out at last, however, the less fortunate donning extra clothing in preparation for spending a night battling with the mosquitoes on deck.

The Ubangi River was too shallow for my boat to proceed beyond Coquilhatville but I found that the *Gent* would be going up-river as far as Batanga, from where I had decided to proceed to Zongo overland. *Gent* was a wood burner, with paddles at the back which spun around sending up a spray to coruscate in the sunlight, a far more homely vessel than a noisy machine-driven affair. All day long a stoker stoked the fire from enormous piles of logs, and every few hours we would stop at odd places on shore to replenish his supplies.

Having made friends with the captain and his wife, I ate most of my meals with them. The food was always varied, always interesting: boiled green bananas, smoked wild pig, mounds of rice with chilli sauce, bukaru, roast Congolese antelope, corn on the cob, fresh honey in the comb bought from riverside villages, and sweet oranges plucked straight from the trees. Chunks of boiled crocodile often appeared on the table, and once we had roast monkey which a man had shot and brought out to the boat. Removing several balls of lead shot which were still lodged in the animal's flesh, I pronounced my verdict: "Delicious!" "Tastes like porcupine," beamed the captain, tossing the sucked bones of a tiny hand over his shoulder into the river.

It was an interesting time of year in which to be travelling through that vast, central African country. Some days were hot and sunny, bringing half-naked village women in grass skirts to bathe in the river where the water was not deep or shady enough for crocs and hippos, while on others a strong wind would turn the placid waters into a wrathful green dragon which would lash the decks with an icy tail, scaring away mosquitoes but causing us to tie up to a tree, for the danger of being grounded was at its greatest during those times.

We reached Batanga just as the river was glowing orange with the dawn. My hand was shaken warmly and a lift was arranged for me to Libenge, a larger village, some miles away.

In the forest between Batanga and Libenge lived a tribe of pygmies. Friendly little people, they stood smiling to be photographed, all half naked, most of the men-folk being clad only in loin-cloths. "Lazy lot!" scoffed the Congolese who was with me, "they don't want to go to school and progress like us, they just like to live here like animals, in the forest."

The immigration officer in Libenge was a charming young man who stamped my passport, took no notice of my luggage, expressed great interest in my travels, and presented me with a letter which asked all police, soldiers and frontier guards 'in all the countries West' to do whatever they could to help me on my way. Some months later I wrote to this man, thanking him for his kindness, and was touched by his prompt reply. "You are the first white person of intellect who has ever treated me in such a way."

On the following day I boarded the *Tousset*, a Brazzaville barge bound for the capital of the R.C.A., and, with the help of a Belgian pilot, we rounded the treacherous sandbanks, to arrive safely at our destination.

One of the transport company's trucks was heading for Baoro three days later, and soon I was seated beside its driver as we rumbled westwards along the rough road.

In Baoro, I stayed with a Swedish couple who introduced me

to an Israeli captain, one of the founders of the Israeli type co-operative village, Bartholomew Buganda, situated five miles from Baoro. "Israel has put a lot of money and machinery into this project," the captain informed me as he showed me around the village, "in order to really help the Africans to become up to date in their habitations, farming methods, and so forth. It has been going on for three years and we have had some very good results, so far. The government are all behind us, because it is solely for the benefit of the Africans, not a colonialist sort of thing!"

Then I was on the road again, travelling towards the frontier of the Cameroons. After passing through Bouar, a hill village built on an area of grey rock, the road wound down to Baboua, almost on the border. In Baboua I had been told to go to the nun's house.

On my first day there, Sister Claire – a nursing nun in charge of the village dispensary – invited me to go with her and meet some of her patients, so we set off together along the sandy track. Many of the houses were enclosed, and Sister Claire told me that the inhabitants were Hausas – moslem tribe. "They put up the barrier to protect their young girls from the public eye," she explained. "There's quite a contrast here, for the pagan women walk around wearing nothing but bunches of leaves!"

Just then, a long procession appeared in a cloud of dust, to file past us and on over a hill. There were hundreds of gaily dressed Hausas, some mounted on prancing horses and carrying spears with which to protect their village chief, who was being conveyed on a chair in their midst. Two of the men were fanning him reverently, while others danced and played musical instruments. "It's all for the feast of the sheep," disclosed Sister Claire. "They'll sing and dance all day and night now. Yet even though they are practising moslems they come to our dispensary to be cured, and their women-folk bring us gifts."

That evening when I went to the dispensary with Sister Claire, I was surprised to see it empty of out-patients for, in the morning, there had been a tremendous crowd. "Mais oui . . . of course!" she exclaimed. "All my patients are watching the feast dancing in the village square. I'll get our padre to take you to see it!"

The dancing was being performed in front of the house of the Hausa chief of the village, who sat enthroned on his spacious verandah, dotted in robes of brilliant blue. Around him stood his retinue and about thirty of his children, all watching the revelry with delight.

Groups of women, naked except for small sprays of leaves tied to their loins, were whirling, shaking, and writhing about in cricles to the beat of tom-toms. For half an hour they danced non-stop to the surging rhythms, the sweat pouring from their chocolate-coloured bodies like water. Every so often a male admirer would step forward and give a coin to his favourite dancer, who would pop it into her mouth for safety, never losing the rhythm for a second.

My stay with the French nuns of Baboua was a memorable one and I realised that for them, every minute of every day was filled with some useful occupation. As well as their dispensary, I often attended the kindergarten school they ran, and the women's sewing sessions, and the knitting group. It was so heartening to see Christians, Hausas, and pagans sitting side by side to learn together.

In spite of their diligence, all the nuns were full of fun, and adored listening to stories about my long journey, while they did their mending and such each evening, before compline. On the morning of my departure for the Cameroons, when we had said a long farewell and promised to keep in touch, Sister Claire put a beautiful card into my hand. "To commemorate the sixth anniversary of your travels," she smiled. "Today is April 4th, 1966!"

Chapter 20

April 1966–May 1966

"Gerard will be passing through today," said Monsieur Zari, "he'll take you on to Yaounde. I can trust him to look after you.' Monsieur Zari and his wife were the only Arabs in Garoua Boulai. Syrian merchants, they ran a shop which seemed to sell everything from pins to pineapples, and was a sort of landmark for passers-by of all nationalities. When Gerard's truck rumbled to a halt near where we were standing, I perceived that he was carrying a cargo of skins, and had a woman passenger in the cabin. "There, off you go, mademoiselle!" shouted Madame Zari, when Gerard had drunk three Turkish coffees behind her counter. "With one of the nicest Cameroonians that you could ever wish to meet!"

In Yaounde, a cool capital set in a damp, green, undulating countryside, Gerard introduced me to his Greek employer who, when I was ready to leave, kindly put me into another of his trucks which was bound for a northern village called Garoua. That night hailstones half an inch thick beat against the windscreen, and after helping Pierre, the driver, to cover our cargo with the tarpaulin, I slept in the cabin while he stayed on top.

The following morning we set off early, awakened by the village tom-toms but at Ekoundouma Pierre turned off the engine and said, "This is my father's village. My taxi-bus should be here and I want to check the accounts."

In Garoua Boulai we stopped at Monsieur Zari's shop, of course, and were invited for a meal of roast venison, recently shot by our host. Then, taking Madame Zari with us as she wished to visit friends in Meinganga, we climbed back into the truck.

That was a long day's driving for Pierre, and at Ossandare,

The first white people to find these bushmen's rock paintings near Citrusdal in South Africa. We trace them . . .

. . . and hunt for more

A Livingstonian encounter with my missionary cousin in Ghana

A typical mode of African rural transport

Hauling water from an open well during a breakdown in Central Africa

he said that he was going to his brother's house to rest and have some supper. "You seem to have brothers all over the place!" I remarked, as we set off through the dark, mud village. "Tribal brothers, not blood brothers," he explained. "We were all circumcised together." Inside the hut we entered sat a middle-aged man, whom Pierre introduced as his brother, the brother's wife, and two policemen. Everyone greeted me politely and with obvious joy, and soon we were all sitting round a table devouring goat's meat, bread, mushrooms in a very hot sauce, and a soup which contained large lumps of river snake. "My favourite dish," cried Pierre, and, although I couldn't agree, I enjoyed the soup and took a second helping.

It was midnight by the time we pulled into Ngaoundere, where we slept for a few hours before pressing on to a village called Guna, where we naturally patronised a restaurant owned by one of Pierre's countless brothers. After food and a rest we travelled northwards through the sultry afternoon, in country said to abound in lions, elephants and buffaloes. Dry, sandy bushlands spread before us to the horizon, divided at intervals by waterless rivers. "Rains begin here next month, thank God!" muttered Pierre, as he stopped the truck to purchase some lumps of dried porcupine from the leper inhabitants of a remote and destitute village. Then some time later, as the sun was turning the savannah into a vast carpet of gold, we entered Garoua.

"Meet Alain, my blood brother, same mother, same father!" smiled Pierre as we stood outside a mud house which was identifiable from the many others like it by the fact that it had a bottle full of leaves standing on a table near the door. "The spray of leaves is to show that we sell local plam-wine here," said Alain, shaking my hand. "We live in a wine tavern, if you like!"

Dinner that night was a jovial family affair, as we sat around an oil lamp at a rough, wooden table. There was dried fish and sesame cooked in banana leaves, plantains, yams, and hot liver soup. Glasses of water from a stone jar in the corner were the alternative to wine, and with practice I became quite skilful at the extraction of drowned flies.

That evening Pierre and I sat outside the house with Alain, his wife, the rest of the household, and some clients who had come to buy and drink palm-wine, chatting comfortably by the light of a candle. "Tell us all the countries you've been to!" said

Alain suddenly, so I began to reel off the names . . . "China, Saudi Arabia, The United States of America, Russia," until Pierre cried, "Stop Wendy, stop! We listen like dogs, for we understand nothing." So then I fetched my world map from the house and conducted an impromptu geography lesson, much to the delight of everyone present. The evening ended with a sing-song in various languages including 'In Dublin's Fair City' rendered by Alain in pidgin English.

My third truck-driver in the Cameroons introduced himself as a native of Chad, called Ahmadu. We drove steadily northward, and the farther north we travelled, the more arid was the countryside. I was surprised to observe fresh piles of elephant droppings in several places. Darkness had fallen when we reached the capital, and a few minutes later we were safely in brother Musa's house.

Welcomed by all as one of the family, I was whisked straight off into a corner of the compound by my host who proudly showed me his latest acquisition there — a newly dug loo. "Should last for ten years — it's very deep!' said Musa with enormous satisfaction. "Our other one's nearly full now, so, when it is, we'll switch over to this one."

The following week Ahmadu returned to Garoua, after giving me 1,280 C.F.A. francs (thirty-six shillings) "to buy a sausage with for your journey", and the next morning I set off for Nigeria with a Togolese friend of Musa's who dropped me at Maiduguri.

"I have a friend in Maiduguri," Bengt Hanovitch had informed me just before I left the Cape. "His name is Joseph Tayi. Go straight to him and he will solve all your problems." There was no address, just a name. Pouring rain drove me to the shelter of a verandah in Maiduguri, and when the Labanese family who owned the house invited me to join them for lunch, I gratefully accepted but didn't mention Joseph Tayi's name.

Next evening I went to a party in the house of some Indian teachers. Rain was pouring down as we said our goodbyes, but one of the guests kindly offered to give me a lift in his car. At the door of my Lebanese hosts, the driver said, "Goodnight, Wendy." "Thank you, and goodnight, Mr . . . er . . .?" I began. "Joseph Tayi is the name," came the voice. "What a coincidence," I exclaimed. "Anyone else could have offered me a lift, but it had to be you!" Unfortunately, Joseph's wife was in Lagos at the time, but during the remainder of my stay in Maiduguri he proved to be a good, reliable friend, just as Bengt had assured me.

Joseph Tayi had to drive to Kano on business some days later, so my transport problem from Maiduguri was solved. "In this part of the world it is wisest to set off early when travelling far," said Joseph as we bumped westwards along the dark road, beneath a misty moon.

As daylight came, the heat was stifling, but we both enjoyed the scenery, first of wide open, sandy bushland, then a sort of 'lake district' with date palms and stony escarpments, which formed a pleasant change. At one village we came to, a little Fulani boy sat playing a haunting melody on a reed pipe beside his grazing cows.

Set on a red, dusty plain, Kano is an ancient moslem city that I shall never forget. An old wall stood around it as it had done since the days when it had been necessary to protect the city from conquering tribesmen, the red mud now starting to crumble a little with age. Through its archways I caught sight of the renowned Haussa horned architecture within. Joseph took me to see the dyeing vats, pits in the ground which had been in use for a thousand years. "The indigo dye they use here is famous," he said, as we gazed at all the blue tunics and veils which had been stretched out along the walls to dry. A crowd of Haussas and Fulanis from the cattle plains and Touaregs from the desert were at that time jostling to choose and buy, the Haussas and Fulanis wearing conical wicker hats over their headcloths as an added protection from the sun.

Traffic was busy in the old section of Kano, but it was not the mechanised kind. There were donkeys, camels, bicycles, and land porters scurrying here and there, yet because it was all unmechanised, the atmosphere was one of equanimity and peace. As we drove back beneath the mango trees to the mission where we would be spending the night, the green copper dome of Kano's modern mosque stood out against the sombre evening sky. I leaned out of the window to get a better look at its majestic beauty and a cool, dry wind from the Sahara blew white dust into my nostrils.

Leaving Joseph in Kano, I hitch-hiked southwards to Ibadan, arriving with a nasty dose of malaria. My hosts there were the Zadoks, Israeli friends of the Tayis. Ibadan at that time was humid, damp and rich in tropical foliage, but with heavy, grey skies and a clamminess which made me, in my malarial state, feel constantly drowsy. However, the Ibadan Israelis were a jolly community to be among, and only two days after my arrival I was invited to one of their annual feasts, this one being a celebration of the spring.

Well again, I moved on to Lagos, which I loved. It is such a nicely arranged capital, with the post office and department stores on one side of the road, and the Atlantic Ocean stretching away on the other, the wide horizon frequently filled with ships of diverse nationalities. It was in Lagos that I stayed with the Deputy British High Commissioner and his wife, and where I suddenly realised that there were some very wonderful people from my own country to meet, as well as those from other nations. Swimming, tea on the lawn of the club, and an International Women's Club meeting made a pleasant change, with added jocularity such as when the electricity was cut off each evening for reasons unknown.

My next destination was Cotonou, Dahomey. I travelled there in a passenger lorry, the driver of which caused quite a palaver with a group of village women, by whipping off all their headcloths at the end of their journey when they told him that they couldn't pay the fare.

Eager to proceed up north before the heavy rains came, I was soon heading for Abomey, capital of the ancient kingdom, with a letter of recommendation for a Madame Behanzin. I found Monsieur Behanzin first, at the Abomey Hospital, where he was a nurse. Before taking me home to meet his wife, Monsieur Behanzin took me on a guided tour of the hospital. Comfort, Monsieur Behanzin's wife, was a friendly person and happily welcomed me into their clean, whitewashed house. The next day my host informed us all that he'd be off duty that afternoon, and suggested an outing to the Abomey Museum.

The museum was situated in the central palace of the old kings, and numerous low, one-storied buildings house the exhibits. In the first room we entered, we saw the thrones of all the kings of Dahomey, dating back to the sixteenth century. The kings had been rather a bloodthirsty lot, it seemed, fond of chopping off their enemies' arms and legs and impaling them, keeping the heads as trophies, and often using the skulls as a base for their chairs. Each king had had his own motto, and these were depicted on a handsewn cloth which was spread above the thrones.

Outside, we came to a royal tomb, which was situated in a thatched house of mud. A bed had been placed over the tomb, and on it were some mats. These were rearranged every so often, I was told, and everything kept in order.

"This is the tomb of King Glele," Monsieur Behanzin informed me solemnly. "He had the distinction of having forty-one women buried alive with him when he died. They did it voluntarily, so that he would have women with him in the next world."

The last thing we saw before signing the visitors' book and leaving the museum was the 'castration yard'. Here, all the male servants of the king's wives were castrated as a precaution against infidelity.

That night we went to see 'small-pox dancing' outside the hut of a witch-doctor. The dancing team consisted of an elderly man who was their leader, three young women, and two young men. They all wore grass skirts which stuck out from around their waists, necklaces made with shells, and in their right hands they each carried a small, silver hatchet. Tom-toms were beating madly and the dancers twirled, cart-wheeled, leapt and shook until the audience was screaming with delight. As they danced, the performers chanted songs to scare away the small-pox spirits, no doubt.

Monsieur Behanzin and I stood watching until it became too dark to see the spectacle clearly, then we returned to the house, where Comfort was preparing supper. "But you're a Roman Catholic; surely you don't believe in all these spirits?" I couldn't help asking my host. "Mademoiselle Wendy, Christianity is really just another French import. Voodoo is our own belief," he replied. "After all, we Africans have got to have something of our own!"

Chapter 21

May 1966–September 1966

"Eighty kilometres an hour is the only safe speed to take on this road," remarked the German girl at the wheel of the Volkswagen in which I was getting a lift to Dassa Zoumé, north of Abomey. "Glad you're here though; useful to have a bit of weight." The road on which we were travelling was of slippery damp red sand, and I murmured a prayer of thanksgiving when we arrived safely at my destination. "Now I must drive on to a village sixty kilometres from here," said the German girl, and disappeared in a cloud of dust.

After a few days with a missionary couple, the Watsons, I went on up through Dahomey to Savé, Parkou, Nikki, Ndali, Bimbereke, and then to Kandi, from where, as there was no other form of transport bound due north as far as Niamey, I decided to treat myself to the luxury of a seat on a Trans-African bus, which proved to be a rusting, rattling wreck.

After crossing the wide river Niger we entered the country of that name, the Trans-African bus rumbling to a halt beside the frontier check-post. The police were still in bed when we arrived, but rather conveniently their beds were all in a line on the roadside, so proceedings were delayed no more than a matter of minutes. By noon that day we were rattling over a sand track which ran through a vast expanse of arid savannah stretching from one horizon to the other.

We arrived in the capital late at night, too late for anyone to go anywhere. The driver had to take his bus into the garage so we all had to descend on to the hard, dusty pavement, but that was as far as we got. We lay down where we were and slept until morning.

On that, my first visit to Niamey, I bunked down with an American Peace Corps couple. The girl was Jewish, and the boy introduced himself as 'Wasp' his abbreviation of 'white, anglo-saxon, Protestant'.

I adored the Niamey museum which was combined with a zoo, and — astonishingly — free of charge. After inspecting the zoo I made my way to the costume section of the museum, where models of Touaregs, Haussas, Fulanis, Djerbas, and Peuls, were attired each in their peculiar form of dress, and it was there that I met the French curator who kindly asked his Nigerian curator, a Touareg called Assaf, to show me round the open air section.

"I always picture Touaregs as veiled men riding camels across the Sahara," I told Assaf as we walked along — "Oh, my father was one like that!" he laughed, "but I've always lived in the city and prefer to wear Western clothes. I've been to Paris, the U.S.A. and Joss in Nigeria. Look, this is a typical Haussa concession. It has houses for the husband's three wives and for his first son, all built separately, and this little grass house on stilts is where the children sleep all closed in, with a screen to protect them from the mosquitoes!"

Next we visited the Touareg tents. They were quite spacious inside with beds made of wooden poles, and numerous leather mats. The Djerbas and Anghais lived in concessions just like the Haussas, though the Djerbas differed in that they slept under the same roof as their children, the parents' bed being enclosed a little and the children sleeping on table-like beds in the centre of the room. In every case, however, the eldest son had a house of his own. Also in the concessions was a circle in which the inhabitants would dance in the evenings, and several miniature houses for chickens.

"Now this is a modernised Haussa residence," said Assaf leading the way to a hut made from mud instead of grass and wood. Inside, it was quite comfortably furnished, with mirrors on the walls and a carved wooden chair for 'Baba' to use.

As in Niamey, I spent my first night in Ouagadougou, capital of the Upper Volta, sleeping on a pavement, again owing to the late arrival of the Trans-African bus. *"C'est le jour!"* cried the person beside me, and although, when I opened my eyes, they gradually focused on a moon and starry sky, I got up and started walking towards what I hoped was the centre of town. At that time in the morning it was hard to tell, for only 'boys' and street cleaners seemed to be awake.

Ouagadougou was larger than Niamey, but one didn't have to continue far along the treed boulevards before coming to wide open swamps and waterlogged African huts; the season of rain and thunderstorms had begun.

To Tenkodogo, some miles south of Ouagadougou, I got a lift with an African priest, who eventually deposited me at the house of some Roman Catholic girls who, like nuns, had sworn not to marry, and were nursing and teaching the Africans as unpaid volunteers.

To Bittou, I got a lift with two German engineers and from Bittou it was my intention to travel down through Togo to Lome, and from there to cross the frontier into Ghana. A bridge on the Oti River had been destroyed in a storm, however, which meant that all Togo-bound transport had to make a detour and pass through Bawku in northern Ghana.

I spent the night in a doctor's house and the lorry I climbed up into on the following morning was filled with impatient passengers, all intent upon moving south and on to better roads before more rain. I didn't care about the squash. I didn't care about anything. I knew that I had a high fever, and it was all that I could do to climb with my knapsack up over the side of the lorry and jump down on to the ground below at each of the frequent customs checks. The relentless sun beat down and sinking into a corner I squeezed my ribs tightly with my arms and tried not to breathe too deeply, in an effort to reduce the pain in my lungs as we bumped along.

"Bawku!" called the driver at last, "that's as far as I go, all change here for the Togo Republic!" What an enormous contrast were the Ghanaian immigration and customs people to their Bittou counterparts. "Sit down," said their superior when he realised my condition. "You must rest here for a while, and our lady police officer will bring you a drink." "Is there a clinic here?" I asked him. "Better than that, we've got a hospital!" beamed the officer, "with three European doctors!" They took me there.

At that moment, however, a shiny black Volkswagen with 'Mampong Maternity Hospital' printed on its side in white lettering scrunched to a halt beside us, and two nuns jumped out. One was short and slim, the other tall and rather corpulent. The latter came bounding towards us, and, catching sight of the label on my water-bottle, exclaimed in a rich Lancashire accent, "You're Wendy Myers – and I'm your cousin!" "Splendid!" I sighed, and tottered weakly off to bed.

The next morning I felt more equal to discussing my family tree, and there was no doubt whatsoever that 'Tomboy Terry' – now Sister Gertrude – was, in fact, my first cousin once removed. Soon we had written a joint aerogramme informing my parents of our Livingstonian encounter – for although I had known that one of my relations was a missionary somewhere in Ghana, the information had ceased at that point.

That night pain kept me wide awake. It was pleurisy, they said. "Don't worry – we'll cure you at Mampong," said Terry gently, and we soon set off. She was a fully qualified nursing tutor. When the dirt road changed to concrete, we parked the car and ate our sandwiches. Then we drove on through low hills which were becoming a little forested now, but this was truly beautiful open countryside, patched with fertile farm fields and with an atmosphere of orderliness and wealth after the rather depressing poverty of Northern Dahomey and Upper Volta.

"Senegal Coukall!" shouted Terry the next morning, as we continued our journey to the south, and from the car window I perceived a black and white bird with reddish-brown feathers on its wings. When it saw us, it understandably uttered a laughing cry. That same evening found us in Mampong, the Ashanti Region of Ghana, and soon I was meeting all Terry's numerous sisters – for apart from running a maternity hospital there, the nuns staffed a secondary school for girls.

So began my period of being 'immured in the convent' as Jean, one of the secular teachers, had jokingly put it. Being a blood relation of Terry's meant that I would sleep in one of the empty 'cells' in the hospital sisters' house, eat with them, and use the 'community room'. There were all kinds of rules to be kept, including absolutely no talking at all during silent meals – or during the 'greater silence' of the night, which started after the office of Compline each evening.

Although I kept the silences as best I could, I didn't have to say all the offices, which was quite a relief when I heard the nuns get up to the sound of clanging bells in the chilling early hours of the morning. My favourite office was Compline, however, and I never missed that. It began at 8.30 each evening, a time when an aura of peace seemed to settle over the sisters' tiny chapel.

Mampong days were crowded and interesting and one morning found me at the school, lecturing the girls on my marathon journey. "Bet you feel just like a sucked orange!" laughed Jean when I'd finished. "Not half!" I said. "Want to hear their oddest question? 'Please, miss, in which country do the people have tails?'"

On Jean's next day off, Mother Superior kindly lent her a car with a driver and told us both to go to Kumasi and enjoy ourselves. Kumasi, capital of the Ashanti Region, was an old town that had been modernised, and sported a new shopping centre surrounded by wide, busy streets. But it was to the ancient covered market, said to be the largest in the world, that Jean and I first made our way.

"The Ashantis used to be the fiercest warriors of West Africa, but today they have earned the distinction of being its shrewdest traders," said Jean as we wandered around the stalls. Near by stood trucks where farmers from Ashanti's purple hill-slopes were busily unloading masses of raw cocoa.

During the days which followed, I often helped Terry by drawing enormous diagrams with coloured pastels illustrating the circulation of the blood and so forth for use in her lectures, and on one occasion I accompanied her when she took a party of her students to the near-by village of Bosofour, where the sanitary inspector gave them a talk on drains and toilets. He rounded off the lecture by taking us all to see a brand new fifty-hole outside toilet which was to be used by no fewer than 150 people.

One of the school sisters was going down to Accra at about the time I had decided to leave Mampong, so it was arranged for me to travel down with her. My pleurisy was now quite better, and I felt healthier — both mentally and physically — than I had ever been before, yet my heart never was so heavy as at that time. It is a rare thing to find a sincere friend, a spiritual adviser, and blood relation all wrapped into one, out in the middle of the African bush.

Accra seemed like another world — after the seclusion of Mampong. There were up-to-date, air-conditioned shops where the Ghanaian sales-girls could wear wigs (of black, straight hair) without being overcome by heat, an enormous

'Black Star Square' – a Nkrumah idea, of course – and, not far away, an Independence Memorial, a huge arch, closely resembling Paris's Arc de Triomphe. It was the old part of Accra, however, which attracted me most, where thick-walled, balconied old houses still hugged the spirit of bygone 'Gold Coast' days. Behind them stretched a long yellow ribbon of sand, where palm trees whispered to the crashing waves, and fishermen mended their nets beside gaily painted piroques. It was there that the thick-walled prison stood, where so many unjustly accused people had been detained during the reign of Kwame Nkrumah.

Before heading north-westwards to the Ivory Coast, I crossed the border into Togo and spent a week-end in Lomé, its capital. Lomé was desperately trying to 'keep up with the Joneses' I was told, the 'Joneses' in this case being Cotonou which had just had a vast new port built; so Lomé had engaged some Germans to build them one like it.

Up in the Brong-Ahafo Region of Ghana, rivers were now swollen with the monsoon rain, and trees in the equatorial forests dripped continuously on to the damp earth below. The countryside on the way to Abidjan, capital of the Ivory Coast, was green and fertile, and I noticed many elaborately built houses with verandahs of carefully carved stone as well as the usual mud huts, with their roofs of thatch or corrugated iron.

Abidjan was large, modern, and very 'Europeanised'. Then I was on my way again, travelling north-westwards through paddy-fields where rice planters from Taiwan worked side by side with local farmers. Forests of tall trees were being felled by huge machines from America, and the other passengers in the Peugeot in which I was travelling were filled with awe as they watched an enormous tree being wrenched from the ground by its roots.

A Lebanese offered me a lift from Man to Toulepleu, and I stayed with him and his family in Toulepleu, and enjoyed a supper of raw liver, salad with curds, onions, stuffed lamb, bread, and honey.

In Liberia, my first stop was Ganta. How refreshing it was to hear my own language spoken again, for this now independent negro republic of West Africa had been founded by the American Colonization Society in 1822, twenty-four years before receiving its independence. It seemed odd to be using

American 'green-backs' again, though British weights and measures were employed.

Some days later found me travelling north-westwards once again to enter Sierra Leone. My first impression of Sierra Leone was of green, undulating countryside and paddy-fields bordered by tall coconut palms, backed by majestic hills of rock. Everything seemed so fresh and prolific, due, no doubt, to the almost ceaseless rain. To Freetown I got a lift with a Protestant minister called Reverend Lumanda, and not far from the capital we came to a wide, alligator-filled river. There was no bridge, and although the current looked to be extremely powerful, the ferryboat worked not with a motor but by means of steel cables pulled by a group of brawny men. As the ferry took only two vehicles at a time, we had a long time to wait for our turn.

Some hours later I was eating supper with the children and Mabel, the Rev Lumanda's wife. "Do stay here with us," said Mabel, and when I asked her if it wouldn't be too much trouble, she got quite indignant and demanded, "What is it — do you mind about our colour?" That settled the issue.

My next destination, I hoped, would be Guinea, where Kwame Nkrumah was still a political refugee at the time. I made several journeys to the Guinean embassy to apply for a visa, but upon each of my visits, the consul, a supercilious young man, who chain-smoked using a long, glittering cigarette holder, always had some reason for delay.

At last he could no longer conceal his unwillingness for me to enter his country, and asked, "You've been to the Congo, Kenya, and most of the other countries in Africa; why do you want to go to Guinea? Why can't you fly over it?" I suspected that the multiple Ghanaian stamps in my passport hadn't helped but, whatever the reason for his inhospitable attitude, the consul thus let his country have the sole distinction of having presented me with any serious difficulties concerning an entry visa. The Guinean Ambassador died some days later and I decided to travel to The Gambia by boat.

The boat was English, and the crew were a cheerful bunch. On the night before we were to arrive in Bathurst I was up on the bridge when a tall ship passed us. An officer fetched the signalling equipment and soon we discovered the other ship to be German. "Very polite, as usual," remarked the captain.

About an hour later, a British vessel came parallel to us and again we 'talked' by means of Morse code. "She's a British oil-tanker," said the captain. "Where are you going?" she signalled. "Going to Bathurst," we replied. "Lucky you!" said the oil tanker. "Talkative blighter!" muttered the captain, as we chugged on through the darkness.

Chapter 22

September 1966–December 1966

" 'The Gambia' – never simply 'Gambia'," said the shipping agent as I stood in his Bathurst office. "This colony, you see, is really little more than the river Gambia, the territory on either side of it never exceeding ten miles."

Fortunately, there was a small yacht, the *Lady Wright*, used for cargo and passengers, on which I was able to book a round trip of five days from Bathurst and back for £3 2s. exclusive of food. This seemed much the best way of taking a peep at The Gambia. What might have proved a very dull voyage on an overcrowded ship was enlivened for me by the radio officer, a young Gambian named Denis Drawers. He had a fiancée named Duchess, and when he wasn't arguing with me, he was phoning or sending telegrams to Duchess. On our return to Bathurst, Denis introduced me to her, a charming Gambian girl hoping soon to enter nursing school.

My first stop in Senegal was in Kaolack, about two hours' journey from the capital. I had travelled there from Bathurst in a ferry boat across the mouth of the Gambia River. My passport had not been looked at, let alone stamped, upon entering the country, however, so I decided to go to the immigration office in Kaolack to save the risk of possible complications later. Stopping in a street which was made up entirely of Lebanese drapers' shops, I asked where it was. "My boy will show you the way," said a man emerging from behind one of the counters. "You can leave your heavy knapsack here, nobody will touch it." That was the beginning of a firm friendship – not only with that one Lebanese and his family, but with the whole of the Lebanese population of Kaolack, to whom they were related.

"You will join us for lunch, of course," smiled the proprietor of the draper's shop, when I returned to collect my knapsack. "I am Zaki, by the way, and here are my wife and children who join me in saying 'Welcome to Senegal!'" That first meal in Kaolack was quite wonderful in every way. The food – chicken, rhoti, shish-kebab, kifte, feuilles du vin, chips, fish heads with rice and melon, yams and salad was superb and, backed by the constant musical flow of Arabic, it reminded me of bygone feasts in Arabia.

The Zakis were moslem Lebanese. I had several delightful days with them during which time I learned to dive. My diving instructor, named Jad, was also the champion judocar of Senegal. Soon I was practising judo again – the only girl in a class of Senegalese and Lebanese students.

I travelled with some of Zaki's prolific family to Dakar where my hosts showed me the sights. Each day their chauffeur would drive us to a different spot. To the artisan area of Dakar, where beautiful wood-carvings, leather-work, and so forth were being made; the sea-front, from where Serpent Island and Goree Island could be seen in the Atlantic waters near the coast, to the beaches of N'gor, the museum, the mosque, and the university. Business also had to be attended to, however, and I spent many hours in trudging around the embassies of Algeria, Mali, and Mauritania.

The second-class compartment of the train I took from Kaolack to St Louis smelled execrably, which was not in the least surprising, for it was crowded with goats and other livestock. In St Louis, doubts were expressed about the possibility of my getting much farther north – "because of the rains, you know". However, a Vietnamese driving instructor, who was about to fly to Nouakchott, kindly offered me a lift in his plane.

Six a.m. the following morning found me speeding along towards St Louis airport with my new Vietnamese friend, to where the one-engined, four-seater plane stood waiting. By the time we'd been checked out at the control tower, it was 7 a.m., and as dawn hadn't long broken the sky was still smudged with the greyness of night. Far below us, waterlogged land stretched across to the broad Atlantic Ocean on our left, and the engine purred steadily on. And then we were in the Islamic Republic of Mauritania.

A quiet capital, with most of its streets still made of the

desert sand, Nouakchott basked in the morning sun, its rows of white-walled, Moorish dwellings gleaming in contrast to an azure sky. The market for camels, sheep and goats was spread out over a wide area of town, and was always the setting, I guessed, for more activity than anywhere else. My first impression of the place was a group of dirty, bored-looking animals, being bargained for by merchants from all over the country. I patted and stroked some of the camels while with much dramatic bargaining Turki, my Mauritanian host and guide, purchased a sheep. Then he pushed it into the boot of the car and we returned to the house.

While the sheep was roasting we played 'ludo' and sipped 'zrig' – a concoction of whey, sugar and water passed around in a communal basin. When the sheep arrived, nestling on a yellow bed of cus-cus, I noticed that the servant who brought it was a negro, not a Moor. Mauritanians still kept negro slaves, Turki had informed me, and in some remote desert villages they were kept as real prisoners by their Moorish masters and could never hope to escape.

My intention being to cross the Sahara Desert on my way to the Mediterranean coast, I found that the best points to start from would be either Gao or Agades, which meant travelling back to Dakar and from there to Bamako, the capital of Mali. Some days later I took my last meal of cus-cus with my Mauritanian family, for the next day I would be travelling southwards again, overland this time, the rains having ceased and the road being dry enough to take light vehicles.

The next morning I carefully folded the *melefa* that I had worn constantly since my arrival in Turki's home, and inside the tissue tried to fold away so many happy memories.

It was fun visiting the Nawafs and the Dkhils once more before going back to Kaolack to take a train to Bamako. I had not yet bought my ticket when Yves, a French schoolteacher friend of Jad's told me about the private school he knew there in Kaolack. The headmaster – a Senegalese friend of his – was short of an English teacher. That was how I became a 'professeuse' teaching English through French in the little town of Kaolack, Senegal.

First of all I was assigned to instruct the sixth grade, then the fifth, and soon after, the fourth. Five hundred francs C.F.A. (fifteen shillings) was my wage per hour, and when I left

Crossing the Volta on the ferry

With some missionary friends in Sierra Leone

Travelling up the Ubangi River in the Congo on a woodburner

On the beach
with Lebonese
friends in
Kaolack,
Senegal

Emerging from church in
Coqhuilhalville with the
Congolese congregation

Wearing Mauretanian costume
(including the necessary false
hairpiece) with my 'family' in
Nouakchott

Kaolack I had another twenty-five pounds to boost up my fading funds.

A biting blast of air swept through the open window of the train as it chugged on through the night in an easterly direction towards Bamako. It was the first real cold that I had felt for months; air from a November Europe which ran a gelid finger across North Africa and over the Sahara to Mali. How I wished that I could stop shivering. I closed my eyes. When I opened them again, kapok, maize, and groundnut plantations were rolling past the windows. The day became very hot, but at 4 a.m. the next morning my teeth were chattering again, and I was glad when at last we were pulling into Bamako station.

I had a letter and a parcel of cigarettes to deliver to a Frenchman in the capital. He introduced me to a Malian family with whom I lived for a few days. The family consisted of Barkah and her children; her husband was in Paris. As each husband had two or three wives, the women lived in a kind of colony and the men came to them for meals.

"Don't you ever miss your husband?" I enquired, as Barkah began to cut up and wash a newly plucked chicken. "Not at all!" she smiled. "I am thoroughly spoiled by all my family here — especially my papa and 'petit papa' (the younger brother of my father). Father has four wives and twenty-nine children, so I'm never lonely."

Sitting on one of the little wooden stools which stood here and there beneath the trees, I looked around me at the busy African scene. By this time Barkah had sprinkled lemon over the chicken and was frying it in a huge, black pot over a wood fire, along with yams (sweet potatoes), tomatoes, and chillies. In a shady corner one old grandmother was busy twisting cotton from some raw tufts to be used for spinning while in another corner a spinner sat with his loom, skilfully producing yards of multi-coloured native cloth. A group of young women were nursing their babies, and others pounded up maize with mortars and pestles, pumped water, or washed clothes. Chickens pecked and children played around my feet. What a very communal life this is, I thought, so different from that of an English housewife. How lonely these women would be with our system.

My intention being to cross the Sahara either from Gao or Agades, I had decided to travel by boat up the 2,600-mile long river Niger, that yellow waterway of Africa which flows from the mountains of Guinea to Akasa, a port on the coast of Nigeria. The river was high at that time of the year, and passenger boats could get up-stream as far as Koulikoro, which meant only a two-and-a-half-hour train journey from Bamako.

After a leisurely journey on the *General Soumari*, pausing at Mopti and Avie, we docked late at night at Kabara, the port of that renowned Malian town, Timbuctu. Annik, my French hostess, lived alone in a huge, stone house in the only tarred road in Timbuctu, that leading to Kabara. An M.A. graduate from Paris with a teacher's diploma, this highly intelligent young woman was employed by the Timbuctu Lycée Franco-Arabe. Bed was welcome; I slept late the next day.

After lunch, Annik disappeared to rest, and then suggested a walk around the town. The shops around Timbuctu's market square were small and dark, the streets narrow, with balconies touching above them so that they, too, were dim. We trudged around in the hot sunshine of the day which was to fade and leave the town bitterly cold during the night. I shall never forget the beautifully carved and studded doors, the tiny windows set in odd places in the mud walls, nor the ancient mosque, which was the first mosque ever to be built in Africa.

The following afternoon two Touaregs came to the house. Tethering their camels to a bush in Annik's compound, they joined us, drank a quantity of raspberry sherbet, and talked about nothing much at all. They were most fetching in their flowing white robes, leather belts with dangling swords, and black veils. Before they left, one of them, Rashid, kindly offered to come and take me for a walk into the near-by desert on the following morning to meet some of the tent people who lived there.

At 8.30 a.m. the next morning Rashid rode up to the door, accompanied by his shepherd. "It takes us an hour to get here," he told me, dismounting and readjusting his sword. This surprised me, as their camp was only two kilometres away. Quicker on foot, I decided, following Rashid as he strode across the sand. The first lot of tents we came to were round-topped and made completely from rush matting. Women and children sat in their shade while goats and camels grazed around. On we walked and came to the camping site of people whom Rashid called Arabs, relations of the Moors of Mauritania, then to some Dagars, Touaregs mixed with negro slaves. All the tent people were friendly but didn't offer us tea as the Mauritanians would have done. "In looks, I can't tell the difference between the Arabs, the Dagars, and you Touaregs," I told Rashid as we tramped back to Annik's house. "Hum," he muttered, "well, maybe not, but we Touaregs can't intermarry with them, only with another Touareg or a French girl!"

The *Mali* – my boat to Gao, was so crowded that I could not even find a place in which to stand on the fourth-class deck, but had to climb with my luggage to the top of some sacks filled with groundnuts.

The next morning some soldiers kindly shared their food with me: coffee, bread and raw yams, while I watched the crocs and hippos getting out of the way as our boat went gliding down the river.

Next day at sunset the *Mali* glided past an abattoir, to arrive in Gao. A group of White Sisters greeted me warmly and I was taken to the house of some girls who were not nuns, but helped the sisters in their work, who eagerly put up a stretcher for me in their patio.

The White Sisters were an integral part of the Gao community, I discovered, and, instead of simply spooning Biblical passages down everyone's throat, these French nuns concentrated on being useful by doing necessary nursing and teaching. Consequently they had far more success, for they drew the Malians closer to them, and the people followed their love of Christ out of interest and respect for the nuns whom they knew to really love and care for them.

I was still in doubt over transport across the Sahara, whether to follow the Gao route or the one from Agades. After some enquiries, I plumped for the longer and more varied route from Agades. So the following evening I set out for Niamey again, squashed into the back corner of a passenger lorry. I attended the Independence Day celebrations in Niamey with an English traveller called Robin Hanbury-Tennison. The following day, we parted company, he to fly home, I to travel overland across the Sahara Desert.

A bumpy road with a 'washboard' surface led to Zinder from Niamey, and Robin's sleeping bag which he had lent me 'for the desert' came in handy as a cushion, while my hunger was taken care of by a large box of goodies which Madame Platteuw, my Niamey hostess, had pushed into my hands at the last moment. The driver pulled up in Konni for the night, and with most of the other passengers I made my bed on the floor of an empty mud house. The next day a breakdown held us up, and it was not until 2 a.m. on the following morning that we reached Zinder.

I spent the rest of the night curled up on Robin's sleeping bag. Next day I encountered two young teachers, a Peace-Corps girl and a V.S.O. who were on local leave from Kano. As they hoped to travel as far as Tamanrasset we decided to walk out of town and wait for a passing vehicle. All day we waited, and at dusk we lit a fire beside which we slept under a friendly moon and some decidely unfriendly vultures. It was not until late afternoon next day that a truck came rumbling northwards along the road, and soon we were perched on top with a host of other passengers all bound for Agades. As the truck bounced between some low trees, thousands of locusts swarmed out in a huge, black cloud. Then the trees finished and we were speeding across bare, brown steppe, from which jagged rocks thrust their sombre peaks against an evening sky.

Agades was a brown town on a brown plain, the walls of its ancient houses 'horned' in the Haussa style. Passports duly stamped, the teachers and I went to the market to buy food for the journey which we hoped to begin later that day. All trucks, we were told, had to stop at the 'Douane' (custom-house) before they could either leave or enter the town, and that place was obviously the best for us to go and enquire about transport. When we arrived there, however, we found trucks galore, but no chief customs inspector, and without him, the police informed us, nothing could move in any direction.

Christmas Eve dawned, the teachers' holiday was slipping away, and so was the validity of my Algerian visa, but no one could move on until the missing customs inspector turned up. Not far from the customs-house was a race-track around which a couple of men were galloping their camels, and on the edge of the track stood a small, one-roomed mud building, which was the betting-office. The biting wind of evening was already blowing great clouds of sand into our faces as we made our way between the camelthorns to that small mud room which offered shelter, and it was there that we spent Christmas Eve, 1966.

A fire was lit, supper was eaten, and carols were sung, until the howling wind lulled us to sleep. There were other Christmas Eves, and there will be other Christmas Eves, but never before or since have I been able to imagine that long-ago scene in the Bethlehem stable so clearly, as there in that mud shack on the edge of the Sahara Desert.

Chapter 23

December 1966–February 1967

He stood before me, gaunt and sinewy, a soiled white *shaish* wrapped about his head, from which a pair of slanting eyes gleamed like those of a wolf. That was the first time I saw Abd el Latif, one of the most fascinating personalities that I had ever encountered during those seven years of travelling about the world, and it was with him that I made my first crossing of the Sahara.

It was the evening of Christmas Day. The chief customs inspector of Agades had just returned from his binge, and was apathetically signing the pile of forms which impatient truck-drivers thrust before him.

Eight-thirty that evening found me clambering with the two teachers on to the truck that I was soon to know so well. Up on top it became bitterly cold, and we weren't sorry when, in a deserted spot sixty kilometres from Agades, a voice from below informed us that we'd be stopping there for the night.

A thickset lad, whom I was soon to know as Hubsi, Abd el Latif's sixteen-year-old nephew, and a driver called Fawaz, collected some wood and soon had a blazing fire going. Cus-cus was heated and shared, and then as the other two didn't speak French they went away to sleep, leaving Abd el Latif, Hubsi, Fawaz and me sitting talking in the light of the fire.

"I know this desert so well," sighed Abd el Latif, rearranging the wood to make a brighter blaze. "I used to be in the F.L.N., a terrorist, you know, fighting for the freedom of our country. For many months I fought in the Algerian Revolution, and was then imprisoned for five and a half years by the French. They tortured me, trying to get information, but I didn't give in. They gave me everything: the water-treatment, broke both my legs, electric wires, but not this eye of mine, this was injured by a grenade." Abd el Latif rewound his *shaish* and barked some instructions in Arabic to Hubsi and Fawaz. "We've got a flock of sheep here," he told me quietly. "I bought them in the south so haven't bothered to declare them in Agades. These Nigerians can do without my hard-earned money! Anyway, we'll be loading them early tomorrow morning. Sleep well!"

The following morning we breakfasted on bread and tea, and I helped to load up the wily sheep. As we drove on, the country became wild and desolate, a sharp wind moaned across it, and our 'road' was just a faint track, winding over a surface of small stones. We startled numerous gazelles, camels and donkeys as we rattled along, and I wondered where they grazed, for I noticed that Abd el Latif and his friends had each brought a hay supply for their sheep.

After a brief halt at a well to take on more water and for the men to wash and pray, we drove steadily on until we came to an area of camelthorn trees, where we stopped for lunch. These men are so organised, I thought, watching Hubsi throw some wood to the ground from a supply on the truck, and the others start a fire going.

Then we were off again, over the ever-changing desert, sometimes of pebbles, sometimes coarse scrub, sometimes a yellow, gravelly sand. We saw no other vehicles and very few people that day.

At 6 p.m. we stopped again as the men who had been fasting all day long were extremely hungry and could now eat. They were just lighting a fire when Abd el Latif discovered one of his sheep to be seriously ill, with a limp and a stiff neck, so before it died a natural death, he ordered Fawaz to cut its throat. Then to my surprise the tyre-pump was inserted between the sheeps' skin and its fat, and the animal was inflated until it resembled a furry, four-legged balloon. Just as it was threatening to burst and make a nasty mess, the pump was withdrawn and the animal's skin removed in one piece. "It will make us a good water-bag when it's dried and sewn up!" said Hubsi, turning to me with a boyish grin.

Later we devoured freshly cooked *mishui* washed down with camel's milk, which we had exchanged for some of our water with a group of nomadic Touaregs, sweet water being a more scarce and estimable drink for them.

The fasting men were happy now they'd eaten, and soon an impromptu orchestra was formed, led by Fawaz who got a very good rhythm by banging on an empty bucket (helped, no doubt, by the fact that he was part negro). Another played the flute (a favoured instrument in Algeria), a third banged his spoon on a tin, while the rest clapped their hands and sang. They were a gay crowd, these men who spent their lives in crossing and recrossing the Sahara, and I was soon to learn how much they helped each other, getting unstuck from the treacherous sand-dunes, for example.

The following morning we all awoke at about 7.30 a.m., when the men lit a fire and made tea which we drank with dry bread. We then set off towards the frontier of Niger where we found the police to be extremely courteous, presenting no difficulties to anybody. Driving on, we came to a stretch of desert which was entirely formed of soft sand, and this had been blown into those classical 'golden dunes'.

By noon we were out of the sandy 'no-man's-land' and on to a surface of tiny stones which stretched most of the way to In Guezzam, the Algerian frontier. After two short stops, once to eat and once because our engine failed, we arrived at the oasis police-post. There, the guards were again an easy-going bunch and Abd el Latif seemed most relieved and in great spirits for the rest of the day. That night, supper was supplemented by bread cooked in the sand. It was warm, brown, delicious and not sandy at all.

Next day at a place one hundred and twenty kilometres from Tamanrasset we pulled up in a valley filled with bushes and coarse grass. The sheep bleated noisily, eager to stretch their legs, which were stiff with cold and one poor animal had to be killed immediately.

Meanwhile those who were doing the *karem* were ravenously watching the sun go down, their hands filled with crushed dates ready to stuff into their mouths as soon as the time came. Then the dead sheep was blown up, skinned and cooked, and we all shared its liver before reloading the sheep and moving on.

Soon the moon revealed craggy mountains looming before us from the desert. We had reached El Hoggar, one of the most beautiful regions of the Sahara, and cold and sleepy, we stopped where we were for the night.

Next day we were off again, rolling along a grey, narrow

track which wound over some low rocky hills, with a backdrop of the weirdly shaped Hoggar Mountains towering before us.

In Tamanrasset the teachers left us. Abd el Latif offered to take me as far as Timimoun, but said that as his sheep were all in such poor condition he wouldn't be leaving for at least two days. I was lucky to find a party of French teachers, on tour for the New Year, with whom I stayed, and the following day went with them to meet the local Touareg chief. Expecting to find the usual cluster of tents, I was surprised to find him living in a village of straw houses with log roofs. The chief was a well-built man, who proved most hospitable. Over the sugared cakes, the noodles and the tea, we talked animatedly of the Vietnam war, the Congo troubles and so forth. Then at last we took our leave and drove back through the cold night air to Tamanrasset.

The next day was the last of 1966, and I was invited to a New Year's Eve party at the house of an Argentinian journalist who had come out to the Sahara to write a book about her country. It was an unforgettable New Year's dinner and five o'clock on New Year's Day morning found me banging on the door of Abd el Latif's truck. One hour later we were all in the truck driving north from Tamanrasset towards In Salah.

In the days that followed, as we drove on, certain suspicions began to form in my mind. Abd el Latif was very reticent about his sheep in the villages and towns, but out in the desert he tried to sell as many as he could to solitary Touaregs that we passed.

One evening, when we had stopped for the night in a mud village, he suddenly presented me with a surprise. "Look!" he said. "I have gathered some roses for you." They were sand roses, shaped and hardened by cold, fierce winds which had swept over the Sahara, brown in colour, exquisitely formed, and quite natural. Holding them, I felt as touched as if they had been of the living variety from home.

When we sighted In Salah, a few days later, all my suspicions were confirmed. Abd el Latif was a sheep smuggler. Well hidden behind the last sand-dune before the town, he stopped the truck and rapidly unloaded about forty of our sheep. Then he whispered instructions to Hubsi and his young friend, and turning to me he hissed, "Get in quickly and let's go! It is illegal for any sheep coming from Niger to pass farther than this point. I get a far better price for them in Timimoun than I would in In Salah, however, so I smuggle them there. That's why I unloaded that lot. Hubsi will drive them around In Salah and we'll pick them up at the other side. The ten sheep that I left in the truck are there to mislead the police."

In Salah was just a sleepy, sandy cluster of orange mud buildings and an ancient castle. After filling up at the petrol station, Abd el Latif called at the market to buy carrots, onions, oranges, and bread for our ensuing journey, then after a fierce argument he gave me permission to go to the post office, muttering, "You attract too much attention and I don't want any delay here."

As soon as I returned from the post office, Abd el Latif ordered me to climb aboard, and we were off, speeding out on to the Raggane road, where we soon met up with our sheep. We loaded them with all haste, and had just set off again when two policemen on 'mobilettes' appeared on the road behind us. Latif was giving me a running commentary on their progress — he could see them in the wing mirror, from which our smalls had been removed — when suddenly we sank into a dune of soft sand. Cursing ferociously, Latif reversed, changed gears and stepped on the gas. With wheels spinning and engine billowing grey fumes, we finally got a grip and left the dune. The police, however, were not so fortunate, and feeling like a real bandit I cheered with the others as they disappeared into the sand. Latif and I had not really been on speaking terms since the post office incident, but he suddenly turned to face me and I saw that his eyes were twinkling. "We almost didn't make it — just because a tourist had to stop and send postcards!" he chuckled, and I knew that I'd been forgiven.

That night was our last for sleeping out on the sand together. It seemed to be the coldest of them all, but the feeling of enjoying life in the company of people I liked provided an inner warmth. The following morning, Latif branched off the main track at Aoulef, to cut across a stretch of unmarked desert. When we got to just outside Adrar he again made a detour with our illegal load, relying on his instinct to keep him in the direction of Timimoun.

When we reached the sleeping town, the sheep were hastily unloaded into somebody's garden, Fawaz's uncle took his belongings and disappeared, and then Abd el Latif turned to me. "When I'm here I stay with Hubsi's parents," he said. "I shall take you there with us, if you wish, that is. But I warn you, these people are very religious, so you must keep calm and behave yourself, no running or shouting . . . And DO NOT tell them that I haven't been keeping the *karem*!"

Hubsi's parents' house was an ancient mud affair with domed ceilings, numerous archways, narrow flights of steps, and narrow, sandy passages connecting each room. After a warm welcome we were invited to seat ourselves on a woven blanket beside a flickering wood fire which had been carried into the centre of the room on a metal tray. As the whole of the adult household was doing the *karem*, we had arrived just in time for their big meal of the day, so after Arabic coffee that was hot, sweet and spicy, we devoured an enormous bowl of cus-cus.

The next morning everyone slept till 10 a.m., understandably enough, for nobody had slept until 3.30 that morning. We were woken by a man walking through the streets banging on a tin to warn people that the day's fasting had begun. From that moment, for those who didn't cheat, there should be no copulating, eating, drinking, smoking, or even swallowing the saliva, until after sunset.

Resolved to keep the *karem* I missed my morning glass of tea, and tried to concentrate on writing my notes until Latif came to tell me that we would be returning to Timimoun.

Twenty minutes past five found us back at the truck, waiting for the siren to go as a signal that we could break our fast. An old *hadji* hobbled up to us and placed some dusty dates into our hands for our first mouthful and those tasted more scrumptious than any dates I had ever eaten. Latif was soon smoking rapidly and chattering contentedly to Hubsi who was supposed to have fasted but had been chewing discreetly at intervals throughout the day. Latif turned a blind eye to this because of his nephew's youth.

Latif decided to drive his truck on to El Goléa instead of taking the plane, and invited me to go with him and spend the feast of Ramadan with his family. I was delighted. El Goléa was 400 kilometres from Timimoun and we stopped only once during the journey – to let a passenger disembark. Abd el Latif's house was one of the smartest in the village. Built of concrete, it had a flat roof (for drying washing, beds in the summer, and so forth), a flower garden at the front, and chickens, fruit and vegetables all thriving behind.

Soon I was being introduced to eighteen-year-old Jaleela, Latif's wife, and all her family. Next day I donned sweaters and kept them on all day for the weather never really got warm any more, and, though bright and sunny, there was usually a chilly wind. Therefore I wasn't sorry when, in the evening, Jaleela invited me to join her in a visit to the village hot bath.

Swathed in long, white veils we trudged over the sand with a host of other women to the public bath, the water of which was supplied by an underground hot-spring. "Days are for men, evenings are for women," chanted Jaleela as we marched along, with me being careful to display only one eye as the others were doing.

Jaleela and the others removed all their clothes in the waiting room, but I prudishly held on to my pants and bra until we entered the next room, which was roasting, and then the bathroom itself, which was almost unbearable. Quickly stripping as naked as the rest, I told myself that if there is a special hell for women, it must be like this. There was screaming, shouting, sweating, swearing, and sloshing of boiling hot and icy cold water all over the place. Crouching beside Jaleela on the only vacant patch of stone floor, I slowly began to scrub. "Rub my back," said Jaleela suddenly, passing me a large, rough, stone. When I had finished, a woman whom I had never seen before seized the stone and began to rub my body fiercely all over removing not only the embedded dirt, but some of the skin as well. I enjoyed that rather delicious sensation, however, and then just managed to stagger over to the cold water barrel in time to refresh myself before being quite overcome by the heat.

The following days were spent in excited preparations for the feast of Ramadan. Sheep were fattened, sequined dresses were sewn together, new suits were bought for little boys, and hands and hair were carefully dyed with henna. I quite enjoyed the sewing sessions which Jaleela attended in her parents' house, where the women would work by the light of a flickering oil-lamp, entertained not by a radio, but by the singing and dancing of their little girls, who had learned such things at wedding feasts.

On the day of the feast of Ramadan, we all rose early and helped to dress the children in their new clothes. Then came the visits and the visiting, and the wishing of 'Happy Feast!' or 'Happy Days!', just as I had done two years ago in Baghdad.

Eating went on throughout that day; nobody seemed to be able to eat enough. That afternoon there was to be dancing and rifle-shooting in the village, and somehow I managed to escape from the gossiping groups of relations and their obstreperous infants to go and watch.

Only 'modern' girls from North Algeria came unveiled to these events which were performed by Algerian men in their national costumes. The rifle-shooting fascinated me most, executed by two lines of men who skilfully loaded heavy rifles and fired them into the ground before an admiring audience.

That night Latif said he had arranged for a taxi to collect me at his house on the following morning. "The driver is a cousin of mine," he added, "so there will be no charge, and I can trust him." After supper, we talked in his smoky mud room. The conversation was in Arabic, and my mind began to wander back to those happy, carefree, desert days of camping, washing, cooking, rounding up sheep, climbing about the truck, and being a bandit's accomplice. Days which I shall never forget, and for which, even now, my heart yearns.

.   .   .

In El Goléa, the desert track came to an end. From there to Ghardaia and right up to the coast, the road would be tarmac. The sun rose as my taxi sped northwards, painting the sand-dunes with a pink and orange glow. Then, suddenly, there was Ghardaia spread over a hill-top, its blue, yellow and white-washed houses gleaming in the sunshine.

Ghardaia will always seem like a fairy-tale town to me, with its narrow twisting streets, winding stairways leading up the hillsides, poky little shops, intriguing passages through ancient archways, and tiny windows from which palefaced children peeped. As always though, it was the people who interested me most. The Mozabites, with their sharp-featured faces, baggy trousers, and white skull-caps, the desert people in their coloured *shaishs* and thick burnouses, women who shyly turned their already veiled faces to the wall as one passed, and little girls with long hair and long knickers, still clothed in their glittering dresses of the fête. While I was thus absorbed in that picturesque old town I bumped into a French girl. Introductions followed, then an invitation to lunch followed by an offer to occupy a spare seat in a car bound for Oran.

It was somewhere between Ghardaia and Oran that I took

my final look at the Sahara Desert, for the last of the bare, brown hills were fading into the distance, as the road wound north-wards through country covered by sparse grass where sheep, camels, goats and nomads became more abundant as the vegetation grew thicker. We drove through Laghouat, the capital of the Sahara region, paused in Tairet to visit the carpet mart and then, as dusk fell, the lights of Oran twinkled a welcome.

I stayed the night in Oran with the French girl and then hitched another lift along the coast to Mostaganem. From there I travelled in style to Algiers in the ambulance of the local fire brigade.

For me the most exciting thing about Algiers was its enormous casbah, where the tangled streets were so steep and narrow that almost every one of them was a long flight of steps, with tiny shops and thick-walled houses leaning on either side. An Algerian boy showed me round, pointing out the tiny windows placed high in the walls, the carved wooden doors with the red stars and crescents painted above them, and the 'hands of Fatima' painted here and there to ward off the evil eye, especially if there were children in the house. When the moon rose and peeped down from somewhere above us, she illuminated a glimpse of long-ago Arabia, so beautiful, so ugly, so happy, so pathetic, all at the same time.

When I was finally in the train which would take me out of the country I had grown to love so much, I felt extremely depressed as it rattled steadily towards the Tunisian frontier.

Some days after my arrival in Tunis, I stayed with a Tunisian 'Mama' to whom I had an introduction. After break-fast one day she said, "This morning I'll show you the *souk*. I want to visit my cousin who has a shop there."

The first shop we stopped at was that of a Jewish silversmith. "I lived here in peace for thirty-seven years," he told me quietly, "until last June, when the police broke into my shop, turned everything upside-down, and locked me out of it. They let me have the keys again later, but I'm going to leave this country soon. It's such a pity," he went on, "for there are many Jews in Tunisia. The president here is a very liberal man, com-pared to most Arab leaders, and we have our Rabbis, our synagogues, our kosher food, and even our Hebrew schools. Yes, I have been extremely happy in this country."

The *souk* of Tunis was quite fascinating. Mama pointed out to me craftsmen embroidering on leather, hammering brass, and shaping gold and silver. She took me into perfume shops as narrow as cupboards, where bottles of scents such as rose, pinks, jasmine, vervain, and musk were on display, and to stalls where rugs, blankets, tissues, necklaces, bracelets, fibulas, ewers, chased trays and shining teapots were spread in an attractive confusion. The streets there were dark and tunnel-like, and in odd corners groups of old men sat sipping endless glasses of tea as they watched the world go by.

The shop of Mama's cousin was exactly opposite the big mosque, a very advantageous position in which to be at prayer-times. In between selling his nuts and raisins and talking to Mama, he served us delicious Arabian coffee.

A day or so later, I took a tram to Carthage. After inspecting the old port, I wandered along to see the thermal baths of Antoninus, now in ruins, where I discovered a man from the Archaeological Institute lecturing a group of students about it all. As we moved on towards the open-air museum on a hill-top facing the sea, I fell into conversation with the lecturer, whose name was Monsieur Jeddi. He told me that he'd be travelling to Sousse in two days' time, and kindly offered me a lift. Sousse lay in the direction I wished to go, on the Tripoli road, and I gratefully accepted. But on the morning we were to set out the road was sunk in dense fog. "And there was I, thinking this only happened in Manchester," chuckled Monsieur Jeddi. "And there was I, thinking that all Arabs had brown or black eyes," I laughed, glancing up into his cornflower blue ones. "But I'm not an Arab, I'm a Berber," he informed me quickly. "We are a racial group belonging to the Hamitic branch of the white race." He continued at some length during which time the fog lifted and we were able to take the road to Grombalia, Monastir, and Sousse.

Monsieur Jeddi's friends in Sousse lived in the old Roman fortress there, for the father of the family was curator of the Sousse Museum. It was fun sleeping in a turret room at nights, after looking from the tiny window to see the long, white beam of light which shone from the tower down to the harbour as a signal to passing ships. On the morning after my arrival my host took me to see the catacombs, and from some loose soil in that underground maze of passages he pulled an ancient jawbone containing rattling teeth. "You can have it," he smiled "Used to belong to a very early Christian whose tomb was in this particular recess." "Sure to be early!" I said, examining the teeth. "No fillings!"

The following afternoon found me in a friend's car speeding along to El Djem where yet another of Monsieur Jeddi's friends was my host. He also was curator of the museum, and he showed me around many of the excavated Roman houses and the coliseum. One morning he took me to the coastal town of Mahdia, where the fishermen used the peculiar method of fishing only at night, by the light of their lamps.

Then, after spending one day in Sfax, the second town of Tunisia, which was founded in the ninth century on the ruins of ancient Taparura, I travelled through vast plantations of silvery olive trees which represented the wealth of that region. From Ben Gadane on the Libyan border I hitch-hiked to Tripoli in a truck with a very dark-skinned driver who spoke both English and Italian.

Thankful to have arrived safely in Tripoli at last, I trudged around the streets looking desperately for a Y.W.C.A., a convent, a girl's hostel, or even the British Embassy, for I was weary, and rather anxious about the rough-looking pack of 'wolves' who were following me and seemed to be gradually closing in. The streets were almost void of any women except one or two who were veiled so heavily that they appeared as black, sexless shapes – and I didn't blame them one bit. Some Libyans even stopped their cars in order to get a better look at me, and there were many catcalls and wolf-whistles.

When I heard yet another sharp hiss just behind me I didn't look around but, clenching my fists, strode on. "Miss England!" suddenly shouted a voice, an unmistakably English voice. There were a couple in a car; they'd seen the Union Jack on my sleeve and guessed my predicament. "We're with the British Military Mission," said the wife. "Hop in!"

That kind English couple were my hosts in Tripoli. They took me for *smorgasbrod* suppers at the American Army Base, drives around the sea-front to view the royal palaces, into the *souks* to see where the intricate filigree work was being done on solid silver, and to visit the museum.

At one of the silver and pearl shops, we chatted for a long time to its owner – a pleasant young man who spoke broken

English with a broad Yorkshire accent, having been a British army cook during the war.

As we were about to take our leave, my host enquired, "I say, wouldn't you like to come and work in our mess?" "Not bloomin' likely!" replied the Libyan with a grin, "I've got enough mess of me own, right 'ere!"

Chapter 24

February 1967–April 1967

I decided to visit Malta on my way to Italy, and took a third-class ticket to Valetta. Leaving my boat I was soon walking past the inevitable statue of Queen Victoria to the Grand Master's palace to see the remarkable tapestry chamber, and the armoury of the knights, and then to the sixteenth-century St John's Cathedral, with its famous masterpieces, including Caravaggio's impressive 'The beheading of St John'.

That afternoon found me cutting through some back streets, where washing flapped from balconies Neapolitan-style and fair-skinned, dark-haired children called to each other in Maltese, a language which sounded to me like Arabic with a few Latin words thrown in. After a brief visit to the National Museum, I made for the post office to wait for an Engish couple whom I had met on the boat coming from Tripoli, for they had, invited me to stay with them. During my days in Malta, my new friends drove me all over the main island, to Rabat, where the marble in the cathedral came from Russia and had gold threads running through it, to Saint Paul's Bay, where the saint had been shipwrecked in A.D. 60, to Mdina, 'the silent city', a town full of mediaeval buildings as well as the stately homes of many Maltese nobility, and so on.

Then I was on board another boat – this time bound for Syracuse. Slowly we moved out of Valetta harbour beneath a moonlit sky. I stayed out on deck until the last little fox-terrier tug had pulled us clear of the port and gone chugging away in the darkness.

Arriving in Syracuse early on a Sunday morning, I set off immediately to try to locate the Youth Hostel there. Becoming hopelessly lost in a maze of streets which closely resembled those of an Arabian town, I could find nobody around of whom to ask directions. The only people awake seemed to be either at Mass, or in bars throwing back spirits, and these latter called to me in a way which didn't tempt me to speak to them

At last, however, an elderly Sicilian asked if he could drive me somewhere. Upon hearing that I wanted the Youth Hostel, he said, "Of course, Signorita! It is seven kilometres from here, out at Belvedere, on the way to where I live. Let's go!"

My new friend lost no time in introducing himself as Signor Tagliarini. I shared a double bed that night with his daughter, Maria, and it was then that I realised how much the South Italians resembled their neighbours, the Arabs. "Our men like fat girls," Maria informed me solemnly. "The girl next door is seventeen and she can't get married; she's about your size and they say she's too thin!" This was cheering news to me, as I had no intention of settling down in Sicily.

On the following morning I journeyed to Catania by train and then by way of Catania and Messina to Palermo, where I received the disappointing news that, owing to a strike, no boats would be leaving for Cagliari that week. Returning to Messina I decided to take the alternative of travelling up north through the toe of Italy, and after crossing the straights by ferry-boat I arrived in Villa San Giovanni.

From that small town I hitch-hiked northwards and the next day found me waiting for a lift at a petrol-station in San Eufemia Lamezia. Having decided to hitch-hike home all the way from that point, I knew enough about South Italian males to take some precautions, and had thus taken the petrol-station people into my confidence. Early that afternoon when an enormous truck pulled into the station, I was informed that my lift to Naples had arrived. "These men are old. You need have no fear!" said the proprietor of the petrol-station nodding towards the driver and his mate – whom I guessed to be somewhere in their late fifties.

As soon as the men had eaten we were on our way, first along a *bruta* road which hugged the coast, then inland across a plain backed by tall, snow-covered hills.

As we rumbled along, the truck-drivers treated me to lengthy descriptions of their homes, wives, and children, one of them even producing photographs of his eldest daughter and asking my advice as to her education. Then, just as I was least expecting it, their conversation began to get extremely personal and after that my journey to Naples was ruined. Even when all the base questions had stopped, there was a 'nasty taste' in my mouth somehow, and I was not over-surprised when, not far from our destination, the man who was driving pulled into a layby. As his friend gazed nonchalantly out of the window he said: "Signorita, you are twenty-five years old. You must have some sort of sexual need. Now please understand that we do not intend to rape you but, if you agree, then we are willing."

At this point the Italian lifted a curtain to reveal a bed at the back of the cabin. "Please," I begged, "just let's get on our way. All girls are not the same you know. And can't you understand that I only asked the petrol-station people to find me a 'safe' lift because I had wanted to prevent something like this? I even promised to let them know if I arrived in Naples without mishap."

The truck-driver stared at me coldly, and then continued to ask me personal things — eyeing the bed all the time. Suddenly I couldn't stand it any longer. I was cold, tired, hungry, and feeling extremely sorry for myself. The tears began to fall and those tears seemed to change the whole atmosphere. A look of fatherly concern swept over the driver's face. "O *scusi*, Signorita, he whispered gently. "We did not mean to make you cry. We were only asking. When you write to those petrol people, you can please tell them that we were good with you. Now wipe your eyes, *prego*, we are sorry." They dropped me off at an all-night supermarket on the Naples Autostrada, where I stayed safely until the morning.

That February I was to discover Naples anew, its fabulous museum, its noisy slums, towering Vesuvius, colourful Capri. An Italian professor whom I had encountered in 1959 drove me to the volcano in his gleaming Alfa Romeo. At 3,000 feet we parked the car and walked up to the crater along a narrow track which ran over hardened black lava to where masses of white, sulphurous smoke were still pouring forth, though the last eruption was in 1944. Standing on the warm summit I felt as though I were perched on the rim of a gigantic cauldron. I could see the ruined Pompeii spread out below, Napoli harbour with its oil refineries, Capri and Ischia guarding the bay.

In Rome I stayed with friends of friends, Signor and Signora Bouzo, whom I had met during my short journey of 1959. On the first day, after the siesta, they took me to see the city that had first captured my heart eight years ago. First we drove past the Hero's Fountain and along the river Tiber to see an island on which some friars ran a hospital. Near by was a dwelling which resembled a miniature castle, Dante's old residence, I was told. Driving up the Campidoglio – the most sacred of Rome's seven hills – we got a splendid view of the ruined Roman forum below, and the ancient, cobbled streets, one of which (the Via Sacra) ran from the Forum to the summit of the Campidoglio.

Night was rapidly falling as we made our way back to the Bonzo's apartment through the pre-theatre rush-hour traffic. Past the Baths of Caracalla where I'd see *Carmen* performed one long-ago summer's eve, then along the Via Nazionale to the Fountain of Trevi where I couldn't resist throwing another three coins, to the Piazza di Spagna.

Before heading for Milano and then Switzerland, I decided to visit the world's oldest and smallest republic, San Marino. I caught a local bus from Rimini, and as we wound our way upwards to Monte Titiano, 2,437 feet above sea-level, the view across the Appenines became quite perfect.

From the forts and palaces of that tiny, semi-communist republic, I hitch-hiked to Bologna through Italy's rich wine country and then along the 'Autostrada del Sole' to Milano, where I went straight to the house of the Baronis, parents of an Italian girl I had met in Bolivia. They took me to the magnificent Scala Theatre to see *La Boheme*.

After two days in Milano I travelled to St Moritz, situated 6,090 feet above sea-level in the Engadine, the most extensive and magnificent high valley in the Swiss Canton of the Grissons. My first impression of the place was hundreds of women in mink coats, and men in sleek new cars – all up there for skiing holidays. Skiing must have been perfect and I wished I had time to linger and learn, but it was then March and I had exactly one month to get myself back to England for April 4th. I had told my literary agent that my journey was to have taken just seven years to the day and, if possible, I intended to keep to schedule.

From the snows of St Moritz, I hitch-hiked with a French-speaking Swiss to the Principality of Lichtenstein. We wound around the snowy mountains that were dotted with wooden chalets, the 'country houses' of Swiss businessmen. At Sevelen, not far from Vaduz, my Swiss friend invited me to dine with him in a 'log-cabin'-type restaurant which was warm, bright and cheerful inside. A massive St Bernard dog, complete with brandy keg, lay sprawled before the roaring fire, while snow piled gradually higher against the frosted window-panes. 'Cosy' wasn't the word!

We arrived in Vaduz at 10 a.m. It was warmer than up in the mountains, but the disadvantage then was that the snow was now rain. The rain persisted throughout the day, and that evening when I went to the cottage of a girl I had met earlier in the day, I was soaked. "Never mind," she said, beginning to prepare a meal. "We'll have a good hot supper and then go to a near-by café to warm up and watch their TV!"

I travelled to Cologne with a German student of architecture who sped along at 120 kilometres per hour, all the while describing to me the numerous accidents he'd witnessed on the German autobahns at night.

There was a sort of mission in the railway station at Cologne, and there I slept with my head on a wooden table. On the following day, a film director gave me a lift to Hamburg, right from Cologne, in his well-worn Czechoslovakian car.

It was still rather early to check in at the Youth Hostel when I arrived in Hamburg, so I decided to go and view some 'pop' art. I set off for the Young Generation Art Gallery, which was situated in the cellar of a large old terrace house. A newly-married couple, Greta and Ludwig, ran the place. Although Ludwig's father had been killed by the British during the Second World War, in a gesture typical of the 'younger generation' he extended his hand to me in friendship, accepting me as I accepted him. They told me that the exhibition of 'pop' art would not be opening until the following week, but by the time they had showed me all the paintings they had on display it was late, and they suggested that I stay as their guest instead of trying to find the Youth Hostel. I gratefully accepted and, after a sausages and sauerkraut supper, my German friends escorted me on a 'Hamburg by night' tour.

I was lucky the next day in getting a lift with a Dutchman from Hamburg all the way to Copenhagen, for I had decided to round off my travels with a visit to Finland and Scandinavia. I found the Danish countryside impressive, with its yellow and red walled farm-houses looking fine in contrast to ploughed fields and soft, green hills. We stopped at a *Kro* Inn for coffee and Weiner *brod* ('Vienna bread'), which is actually a sort of cake, arriving in Denmark's capital just in time to see the green statue of the sad 'Little Mermaid' standing out against a background of shipyards and silhouetted against the evening sky.

People had warned me that hitch-hiking would be difficult in Sweden, but after taking a ferry from Helsingör (Denmark) to Helsingborg (Sweden) I had many lifts, and was eventually being driven through pine forests which stood dark green against fields of snow, past frozen ponds and lakes right up to Stockholm, by a twenty-year-old Swede who was going to start a new job there.

The Youth Hostel in Stockholm was actually a converted yacht called *Al Chapman* originally the *Dunboyne*, a fully rigged sailing ship built in the yards at Whitehaven, England, in 1888. It proved to be one of the most comfortable Youth Hostels that I had ever stayed in.

Feeling grubby after my journey from Copenhagen I found the idea of a *sauna* bath especially tempting, and the next morning I paid my four Krone (about five and eightpence) to enter the *Sturbadet*. Leaving my valuables with the receptionist, I undressed in a cubicle and entered a hot steam room. After sweating there for an hour I took a hot shower and then swam for two hours with a lot of naked women in the pool. Returning to the hot room again I stayed until I was almost fainting, when I took a hot shower, then a cold one, dried, dressed, and left the *sauna* to find Stockholm enveloped in a blizzard.

Ravenous, I went into one of the department stores and bought myself a cheap lunch of milk, buns and chocolate. By the time I emerged again the sun was shining from a cloudless blue sky, so I was able to have my meal sitting on a wooden stand overlooking an open-air ice-skating rink, where scores of children moved lithely over the glistening surface.

I crossed the Baltic Sea from Stockholm to Abo/Turku (Finland) on the M.S. *Ilmator*. From Abo/Turku I hitch-hiked to Helsinki with a Finn who imported guns and ammunition, yet in spite of so delicate a cargo, he sped over icy roads at 160 kilometres an hour, confiding, "I used to be a champion ice-racer!" I tried to concentrate upon the stately pines and the snow-covered wooden houses we passed but was not exactly sorry when at last we arrived in the capital.

Not knowing the address of the Youth Hostel there I asked to be dropped 'somewhere near the tourist office' and was then guided to a tall block of flats. Upon knocking at one of the closed doors, I discovered that there was no tourist office there, and that the flats were, in fact, accommodation for students of the State University of Helsinki. "However," said the girl who had opened the door, "if a place to sleep is all you're looking for, you can make yourself comfortable on our floor. I see you have a sleeping-bag."

Breakfast the following morning was horse-meat sandwiches and coffee, rapidly prepared by the girl, Ula, who then had to rush away to shop for candles and paper plates, as she was one of the organisers of a university ball planned for the following week. We went into the centre of town together and then separated, as I wished to visit the National Museum which was housed in an old church. I thoroughly enjoyed its fine exhibition of mediaeval gilded paintings, furniture, and so forth, and then went to the railway station and bought a sixpenny sausage for my lunch.

Evening found me at Vaasa, and there a couple who gave me a lift surprised me by speaking good English with just the trace of an Irish brogue. Introducing themselves as Mr and Mrs Skoglund, teachers in a near-by village, they invited me to spend the night at their house. After dinner, they took me to see the second largest mink farm in the world. Rows of metal cages held silver minks, black minks, violet minks, beige minks, and white minks. Their owner handled them with leather gloves – which they all bit into, screeching with understandable fear. "At five months old they have their necks broken and are skinned," he informed us cheerfully. "Pigs eat their flesh and the skins are sent off to be auctioned in Copenhagen. About sixty or seventy of them are required for one lady's coat. They spend their whole lives in these battery-like cages and I feed them on a meat-mixture diet."

Time was running out and so with great reluctance I refused invitations to spend more time in Vaasa. On the following morning my host drove me out on to the road to Oulu. In Oulu I was the guest of teachers again, this time a Frenchman married to a Scots girl, and neither of them had much to say in favour of the Finns. "Finland gets so monotonous after a while," declared my French host. "All this snow, for one thing; and then, although the Finns aren't 'naughty' at all like the rest of us Europeans, neither are they 'sympathique'. They're just plain boring and so hard to get to know. First they were under the Swedes, then the Russians, so naturally they've got a bit of a complex about being such a newly independent country. Then their language is so different from the Scandinavian tongues, and they have no special monuments of literature of their own. The Swedes brought a lot of their culture over here, but all the Finns seem to have learned from us in Western Europe is alcoholism and drug taking, especially the university students." I didn't agree with a lot of this, but said nothing. My host was a very opinionated little man.

The next morning found me travelling towards Rovaniemi – the capital of Lapland. The snow became deeper as I penetrated farther north, and blizzards were blown up by biting, Arctic winds which made my toes and fingers go numb and painful. Walking along the road, wondering about the dangers of frostbite, I was highly relieved when a van drew up beside me and a local 'pop' group who were also heading for Rovaniemi offered me a lift.

My host in Oulu had given me a message to deliver to a Filippino doctor in Rovaniemi, who took me straight to his home, where I met Kaisa, his young Finnish wife. That evening, just before dark, the doctor and his wife took me for a drive eight kilometres north of Rovaniemi to where a notice said that we were now on the Arctic Circle. The next day, Kaisa and I left the new block of apartments which had been erected for the hospital staff, and walked into town. After mooching around the shops and picking up one or two gifts for my family, we went into a *baari* filled with rugged-looking men from the country, and drank mugs of steaming hot chocolate. We then returned to the apartment and had a *sauna* bath, beating ourselves with bunches of leaves to sweat even more profusely, in the true Finnish way.

Kaisa prepared reindeer meat for our late lunch with the doctor, plus another Finnish dish called *hernekeitto*, pork and peas all mixed up together in a sort of stew, and a desert called *mami*, a brown stodge, eaten with fresh cream. All were delicious, I thought.

From Rovaniemi I would be travelling southwards again, with only twelve days in which to get home. The doctor and Kaisa put me on to the Kemi road, where I soon hitched a lift to Tornio, a town on the Finnish/Swedish border. Crossing over, I observed how the road wound around in a figure eight, so that cars could easily change from the right-hand driving of Finland to the left of Sweden.

It was then that what looked like a middle-aged Swedish businessman stopped his car, and motioned for me to hop in. He couldn't have introduced himself as he spoke nothing but Swedish but some things don't need words, and some time later I noticed that he was eyeing me lustfully, releasing protracted sighs, and fidgeting. Those were the signs I had come to know so well, and sure enough, before long he took a note from his breast pocket tapped me on the knee, and pointed to himself. Thinking rapidly, I looked wide-eyed and pretended that I had no idea what he meant at all. Misunderstanding the reason for my hesitation, the man replacing the single note and took out a wad. I didn't feel flattered one bit. Acting quickly, I whipped out my handkerchief, held it to my mouth, and made some very realistic vomiting noises. The man stopped his car, looking extremely puzzled, and I shot thankfully out into the road. As we parted, I think we were both looking utterly disillusioned with one another.

My next ride was with two enormous Finns, who hauled out a map and indicated that they were going south right past Sundsvall. They drove fast and round about lunch-time untied a dirty cloth to reveal chunks of salted reindeer meat, raw and cooked. Hacking off wedges of it with a huge knife, they fed themselves and silently passed pieces of it back to me. Sundsvall was sleeping when we arrived, but a wandering student took me to his parents' wooden house where I slept on the floor of the boxroom.

Next day, the roads were crowded with Easter holiday traffic. At six in the evening, in a dense blizzard, I was dropped at a place called Ann and began to walk quickly along the road to prevent myself freezing up. An elderly Swede, a schoolteacher, came to my rescue. I spent Good Friday with his family, and saw his small but well-appointed school.

On Easter Saturday I had to be on my way again, and was fortunate in getting a lift as far as Gjövik with a vet, who spent a long time in telling me about the large number of skiers who had got lost and died in the snow already that Easter. I spent the night with the vet and his family and left Gjövik for Oslo after breakfast on the following morning. I felt an urge to attend an Easter Sunday service, and was wandering around the streets of Norway's small, unpretentious capital in the hope of finding an English-speaking church when I bumped into a British major and his family. The result of this encounter was an invitation to stay in their house. They were Roman Catholics but took me to the Anglican church that evening, and the next morning dropped me on the Peninsula of Bygdy where I spent a happy day exploring the museum.

First of all I went to see the three Viking ships which had been excavated from the banks of the Oslo fjord. In one of them, the remains of a queen, her old woman servant, a cart, three sledges, fifteen horses, four dogs, and one ox had been discovered. Then I went along to see the Kontiki Museum, where stood the balsa-wood raft, made in 1947, which crossed from Callao to Polynesia, thus proving that Peruvian Indians could also have made that journey in bygone days.

At the British Embassy in Oslo I had collected a letter from my London agent. The letter informed me that he had sold my exclusive story to a newspaper and that I was to speak to no journalists from now on. I phoned from Copenhagen and arranged to meet him and somebody from the press in Amsterdam on March 31st.

From Copenhagen to Hamburg I hitch-hiked, first with a young Dane and then with a German on the back of his motorbike. Words were few and far between. I became so stiff with cold during our brief journey together that I practically had to be chipped off the thing — and was just standing on the verge, rubbing my fingers to get them to bend a little, when a car pulled up and I found myself Hamburg bound with a corset salesman who kept asking, in that special 'lingerie' voice, "and how is that cold, inner feeling now?"

In Hamburg I stayed with my 'pop' art friends once more, and then set off for Amsterdam on the morning of March 31st. Canals, fields full of shaggy Shetland ponies, barges, houseboats, windmills, dykes, and then the Polderlands of Western Holland, which lay four to five feet below the level of the sea. "God made Europe but the Dutch made Holland!" laughed the man who dropped me at a tram stop in the Dutch capital. I met my literary agent and the press reporter in the American Hotel late that night, and the following morning they hired a local photographer who took pictures of me on barges, beside barrel-organs, and such.

That afternoon, when, thanks to the hotel phone, I had spoken to my parents for the first time in seven years, my new friends and I went ambling through some neat Dutch back streets alongside the canals where the very organised brothels stood. The girls lived in prim-looking houses with lace curtains fluttering at the windows and posies of flowers set attractively here and there. The windows were opened wide at the knock of a prospective client and, if terms were agreed upon, the shutters were tightly closed. All so tidy and discreet; so very Dutch, one could say.

The next morning I was alone again, and on the road bound for Brussels; thence I would be crossing the channel to England. At the Youth Hostel in Brussels, a newspaper was waved before my eyes by a little girl who shouted, "Are you Wendy?" My photo was 'out' all over England. Wendy Myers eating a cheese sandwich on a barge in Amsterdam.

On the morning of April 3rd I arrived in Ostend – to enjoy a day on the beach, which was still crowded with Easter holiday-makers. I booked into a Youth Hostel, and then went for an evening stroll beside the grey Atlantic. Tomorrow, God willing, I would be safely home after my journey of seven years all over the world. I felt less of the 'shock' of this occasion than I thought I might, because my agent and the press had given me so much to think about during the past few days.

I only hope that they are not too disappointed with the 'goods' they came to see, I thought, and that I shall be clever enough for them. Sometimes I feel that what I have done is nothing spectacular, that any other girl could have done the same thing, so why all the fuss? Maybe I felt this way because travelling alone in all parts of the world has come so natural to me, I can be completely 'at home' in almost any society, for I have always tried to identify myself with the people of the nationality concerned to see things through their eyes. I am lucky in this respect and in another also, in the fact that I can accept danger as a part of my life, and not let bygone terrifying experiences overcome my resolution to continue to do what I eel is a worthwhile thing.

Why was my journey worthwhile? Because, for one thing, it has given me an opportunity to survey the world and the many changing scenes of life, of which I, as a human being, am part. Names written on maps, places mentioned in books or on the news, come alive for me now, and I also feel a tremendous sense of freedom in not having one town or one country only to call my home, but the globe itself. Sometimes I do regret not having had a university education, yet maybe for a person of insatiable curiosity such as I, experience really is the best teacher and can certainly be a very strict one at times.

How quickly these past seven years have slipped by! At times I forget that I am already twenty-five years old. Life still surprises me, thrills me, and delights me – as much as when I was a wide-eyed little girl.

When I set foot on English soil again tomorrow for the first time since April 1960, I know that I shall say a prayer of thanks for my safe homecoming. I still believe in God even though it doesn't seem to be the fashion nowadays among the young people of Europe. Well, I don't much care about fashions, anyway.

.   .   .

"The white cliffs! The white cliffs!" It was the morning of April 4th, 1967, and before me across the wave-crests loomed the white cliffs of Dover. English schoolchildren beside me on the ferry were gleefully shouting and I wanted to shout with them, for I too was thrilled to see again that very English spectacle after so many years. But then I was breathing very fast and hot tears rolled down my cheeks, for I loved these children of my own dear country, I loved those white cliffs, and I was so glad to be coming home.

Epilogue

"But you've made it all seem just like a trip to Brighton!" was the first remark of someone who read this account. My reply to that was, "Well, it was no more difficult for me than going to Brighton. I can't make things up that didn't happen, can I?"

There were hardships, of course; going without food for three days in China to economise, being attacked in the Argentine, robbed in Hong Kong, walking the skin off my feet in New Zealand, crouching beneath a hail of bullets in South Vietnam. But all these difficulties, and more, were absorbed by the most amazing and heartening hospitality of the people I met. People have vacated their beds for me to climb into, gone without food so that I might eat, saved my life, taken me with them whilst moving house, begged me to stay with them for ever.

I travelled to odd little corners of the world expecting to find good, ordinary people, and I found them. There were mamas and papas, chic girls and obstreperous youths, babies doted upon, old people revered. There were holy men, twaddlers, teachers, students, 'moderns', and 'old-timers'.

Their ways of life were often quite different, moulded to suit their climate and adapted to their environment, but the laughter, the tears, the pain, and the peace, were always there, just the same as in England.

One of the most depressing observations I made during my travels was the extent to which countries criticised each other. "You're going there next? Well, you won't like their food!" "That's your next stop? Their hospitality isn't a patch on ours!" "To that place? Well, take care, they're all just a lot of thieves and cut-throats!" This sort of remark was universal, I found. So was the complete ignorance of peoples and places shown by many so-called well educated folk. "What part of London is

England in?" "What language is it you speak there?" came the queries of some Latin American students. And on our side, the wife of a British diplomat eyed me at a party one evening and gushed, "So you've been to Bolivia! Isn't that one of those horrid little Balkan states?"

As the years went by, my passports piled up. I went through seven of them in seven years. When I had five sealed together, they evoked some interesting remarks and often a visa *gratia* – as a kind consul's expression of admiration for my venture.

My note-book-diaries piled up too. These were extremely precious to me as, without them, I should have faced great difficulty in writing this book, so as soon as one was filled I would search for a person of integrity who happened to be leaving shortly for London, no matter what his nationality, and give him the note-book to deliver to my parents by hand. People were only too pleased to have a family to go to in England and on no occasion did I have to rely upon the post.

This was a precaution which perhaps was quite unnecessary, for the postal services throughout the whole world proved excellent according to my parents to whom I wrote at least every three days throughout those seven years. The only exceptions resulted from certain desert, boat and train journeys.

Money came and went, my spasmodic earnings being boosted by the odd cheque from home plus money gifts from friends *en route*. To refuse the latter would have caused offence but I, in turn, send letters, cards and photos to everyone whom I have ever met during my travels.

I hitch-hiked mostly, which cost nothing, and the public transport I took when necessary was of the humblest kind. If I was prepared to sleep anywhere, fight heat, cold, mosquitoes, and eat local food, then I was accepted and protected by the people with whom I travelled. Trust begets trust, respect begets respect, was one of the primary lessons I learned.

"But don't you worry about their smell? Their language? Their colour?" I was frequently asked. "To be quite honest, I never noticed it," I would as frequently reply. When I look back, I truly cannot remember the colours of half my foreign friends, nor the language in which we conversed. And as for smell, I'm sure that after missing a bath for several days – as I often did – I smelled twice as bad as some of them were supposed to!

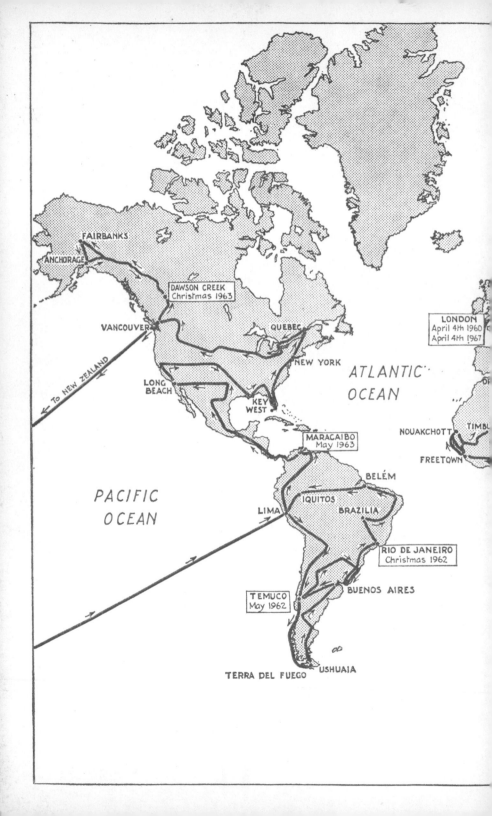